HEZBOLLAH

HEZBOLLAH

BORN WITH A VENGEANCE

Hala Jaber

Columbia University Press   New York

Columbia University Press
Publishers Since 1893
New York   Chichester, West Sussex
Copyright © 1997 Hala Jaber

Library of Congress Cataloging-in-Publication Data
Jaber, Hala.
    Hezbollah : born with a vengeance / Hala Jaber.
        p.   cm.
    Includes bibliographical references (p.   ) and index.
    ISBN 0–231–10834–6 (cloth)
    1. Hizballah (Lebanon).   2. Israel-Arab Border Conflicts, 1949– -
-Lebanon.   3. Islam and politics—Lebanon.   4. Lebanon—Politics
and government—1975–   . I. Title.
DS119.7.J33   1997
956.92—dc21   97–3053

⊗

Casebound editions of Columbia University Press books are printed on
permanent and durable acid-free paper.

Printed in the United States of America

c 10 9 8 7 6 5 4 3 2 1

To the three people who have made me who I am: my
parents and my husband

Contents

Plates

between pages 112 and 113

Maps

Acknowledgements

One man made a particular contribution to this book that towers above all others. In fact none of this would have been possible without his support, encouragement and more importantly his faith in me, my ability and the necessity to write this book. For more than two years he acted as the force behind my drive, selflessly urging and providing me with the means and space to complete this book. I am of course referring to my husband Steve Bent, who not only put his life on hold for the last three years as I researched and wrote *Hezbollah*, but who never once complained (well, maybe once or twice) when I spent eight consecutive months away from him and our home, to conduct much of this research in Lebanon, not to mention the other shorter trips here and there. He was and continues to be my staunchest advocate and the one person I knew I could always count on for strength at times when mine simply deserted me. You will always have my love.

Special thanks must also go to Yunis Awdeh, an old friend and a first-class Lebanese journalist, without whom this book might also not have materialised. Yunis did not assist in the writing, nor did he read the manuscript, or even correct its mistakes: instead he used his personal and special relationship with the leadership of Hezbollah, which he had carefully and painstakingly nurtured over many years to a high level of trust, to provide me with unparalleled access with the leadership of the Party of God. *Hezbollah: Born with a Vengeance*, might not have been possible without his involvement and as such it is as much his book at it is mine. For that and for laying the grounds that would eventually gain me the trust of the Party of God's leadership and for all the hours he gave up to join me in many of the long hours of interviews that were eventually set up with the officials, I owe him more than I will ever be able to repay.

Many others deserve my thanks: my loving friends in Beirut, Dr Ghassan Doughman and his wife Deema as well as Dr Fuad Murad and his wife Lydia and their families who took me into their homes, fed, inspired and took care of me and practically adopted and helped me survive the many months spent in Lebanon during the course of my research. My childhood friend Tarek Sulaibi, who spent many a night helping me transcribe and translate the reams of Arabic tapes of interviews into English. To my cousin Susan Wansa and her family for continuously reassuring me during the course of writing this book; to my best friend Diana Abdallah for always being there and for never once failing to support me, and to her wonderful husband Michael Limb – both welcomed me in their home in Dubai and created an atmosphere to help me write yet another chapter of the book. To Richard Holliday and his wife Sue Mills who saved me and Steve and especially the book when we became homeless; to Askold Kruschelnitsky, who so generously spent long hours reading much of my manuscript and pointing out valuable objective points and advice; to Paul and Newby Palmer for always heartening me; to Lena Kara, my old friend and veteran war comrade who also put me, my mobile library and family up at her flat during our last week of homelessness and where I finalised the last chapter of the book; and to all the other unnamed friends and relatives, I extend my sincere thanks for their unequivocal support, backing and advice during one of the most critical periods of my life. There are others to whom I also owe a more traditional debt: to my parents, my sister Rana and brother Zu, and to little Lara for always believing in me and continuously endorsing my quests, I will eternally be grateful.

To my agent Anthony Goff of David Higham for

acknowledging the subject matter of this book and for always seeking my best of interests I owe special thanks. Equally to Clive Priddle, my editor who remained a pillar of strength and a source of wisdom during the course of bringing together *Hezbollah*. I thank him wholeheartedly for never once complaining and for refusing to give up despite the delays and problems I must have caused him. I can only say thank you. His support and encouragement over the last year and his continuous presence to help and guide me through the web of overwhelming material was invaluable.

Finally, I would like to say a very special thank-you to Jo Glanville, who took on one of the hardest tasks of all – that of sub-editing the endless maze of *Hezbollah*. Jo's ability to carefully sieve through the hundreds of pages of manuscript, her aptness in comprehending the arguments put forward, her efficient research, her expertise and love for the subject and her initiative in suggesting contributions to certain aspects of the book turned what initially seemed like a very complicated subject into an enjoyably readable manuscript. She succeeded in doing so within a short space of time, and continued to be cheerful, not once complaining despite all the difficulties that I caused her. To her too, I owe a debt I can never repay.

To those sources in the book who gave me invaluable information and explanations, but who did not want to be named for security reasons or because of their sensitive positions in the military, intelligence or even political levels, I also extend my gratitude. Only they know who they are.

To Terry Anderson, who first hired and gave me my first taste of journalism, and to his wife Madeleine, for welcoming me in their home in New York as well as helping put me in touch with some of the sources in this book and for sharing their invaluable knowledge and insight, I owe special thanks. Equally I thank Terry Waite for sharing his individual insights.

My thanks also extend to John Fullerton of Reuters for his help now and during my years with the company and to all the other Reuters colleagues who did not want to be named, for so generously and willingly putting their knowledge at my disposal during the course of *Hezbollah*. Samir Sabbah of Reuters television has my full appreciation for all the time and knowledge he shared with me a I pasted together some of the important events in this book.

To all the above and those unnamed I say if this book happened it is because of your help. If it is good it is because of all your contribution. If it is not I solely bear the responsibility.

Introduction

Every evening, four-year-old Mohammed watches the same video. He puts the cassette on by himself and calls his baby sister to join him. It is a short film, primitively made, which lasts no more than five minutes. There is a row of buildings in a bleak landscape and then, suddenly, an explosion. 'There's my daddy,' says Mohammed.

Mohammed's father, Salah Ghandour, rammed a car packed with 450 kilograms of explosives into an Israeli convoy, in South Lebanon, on 25 May 1995. He blew himself to pieces and killed twelve Israeli soldiers. Hezbollah filmed the event, just as they record all their major operations, and distributed the video to all the media outlets in the country. The next day, most of the television stations showed it on the evening news.

The Lebanese government hailed Salah as a hero; the Israeli government denounced him as a terrorist and launched an investigation into its army's security measures in South Lebanon. Salah's twenty-three-year-old wife, Maha, spoke of her pride.

From her modest home in Beirut, Maha, a small, pretty woman, recalled the last few days of her husband's life. Like most Shiites who live in the capital, Maha and her family settled in the southern suburbs of the city. Much of the land was once owned by the Christian and Sunni middle class, but these days the neighbourhood is known as the 'Belt of Misery': 800,000 people, mainly poor Shiite peasants and farmers, are crammed into 28 square kilometres. They are refugees from South

1

Lebanon who fled in the wake of Israel's invasions and subsequent occupation.

There are no road maps of the area and no visible street signs. The residents have named many of the streets themselves; some commemorate martyrs like Salah. The structures here defy all laws of architectural principle and the concept of planning is totally absent. New storeys are always being added to unfinished buildings to house yet another relation who has fled to Beirut. Blocks of flats up to eight storeys high, one side collapsed like a deck of cards, are still home for the desperate.

It is an endless maze of alleyways and winding lanes, cluttered with mounds of smouldering garbage, whose smoke mingles with the aroma of roasted chicken and charcoal-grilled skewers of *lahem mishwi*, lamb kebabs. Above the streets hangs a great web of cables, strung like spaghetti from pole to pole and building to building, forming the neighbourhood's makeshift power supply. Some residents hook up to private generators; others plug into the national electricity source, illegally.

Murals and giant posters of Khomeini, Khameini and Hezbollah's martyrs adorn the neighbourhood. Black flags of mourning and the green and yellow flags of Islam and Hezbollah flutter from almost every street corner and balcony. Banners denouncing Israel and pledging to reclaim al-Quds, Jerusalem, are a common sight.

It was here that Maha met Salah in 1989. They fell in love and he asked for her hand in marriage. Theirs would not be a long engagement. Salah was an active member of the Islamic Resistance and had to spend much time in the South, planning or taking part in the steady flow of attacks against his enemy, Israel.

Maha was never in doubt about the destiny her husband had embraced:

Two weeks before his martyrdom I had a feeling that this would be my last year with him. It was an instinct I had. He had always told me to be prepared for receiving news of his martyrdom. That last week before he infiltrated into the security zone in the South, where he carried out the attack, I conveyed to him my fear and worries. I said, 'My feelings tell me I won't be seeing you again.'

Salah then looked at me and said, 'Your feelings are in the right place.' When I asked him why, he confided in me that he would be carrying out a martyr's attack. I could not help saying, 'Please don't leave us, what about Zeinab, our four-month-old daughter?' Salah then said, 'I never expected you to say this to me. You have always known that this would be my fate.' So I closed the subject.

Two days before his departure Salah told me that if he did not get the go-ahead to carry out the attack he would go to Mecca to perform the pilgrimage. We left the South where we had been staying for the last couple of months and where he was obviously planning and studying the details and area of the forthcoming attack and drove back to Beirut. On the way back, Salah stopped and produced a video-camera which he used to film the kids and himself. He told me, 'Don't worry, I shall put my last will on film for you.'

We arrived in Beirut and carried on with our lives, but there was not much time left. Two days later as I bade him farewell, unaware that the time had arrived, Salah looked at me tenderly and said, 'You know I will not be returning, so take care of yourself and my children.' I asked him, 'Aren't you going on the *Hajj*, the pilgrimage?' His last words were, 'I don't think I will make this pilgrimage,' and he left.

I knew that this was the only way for him. Even if I had tried to stop him I would not have succeeded. It was the end. Salah had been dreaming of this for a long time. He had been thinking about it and hoping to be allowed to carry out something like this for ages and he finally had the chance and opportunity; there was nothing more to say. He only had one goal at the end and that was to kill the largest number of the enemy.

'You see he had been pleading and asking the leadership to allow him the privilege of carrying out a mission of this type for the past three years. He believed he had to defend and fight for his land and countrymen and this was the best way for him to do so.

Maha steadfastly went through the story, while behind her on the wall a modestly framed portrait of Salah watched over her. The living room has become a shrine to the memory of her husband. Prints of the last photograph taken before his death decorate the walls and mantelpiece of the room.

It was indeed Salah's persistence that finally persuaded Hezbollah to choose him as the human detonator for the mission. Hezbollah revealed in a press conference that it had deliberated long and hard on whether Salah was the right candidate: they were reluctant to send a married man and father of three children on such a mission. But Salah had been determined and had argued that if Hezbollah limited such missions to bachelors, and disqualified candidates because of their marital status, they would in effect be discouraging many of their male followers, who believe in self-sacrifice, from carrying out a principle command of Islam, that of marriage and having children. It was an argument the Party of God could not win.

The day the news of the attack broke in Beirut, Maha was at her in-laws, two floors below her flat, chatting with Salah's brother:

I heard that an operation against the enemy had taken place. My brother-in-law, who was here at the time, said to me he was sure that the martyr was a young bachelor. I just looked at him and replied, 'No, he isn't. He is married with three children.' My brother-in-law looked at me, obviously surprised by the certainty of my response, and said, 'How do you know this?' I replied, 'Wait and see.'

I remember then going to my room to perform the afternoon prayers and, while I was doing so, officials from Hezbollah rang our doorbell and came in to break the news to us.

With a calmness uncommon amongst Shiite women, who usually break down into a fit of wailing and sobbing when recalling the death of their loved ones, Maha added:

> Although I was emotional at losing the dearest person in my life, I was filled with joy because he had died while carrying out such an operation. It is something for us to be proud of, something that makes us raise our heads high with pride, especially because he succeeded in alarming and startling Israel like he did.
>
> Really I don't feel like I have totally lost him, because I see him daily in my sleep. He comes to me then and tells me about the attack and details of his last moments and feelings before his martyrdom. You know, he always told me that if and when he died I would never feel lonely or suffer a sense of loss, because he would come to me in my dreams and, thank God, he does so nearly every night.
>
> Salah's act and those of the [Islamic] Resistance are what make Israel live in a state of panic and insecurity. My husband's attack only confirmed and proved to Israel that the Resistance can reach it wherever it may be and whenever it wants. It has made Israel realise that it cannot have the security and peace it thought it enjoyed as long as it continues to occupy our land. That in itself is of value and importance. You see, as long as Israel remains on our land there is no solution, but to resist with whatever means are available. The West also carries part of the blame, because if it did not support and back Israel then none of this might have happened.

If Hezbollah had hired a public relations official to propagate the reasoning of their war with Israel, they could not have chosen a better candidate than Maha. But this was not the case. She was simply a widow and mother, who had known and believed in her husband's chosen path from the day she agreed to marry him. Even though she had struggled with matters of the heart and mind, Maha had obviously come to terms with the fact that Salah's end was inevitable.

As her four-year-old son Mohammed tugged impatiently at his mother's *chador*, clearly aware that it was time for his lunch, she said, 'It is always sad when people lose their loved ones, but my husband died for his land and country.'

Few of us can ever fathom or even begin to understand the kind of conviction that will young men like Salah to seek such a horrifying end. It is easier for us to make sense of it by claiming that such men must be so poor, so desperate and so stupid that a few words promising them paradise and eternity is all it takes the mullahs to recruit them as human bombs. Yet to Hezbollah's adherents it is a means of war, deeply rooted in a sacred tradition of martyrdom.

Salah's last wish and testimony was that his son Mohammed should become a Resistance fighter. 'If my son wants to follow in his father's footsteps, then of course he can go,' said Maha. 'I can live with that and will fulfil Salah's wishes.' In the meantime, Mohammed will continue to replay the last few minutes of his father's life as his bedtime viewing.

1

The Shiites Strike Back

*Permission for warfare is given to those upon whom
war is made because they are oppressed and most
surely Allah is well able to assist them.*
                    Surat al-Hajj, 39, The Quran

At 11.05 a.m. on 6 June 1982, a group of Dutch UN soldiers
on guard duty at the Hamra bridge in South Lebanon saw
thirteen Israeli centurion tanks come roaring towards them. It
was the start of Israel's invasion. The six UN soldiers rolled the
huge stone blocks, which protected their checkpoints, on to the
road and successfully halted the vanguard of the advance.
Elsewhere, in the village of Sheeba, some Norwegian UN soldiers
attempted to cut off the road with two Jeeps, but the line of
tanks flattened them both in seconds. The UN soldiers' stalwart
efforts were hardly sufficient to deter several thousand tanks
and armoured vehicles from their purpose.

Israel's invasion was the brain-child of Ariel Sharon, the
minister of defence in Menachem Begin's government. Its stated
aim was to drive the Palestine Liberation Organisation (PLO)
from Israel's northern border. The PLO had been using Lebanon
as the base for its raids against Israel since the late sixties and
Israel's northern settlements bore the brunt of the attacks. The

Israelis called their campaign 'Operation Peace for Galilee', an Orwellian code-name which concealed Sharon's ambitious plan to destroy the PLO's power base and impose Israel's political will on the country. In seeking to fulfil his aim, Sharon traumatised Lebanon, shocked the Israeli public and succeeded in creating a new enemy to harry Israel's northern border: Hezbollah, the Party of God. Unlike Yasser Arafat's cause, which was based on secular principles, Hezbollah was founded in the name of Islam. Its members are Lebanese Shia Muslims, a group which has been pushed to the back of the queue for most of Lebanon's history. The extraordinary rise of Lebanon's Shia Muslims in the past thirty years from a state of neglect and dispossession to political influence and recognition is fundamental to Hezbollah's story.

Israel's invasion had followed fast on the heels of the most significant event in modern times for Shia Muslims: the Iranian Revolution of 1979. The triumphant return of Ayatollah Khomeini and his establishment of an Islamic Republic in Iran were an inspiration for the Shiites of other countries, who had long suffered discrimination under dominant Sunni Muslim rule. The split in Islam between Sunni and Shia dates back to the early days of the religion. At the death of Mohammed, the Sunnis took power, but the Shiites claimed to be the true heirs of the Prophet. Their history is a curious combination of revolutionary spirit and political withdrawal: their first leaders died as martyrs fighting for their inheritance but later, in order to survive in a hostile environment, the Shiites developed the theological principle of *taqiyya*, religious dissimulation, which allowed them to conceal their religion. In Iraq, where the Shiites form the majority, they were ruthlessly crushed by Saddam Hussein during the seventies and eighties, as well as in the wake of the Gulf War. In Lebanon, where the Shiites were concentrated in the Bekaa Valley and the South, they were a backward, rural community. By the sixties, they had become the largest sect in the country, but while the rest of Lebanon flourished economically and Beirut won fame as a cosmopolitan capital, the Shiites remained locked in a time warp, the underdogs of the population.

The Shiites are one of eighteen different religious confessions in Lebanon, which include Sunni Muslims, Christian Maronites, Greek Orthodox and Druze Muslims. Like the Shiites, the Druze and Maronites are both minority sects within their respective religions. The Maronites were persecuted by the Byzantines for not conforming to Orthodox Christianity; the Druze are an offshoot of the Ismaili sect of Shia Islam. Under the Ottoman Empire, the area of Mount Lebanon had been an autonomous region dominated by the Christian Maronites. After the First World War, the Maronites put in a bid to expand their territory. They were fortunate to have the ear of the French, who had won the mandate for Syria and Lebanon. France had been the Maronites' historical protector since it had come to their aid when fighting had broken out in 1860 between the Christians and the Druze. Again, in 1920, France proved itself the Maronites' champion: it expanded the boundaries of Lebanon to include the South, the Bekaa Valley and part of the coastal plain, which had all belonged to Syria. The new areas contained a large population of Sunni and Shia Muslims. The Sunni Muslims considered themselves Syrians and did not wish to be part of Lebanon. Shrewdly, the Maronites courted the Shia Muslims, who had long lived in a backwater of the Ottoman Empire in the South of the country, and persuaded them to back their cause. They were convinced, correctly, that the Shiites would not wish to be part of Sunni-dominant Syria.* It also served the interests of the French to separate the Shiites from the Sunnis in order to thwart the Muslim opposition. Ironically, thanks to their actions, the Shiites emerged as a distinct group in Lebanon for the first time. In 1926, France permitted the Shiites to establish their own religious courts and to practise their religion freely. Under the Ottomans, the Shiites had been forced to celebrate their most sacred religious festival, Ashura, in secret.**

---

* See *An Introduction to Shi'i Islam*, Moojan Momen, p. 265
** See 'The Shi'is and the Lebanese State', Joseph Olmert, in *Shi'ism, Resistance and Revolution*, pp. 191–2

France's decision to expand the territory of Lebanon was to have grave repercussions. Its protégés, the Christian Maronites, emerged as the dominant force in the new state. Power was divided between the confessions: the president was to be a Christian Maronite, the prime minister a Sunni Muslim and the speaker a Shia Muslim. The ratio of Christian deputies to Muslims was fixed at 6:5 to reflect the supposed demographic predominance of the Christians. The proportional distribution of power, known as the National Pact, was based on the National Census of 1932, in which the Christians formed a 54 per cent majority. Even at the time, suspicion was cast on its validity and the Christians refused to allow another census. The arrangement guaranteed the Sunnis and Christians the leading political and military positions and the top civil service posts. The political system was further complicated by the domination of clans, led by godfather figures such as Pierre Gemayel, who founded the Christian Maronite Phalangist party in 1936. The pro-Western orientation of the Christians ultimately came into conflict with the pan-Arab ideology of the Muslims and civil war erupted in 1958. President Chamoun had attempted to fix the elections and the Muslim and Druze population rose in revolt against the Christians. Chamoun turned to the US for help under the Eisenhower Doctrine, which promised US military and economic assistance to Middle East states which were threatened by international communism. In those early days of emerging Cold War alliances, it was not too difficult for Chamoun to equate Egyptian President Nasser's pan-Arab socialism with communism, particularly since the Soviets had begun supplying Egypt with arms in 1955. The US Marines intervened in the fighting and order was restored with the election of Fouad Chehab, the leader of Lebanon's army, as president.

The Shiites, meanwhile, continued to trail behind the rest of the country. The government neglected them and the Shiites' own feudal, landowning leaders were more interested in their personal pursuit of power than the welfare of their community. The Shiites not only lacked representation, but the basic

necessities of modern life, such as schools, hospitals, roads and running water. In comparison with the prospering areas of the Sunnis and Christians, their standard of living was medieval. When their political awakening finally came, it was not a Lebanese leader who brought the Shiites out of their obscurity, but an Iranian cleric. Musa Sadr was invited to be the religious leader of the Lebanese Shiites in 1959. He was born In Qom, Iran, and educated in Najaf, Iraq – two of the most important theological centres of Shia Islam. A charismatic figure, he was friends with Ayatollah Khomeini and President Assad of Syria. He even gave Assad political legitimacy when he came to power in 1971: as a member of the minority Alawi sect, Assad's authority to lead Syria was challenged. Sadr issued an edict, *fatwa*, that the Alawis were Shia and secured Assad's position.*
Within a decade of his arrival in Lebanon, Sadr became the Shiites' champion and succeeded in giving them a sense of communal identity. In 1967, he founded the Lebanese Shiite Islamic Higher Council, *Majlis al-Shii al-Aala*, of which he was appointed president. The institution allowed the Shiites to follow the example of other religious communities for the first time and gain official representation. Thanks to his efforts, the government set up the Council of the South to develop the neglected Shiite regions. In 1974, Sadr created the Movement of the Deprived, *Harakat al-Mahroumeen*, a socio-religious movement which forced the Lebanese government to grant the Shiites full recognition and immediately won success with the masses. It also provided Sadr with a platform from which to mobilise the Shiites and to pressure the government for reform. He formed close links with most parties and factions in Lebanon, but was deeply resented by the traditional Shiite leaders.

His time in Lebanon was a pivotal era. In 1968, the PLO began making raids into Israel from South Lebanon. A refugee population of Palestinians had lived in Lebanon since the

---

* See *The Vanished Imam*, Fouad Ajami, p. 174

establishment of the state of Israel in 1948. After the Six Day War in 1967, their numbers had swollen to 350,000. By the early seventies, Lebanon had become the PLO's only base, following its expulsion from Jordan. The Palestinians became deeply involved in the internal politics of Lebanon and the question of the PLO became the hottest issue on the agenda, further polarising the Lebanese community. The Christians feared that the presence of the Palestinians would disrupt the balance of power and provoke an Israeli invasion, but the Sunni Muslims supported the PLO. Radical and Arab nationalist parties, united in the National Movement of the Druze leader Kamal Jumblatt, demanded that the Palestinian commandos be given the freedom of movement to continue their operations from Lebanon. The Christian Maronites started to take matters into their own hands and their Phalangist militia began clashing with the Palestinian commandos.

As Israeli reprisals against the PLO intensified, Musa Sadr demanded protection for the Shiites in the South. The Shiites had begun to abandon their villages and move north to escape the war zone. Under the slogan 'Arms are an ornament to men', Sadr set up training camps so that the Shiites could learn to defend themselves. He established close ties with the Palestinian Resistance, but relations became tense as the Shiites' suffering increased: Sadr accused the Palestinians of creating anarchy in the South and relations between the Shiites and Palestinians deteriorated.

While Sadr demanded full political rights for the Shiites, Sunni Muslim and radical parties were also calling for equal representation and an end to the confessional system. Under the pressure of the Israeli attacks and the activities of the Palestinian commandos, the bitter grievances of Lebanon's confessional groups erupted and civil war broke out in 1975. Sadr's followers started their own militia, Amal, an acronym of *Afwaj al-Muqawama al-Lubnaniya*, Lebanese Resistance Detachments, which means 'hope'. The PLO provided supplies of arms and training. Kamal Jumblatt's radical National Movement lined up with the Palestinians against the Christians and would have defeated them if Syria had not come to their aid in 1976.

Syria's military intervention put an end to the first savage round of the civil war, which was to continue until 1990. Two years later, in March 1978, Israel launched 'Operation Litani' and invaded the country for the first time, following the PLO's attack on a bus inside Israel. The United Nations Resolution 425 called for Israel's withdrawal and for a UN force to be established in Lebanon. The United Nations Interim Force in Lebanon (UNIFIL) duly arrived, but Israel continued to control part of South Lebanon with the help of a proxy Christian militia, the South Lebanon Army (SLA). The militia was founded by a Greek Catholic army officer, Major Saad Haddad. The SLA still occupies the area which Israel has declared a 'security zone'; it constitutes 10 per cent of Lebanon's territory. Lebanon had become a backyard for the power struggle between Israel and Syria. Both countries sought to control Lebanon's political future and ultimately Syria was victorious: by the end of the civil war, Syria had established its hegemony over Lebanon. As Patrick Seale sums it up in his book *Asad*: ' "Greater Israel" went to war against "Greater Syria", both controversial concepts of uncertain definition but which certainly ruled each other out.'

Five months after Israel's invasion in 1978, Musa Sadr suddenly vanished on an official visit to Libya. He was last seen on 31 August just before he left his hotel in Tripoli for a meeting with the Libyan leader Muammar Gaddaffi. Nothing has been heard of him since and Libya has always claimed that he left the country and took a plane bound for Rome. Sadr's mysterious disappearance echoed the fate of a central figure in Shia theology: the Twelfth Imam, considered the rightful leader of Islam, who vanished in the ninth century. Shiites await his messianic return on the Day of Judgement. Already a saviour of the Lebanese Shiites, Sadr was elevated to the status of a martyr. The cataclysmic succession of events – civil war, Israel's 1978 invasion and Sadr's disappearance – was capped by the Iranian Revolution in 1979. The fate of Sadr and the triumph of Shia Islam under Khomeini, at a time of civil ferment in

Lebanon, was a potent political and theological cocktail for the Lebanese Shiites. Sadr had politicised the Lebanese Shiites and the Iranian revolution had catapulted Shia Islam on to the world stage. When Israel invaded for the second time in 1982, the force which ultimately emerged to resist its occupation was the child of these ground-breaking events.

Observers in South Lebanon describe the first few months after Israel's invasion in 1982 as a reasonably calm epoch in which little resistance was made against the Israelis. Amal, which had become the main force and representative of the Shiite population, had taken a moderate stance towards the newcomers and the southerners even felt a certain affinity with the invaders. They were grateful to the liberators for freeing them from the heavy-handed Palestinian reign which had terrorised their villages and population for many years. The PLO had become a state-within-a-state in South Lebanon and its officials were accused of rape, robbery and extortion. Prior to Israel's invasion, the forces of Amal and the PLO had begun to clash. Amal was headed by Nabih Berri, a lawyer who was born in the expatriate Shiite Lebanese community of Sierra Leone. He represented a new Shiite middle class and had succeeded in steering Amal away from its clerical origins towards a more secular platform.

The removal of the PLO from the South therefore appeared to be of mutual benefit to both the Israelis and the southern Lebanese. The weariness of the southerners from the years of suffering under their Palestinian masters was reflected in their show of welcome and gratitude to those who had freed them of their tormentors. Israel's accomplishment in ridding the South of the PLO guerrillas also brought with it material prosperity. Refugees returned home to their villages and the construction industry boomed as many visualised personal economic benefits from contact with Israel. Nearly all believed that the occupying forces would leave Lebanon after a few months. Ironically, Israel, Berri and the southern Shiites all wanted the same thing – an end to the Palestinian presence and guerrilla activity in South Lebanon, as well as security across both borders. Some Israeli officers suggested cultivating the Shiites as allies. If the proposal had been adopted, Israel could have secured the southerners as staunch guardians of the border. Instead, it turned them into one of its deadliest enemies.*

The change in attitude occurred slowly as the Shiites became aware that Israel was reluctant to leave Lebanon and appeared set on staying for a long period of time, despite having achieved its main objective of driving the Palestinians from the South. In early 1983, the Israel Defence Forces (IDF) issued the first draft of their plan to form the 'Organisation for a Unified South'. The scheme was in effect similar to one used in the West Bank whereby committees would be established in the main villages and towns to administer the area. In Lebanon, these committees were backed by a newly formed militia, recruited by the IDF from the residents. The force was called the 'National Guard' and was armed and trained by Israel. The purpose of this newly acquired organisation and militia was, first and foremost, to protect Israel. Its other duties included patrolling the South and preventing the return of the Palestinians and local opponents.

Determined to achieve their plan, the IDF began pressuring families to join the scheme and threatened reprisals against relatives whom they were holding in the infamous Ansar prison in South Lebanon. If the Lebanese signed up, they were guaranteed the quick release of their loved ones, and were promised social and financial assistance. Those villages who refused to join the scheme were told that a militia of outsiders would be imposed on them.** From this point onwards, in the view of most Shiites, those same Israelis who had earlier been seen as liberators were now regarded as occupiers. The alarm bells began to ring in a community which was renowned for its fierce sense of independence. Turning a blind eye to Israel's trespass on their land for the sake of the common aim of expelling the PLO was one thing, but becoming their surrogates

---

* See *Israel's Lebanon War*, Ze'ev Schiff and Ehud Ya'ari, pp. 239–40
** See *Sacred Rage*, Robin Wright, p. 221

and allowing Israeli domination of their lives and territory was totally unacceptable to the Shiites. They had, after all, fought their Muslim Palestinian brothers for those very reasons.

The mistrust awakened years of dormant fear that Israel had the same designs on South Lebanon as it had had on Jordan's West Bank and on Syria's Golan Heights, both seized during Israel's 1967 war against the Arab states. When the Zionists had presented their territorial demands at the Versailles peace conference in 1919, they originally asked for Israel's northern border to extend as far as the Litani River in Lebanon. France, keeping an eye on its own interests in Lebanon and Syria, rejected the Zionists' demands. The Zionists' chief concern was water: Chaim Weizmann, the president of the Zionist Organisation and later president of Israel, wrote to Lloyd George in 1919 about the vital importance of water for the future of Palestine and the need for the Litani River. At an international symposium on water held in Amman in 1984, Israel's invasion and occupation of Lebanon in 1982 was viewed in this historical perspective. Salah Halawani, former director-general of the Litani Water Authority, Lebanon, argued that while Israel justified its actions with the need for security, the pursuit of further water resources may also have been one of its objectives.[*] Some Lebanese officials have claimed that Israel is taking water from the Litani for its own purposes, although there in no hard evidence. Israel, however, has denied that it has any designs on the Litani.

Israel's political ambitions for Lebanon were rooted in its early history. In 1948, David Ben-Gurion, the founder of the state of Israel, spoke of creating a Christian state in Lebanon which would form an alliance with Israel. This was also Ariel Sharon's plan in 1982. The Israelis had been supporting the Maronites since 1976 and had provided them with arms even

---

[*] See Salah Halawani, 'Lebanese Development Project and Israel's Pursuit of the Litani and Hasbani Waters' in *Israel and Arab Water: An International Symposium, Amman 25 and 26 February 1984*, Eds. Abdel Majid Farid and Hussein Sirriyeh, London, 1985

before the civil war: the two parties' hatred of the PLO united them. It has been estimated that during Yitzhak Rabin's 1974-77 government, the Maronite militias received 150 million dollars from Israel. Support was increased under Menachem Begin's government which took office in 1977. The Christian militias had begun to clash with Syria: Syria's army in Lebanon had the status of a peacekeeping force, but the Maronites had come to see their presence as an occupation and turned to Israel for help. Begin appeared to identify the historical persecution of the Jews with the situation of the Christian Maronites. He referred to them as a persecuted minority and said that genocide must be averted. The Christian militias duly received training in Israel itself.★

Although the Shiites had suffered problems from the presence of the Palestinians in South Lebanon, they had never stopped sympathising with their plight. Everyone grew up learning about the 'cause', as it was known in the Arab world. Children heard about it as frequently as their bedtime stories and social events often turned into all-night debates on the subject. Many Shiites had joined the PLO's rank and file and participated in the earlier resistance against the Israelis. Most had also received their first taste of military training from the Palestinian experts who ran scores of military camps in Lebanon.

If the Shiites had learnt anything from the Palestinian experience, it was that fighting was the only way to prevent Israel or anyone else from taking their land. Everyone remembered how the Palestinians were driven out of their homeland when the state of Israel was founded. Most had heard how the refugees had believed their displacement would only be temporary, but it had lasted nearly four decades. Above all, the Palestinians' ordeal had taught the Lebanese not to abandon their villages and homes: confrontation and opposition were the only answer.

And so the resistance began. Initially it was a limited number

---

★ See *Israel's Lebanon War*, p. 18

of people engaging in small-scale protests, from boycotting the Israeli products which had poured into the Lebanese markets to attacking the homes of Lebanese collaborators and planting home-made roadside bombs against the Israeli patrols. From the summer of 1982 until early 1983, there was still no organisation directing this. It was a spontaneous movement which had been started by a minority of civilians, motivated by a sense of nationalism and determined to reject Israeli domination. They were soon inflicting one casualty per day among the Israeli lines.

When the occupiers began tightening the noose to ensure the submission of the Shiites, their stay in Lebanon became doomed. On 16 October 1983, the Israelis committed the final provocation. The Shiites were commemorating Ashura, the most sacred religious festival in Shia Islam, in the market town of Nabatiyeh. It is the traditional gathering centre for the annual procession in which thousands of people and villagers gather to mourn the slaying of their Imam Hussein in Karbala, Iraq, 1,300 years ago. The ceremony, attended by 50,000 southern Lebanese, was at its height when an Israeli military convoy drove into the town. The Israeli commander insisted on driving through the crowds, infuriating the Muslims who saw the act as an outrageous violation of their holy day. The Israelis, on the other hand, regarded the crowd's behaviour as a rebellion against their authority. When the convoy forced its way through the throng, people reacted furiously at the intrusion. Screaming abuse at the invaders, men, women and children threw stones at the soldiers, set fire to tyres and placed obstacles in front of the moving line of vehicles. In the mayhem that followed, an Israeli truck was overturned and set alight. The soldiers who were caught in the midst of the hysterical crowd called in reinforcements and started shooting. Two Shiites were killed and fifteen others injured.

Sheikh Mehdi Shamseddin, head of the Higher Shiite Council in Beirut, issued a *fatwa* immediately after the incident calling for 'civil resistance'. While it was not a demand for an all-out war against the Israelis, the moderate sheikh's cry was the first official call for confrontation and one which would soon be reiterated by others. Each time the Lebanese committed a successful attack against the Israelis, the occupying forces intensified their harsh campaign of repression against the residents. The reprisals rallied further support for the resistance and drove larger numbers of people to join its ranks. During the following year, the Israeli forces isolated South Lebanon from the rest of the country by limiting passage from Beirut to only one point of entry. It was a punishment and a desperate attempt to stop the infiltration of resistance fighters from Beirut and the Bekaa.

This measure had a grave impact on the economy of South Lebanon. The inhabitants' livelihood depended on the sale of their fruit and vegetable produce to the capital and northern areas of Lebanon. Most could only watch resentfully as their harvest rotted. Raids were carried out on villages suspected of harbouring resistance fighters. Anyone who was suspected of knowing or being related to someone within the resistance was arrested. It became common to see truckloads of prisoners, as hundreds of people were rounded up from their homes and detained without charge in Ansar prison.

The tiny core of activists began swelling into large numbers. An official resistance organisation was formed called the Lebanese National Resistance (LNR), dominated by Amal. Many of the resistance fighters were Amal members and officials, but the southerners applied a more radical and zealous approach to that of the leadership in Beirut, which at the time had little communication with the area and even less power over the residents. Pictures of Ayatollah Khomeini had begun appearing in some villages, including Maarakeh and Jibsheet, announcing the arrival of a movement which derived its influence from Iran and not from the secular path of Amal. Hezbollah was beginning to make its presence felt, but it was not until 1985 that the group announced its existence and the formation of its military wing, the Islamic Resistance, *al-Muqawama al-Islamiyah*. Until then, its fighters worked under the umbrella of the LNR.

The leaders of the nascent Islamic Resistance were clerics who had trodden the same path as Musa Sadr and studied in Najaf. A centre of theological learning, Najaf became the ideological hub of Shia Islamic thought in the sixties and seventies. It was there that Ayatollah Khomeini outlined the ideas which were to form the basis of Islamic government in Iran after the revolution of 1979.* Following Israel's invasion in 1982, Iran sent 1,500 Iranian Revolutionary Guards to Baalbeck in the Bekaa Valley.**

The radical Lebanese clerics now had the means to spread their own movement in Lebanon. The Bekaa became their base until they moved their headquarters to Beirut. The movement's adherents included Sayyed Hassan Nasrallah, who defected from Amal in which he was a politburo official and was to become the head of Hezbollah in 1992. He outlined Hezbollah's prime objectives in its first months of development in an interview with the newspaper *Al-Safir*:

> It was then a resistance movement and nothing else. We were a young movement wanting to resist a legendary army. This kind of direction required special kinds of men who would not worry about their homes being destroyed or about becoming hungry, thirsty, wounded or injured. The need was for men with the spirit of *jihad*, self-sacrifice and endless giving. The only name that befits a group born with such motivations and spirit, a group which has pledged itself to the Almighty God and which takes decisions of self-martyrdom when resisting its enemies, despite the huge military and fighting imbalance of power between them, is the name Hezbollah [Party of God].

Hezbollah's initial goal was to launch a revolt against the Israeli occupation, which would eventually grow to embrace the task of ridding Lebanon from the presence of Western forces and

---

* See *The Islamic Threat: Myth or Reality?*, John L. Esposito, p. 147
** Ibid.

influence. These aims would be conducted under the banner of Islam, the sponsorship of Iran and with the blessing of Syria. Both countries would mutually, if for different interests, nurture its growth.

Israel swiftly turned on the clerics who were leading the Resistance. Religious leaders were deported from the area and some were assassinated. The Israelis held them responsible for inciting the villagers with their fiery sermons and for turning the Husseiniyahs, the Shiites' social and religious centres, into resistance bases and safe houses. One such figure was Sheikh Ragheb Harb, shot in the head with three bullets as he walked home on 12 February 1984. He had been watching the evening news at his neighbour's house in Jibsheet.

Harb, remembered by most as the first instigator of resistance activity in South Lebanon, ranks high on Hezbollah's list of martyrs. His name means 'war' and he had become a powerful figure in the South, preaching vehemently against the occupation and calling on people to rise and resist. He was an instrumental link between the South and Hezbollah's base in the Bekaa, spreading Islamic doctrines and recruiting the southerners for military training and membership. He was well known as the brains behind the attacks made against Israeli soldiers and members of the National Guard. Under his supervision, Jibsheet was transformed from an insignificant, sleepy village into one of the fiercest Resistance strongholds facing the Israelis to this day. It is currently one of Hezbollah's bastions in South Lebanon and a regular target of Israeli aggression. Most of its residents are affiliated to Hezbollah's Islamic Resistance.

Harb is said to have received scores of death threats and warnings from the Israeli forces who arrested him on 18 March 1983. He had refused to give in to the warnings and instead turned his village mosque into the command headquarters of Resistance activities. He was continuously aware of the danger but strongly believed that he and his people had an obligation and a right to oppose the occupation. His townsfolk remember him saying frequently, 'Israel will kill me and shed my blood.' Shortly after news of his murder spread to the neighbouring towns, villagers began arriving at Jibsheet in a show of grief and anger and were confronted by the troops of the South Lebanon Army. Six people were injured and one was killed. The Israel Defence Forces immediately imposed a curfew on the area and sealed off all entrances to the village, but they could not deter the thousands of people who arrived in Jibsheet the following day to attend Harb's funeral.

The Resistance began to employ a deadly weapon: young Shiite fighters volunteered to drive vehicles packed with explosives into Israeli targets and went to their deaths as human bombs. No one had ever deployed such tactics before. After Harb was shot, Bilal Fahes, an active member in Amal and one of Nabih Berri's personal bodyguards, went on a lone mission. He was eighteen years old and had been raised in Jibsheet. He had been arrested and imprisoned by the IDF in the early stages of the invasion and was released after a few days. On 6 June 1984, Bilal was seen sitting in a white Mercedes car by the lemon groves on the Zahrani–Tyre coastal road, awaiting the arrival of an expected Israeli convoy. He could be heard whistling. As the convoy came along the Zahrani–Tyre coastal road, Bilal thrust his car into the target detonating 150 kilograms of explosives. The force of the blast threw a huge armoured personnel carrier twenty yards across the road and into the wall of the orchard. Israel reported nine soldiers injured.

As newly trained fighters infiltrated the South from Beirut and the Bekaa, the circle of violence rapidly increased between the Israelis and the Lebanese. By mid-1984, seven villages, including Jibsheet and Maarakeh, had become known as the 'arc of resistance': Israeli soldiers dared enter them only during daytime with massive back-up. Khalil Jarradi, a local theology teacher, led the operations from the Husseiniyah of his village, Maarakeh. Hundreds of men, some as young as thirteen or as old as sixty, were arrested and detained from these villages and consistently asked about Jarradi's habits, hideouts and companions. Jarradi himself had escaped detention several times and enjoyed boasting how, on one occasion, soldiers had come looking for him in one of the Husseiniyahs in which he happened to be sitting and reading. One soldier apparently stood in front of him, but failed to see Jarradi whose face was concealed behind the Quran.*

Jarradi frequently challenged Israel's presence, boasted of his participation in attacks and dared the soldiers to find him. In an interview with the newspaper *Al-Safir* Jarradi said:

> We challenge the Israelis to come into Maarakeh or one of the seven villages in a small unit without four thousand soldiers and helicopters. We have a firm belief in our land. It is rightfully ours and we have the right to defend and liberate it from the occupiers. The Resistance is not led by commanders, it is directed by the tenets of Islam.

When asked what had contributed to the transformation of his hometown Maarakeh into a symbol of resistance Jarradi answered: 'It is faith. No one might believe us, but it emanates from our faith – that wondrous weapon, which no armaments in the world can destroy, united our town's residents, despite the fact that they had belonged to different political parties and affiliations before the invasion.'

A few days after he spoke to the newspaper, Israel launched a massive dawn raid on the village of Maarakeh followed by similar incursions in other villages in South Lebanon. About 800 soldiers, backed by dozens of armoured personnel carriers, five tanks, thirty trucks, two bulldozers and given cover by low-flying helicopters, piled into the village. United Nations witnesses confirmed reports that the soldiers went into the Husseiniyahs and tore up copies of the Quran which were later found with boot marks on their pages; police dogs, deemed impure and unclean in Islam, were also brought inside the Islamic centres. Relief agency workers reported that the Israelis mixed sacks of different grains together, rendering them unusable, as well as combining kerosene with cooking oil.**

---

* See *Sacred Rage*, Robin Wright, p. 226
** Ibid. p. 230

They left with seventeen men, but without Jarradi. On 4 March 1985, a day and a half after the raid, a bomb planted directly under the Husseiniyah's back room in Maarakeh, which was the main meeting place for Resistance leaders and co-ordinators, exploded. The blast killed twelve people and injured thirty-four. Khalil Jarradi, who had returned to his village after the raid and was chairing the meeting, was found dead under the rubble of his office. The gallant reputation which the twenty-five-year-old fighter had gained during his lifetime was sanctified after his death. Jarradi became a symbol of heroism and for thousands of Shiites he became the definition of resistance itself.

The earlier modest call for a 'civil resistance' against the occupiers was now transformed into a call for an all-out *jihad* against the Israelis. The holy war was finally declared. The spontaneous resistance against an occupation had become a lethal crusade with wider dimensions.

Six days after Jarradi's murder, on 10 March 1985, a young man drove a red pick-up Chevrolet, containing 900 kilograms of explosives, into a military Israeli convoy just two miles away from Israel's settlement Metullah, north of Galilee. The convoy was taking soldiers back from leave in Israel to their military bases in Lebanon. The bomber, who was identified only by his alias 'Abu Zeinab', and believed to be from Israel's 'security zone', killed twelve soldiers and wounded fourteen others. The fact that the attack took place so close to Israel's northern settlements and border with Lebanon unnerved Israel. It confirmed Israel's worst fear – that the spirit of the Resistance had extended to the 'security zone', where Israel had believed itself to be safe and in the least danger from its Shiite foes. According to Israeli newspapers, the surviving soldiers of the attack believed the death toll to be higher than the official number. Hezbollah's Islamic Resistance had begun to operate out in the open and claimed responsibility for the attack. Another new organisation, Islamic Jihad, also claimed responsibility.

The anniversary of Jarradi's death is commemorated every year in the village of Maarakeh by thousands of Shiites and religious leaders. His old speeches, now on tape, are played on the mosques' loudspeakers and continuously listened to by young fighters keen to follow in his footsteps. Even southern children, when asked who their hero is, will immediately say, 'Jarradi, of course.'

Israel denied accusations that it was behind his murder, contrary to the belief of the observers and inhabitants in the South. For years, the Israeli military and intelligence have believed that they could curb the Islamic Resistance in the South by eliminating its leaders. Furthermore, the Israeli government has worked on the assumption that penalising the population for the attacks of the Resistance would eventually provoke the villagers' wrath against the Muslim fighters. In both cases, Israel's strategy backfired. The leaders it eliminated became the idols of the people who, in turn, became further radicalised. After each Israeli reprisal, their grief, anger and frustration strengthened their determination to continue the fight.

The Israeli invasion in June 1982 had penetrated as far as Lebanon's capital and submitted West Beirut to a devastating siege. The PLO was evacuated in August under the supervision of multinational forces and in 1983 Israel had begun its retreat through Lebanon and withdrawn to the Awali River, north of Sidon. The Israel Defence Forces came under increasing attack from the Shiite Resistance fighters, who played a significant role in forcing Israel's retreat. In February 1985, Israel concluded the first stage of its withdrawal to the Litani River and declared an 'Iron Fist' policy over the 900-square-mile area it still controlled.

The region comprised the Shiites' heartland which boasts the longest history of military resistance. The area, a collection of hilltop villages just outside Tyre, known as Jabal Amel, was the cradle of Lebanon's Shiites. It had historical links with Iran through family ties and, most importantly, through religion. It was here that Amal's founder, Musa Sadr, built a religious school which had hosted some of the men who would be key players in the Iranian Revolution. They included Mustapha Chamran, who had worked closely with Amal before the Shah's overthrow. He had also received military training in the Palestinian camps of Lebanon. On his return to the Islamic Republic after the Revolution he served as chairman of the Higher Defence Council and minister of defence during which time he co-founded the Iranian Revolutionary Guards. Sadr's school had also taught some of the men who would later found Hezbollah and lead the revolt in South Lebanon. From this area came many of the Shiite clerics who had travelled for further religious studies to the holy cities of Qom, Iran, and Najaf, Iraq, where they had established good relations with many of the Iranian clerics who later became government officials in the Islamic Republic.

Israel's withdrawal coincided with the public debut of Hezbollah and the first anniversary of Harb's murder. The day after the Israelis pulled out from Sidon, truckloads of Hezbollah members began arriving in the area. Some came to parade and openly declare their presence and others to find ways of infiltrating the occupied area beyond the Litani River. The Israel Defence Forces' new regulations banned motorists from driving their cars alone, in an attempt to prevent human bomb attacks. Motorcycles were also forbidden. Cars parked on roadsides were blown up and an indefinite curfew was imposed from sunset to sunrise. 'Free-fire zones' were also established which in effect gave the Israeli soldiers and patrols *carte blanche* to shoot at anyone and anything that moved in the area. To emphasise their seriousness, the Israeli forces launched mass raids on most villages, rounding up hundreds, killing some in the process, and deporting many from the area. Orange and lemon groves along the coastal road were destroyed and then scorched. Many families who refused to co-operate with the Israel Defence Forces had to suffer the destruction of their homes.

Western news agencies and journalists in Beirut received telexes from the Israel Defence Forces warning them against visiting the region from the Lebanese side. Those wishing to do so had to apply to the military which would escort them from the Israeli border. Journalists caught without IDF approval would be arrested. Nearly all those covering the war from Beirut refused to comply, deciding to take the risk and travel South, rather than undergo Israeli censorship and face limitations of access. Some journalists were detained or arrested, others were threatened and even deported. A local crew, working for CBS, the American television network, was shelled by an Israeli Merkava tank. The Israelis claimed that they mistook them for the Resistance and their camera for a rocket launcher, despite the huge sign plastered on top of the vehicle indicating that they were journalists. Two members of the crew were instantly killed, one cut in half by the blast. The driver was crippled for life.

The 'Iron Fist' policy that was launched in the South resonated in Beirut and provoked moderate politicians to alter their stance. Even Nabih Berri, the leader of Amal, who until then had behaved with restraint and had adopted a less militant attitude towards the occupation, finally lost his composure. He vowed angrily that Israeli villages across the border would be targeted every time a Lebanese town was attacked. Berri's outrage reflected the change of mood amongst the once moderate Shiites. The original mission of the Shiites to rid Lebanon of the Israelis had entered a new phase.

On 6 June 1985, the third anniversary of its invasion, Israel fulfilled its last stage of withdrawal and retreated to the 'security zone'. Scores of villages remained under occupation in the zone and have been in that predicament since 1978. The Lebanese National Resistance took a slight respite after that phase of withdrawal and Amal's policy in South Lebanon, largely inspired by its local leaders, became more pragmatic in its outlook. It took the line that if the South was not used as a fountainhead for attacks against the Israeli forces then its residents would not be subjected to reprisals. Hezbollah's Islamic Resistance, however, became more visible as it increased its attacks.

The militant group had completed the final leg of its journey to South Lebanon. From the Bekaa Valley, where it first came into being, it had moved to Beirut where it based its central headquarters. It now established the name of the Islamic Resistance as the force responsible for fighting Israel and its surrogates, the South Lebanon Army. Timur Goksel, UNIFIL's spokesman since 1978, recalled the Islamic Resistance's methods. 'They [Hezbollah] were very amateur, foolhardy in many ways, but very brave. They just walked into the line of fire and were cut down very badly. It was just like watching the Iranian assaults against Iraq.'

On 17 February 1986, the Islamic Resistance dealt a severe military blow against Israel when a group of its combatants captured two Israeli soldiers near the town of Qounin. The two infantrymen, Yossi Fink and Rahamin Alshiekh, were captured while on patrol. The following day, Beirut Radio reported that both had been seriously wounded and were receiving treatment. Shortly after that a picture released to local newspapers showed one of the soldiers lying on a bed with a drip. The second infantryman was also seen stretched on a camp bed, but he appeared motionless. The soldiers are thought to have died of their injuries.

Israel has continued to denounce the capture of its soldiers and has made attempts to include them in negotiations for the release of Lebanon's foreign hostages. Hezbollah, however, has insisted that the soldiers were not taken as hostages, but were captured as prisoners of war while performing an act of aggression in occupied territory. It has said it would release the bodies of the two men in exchange for Lebanese prisoners who are being held without trial in the notorious Khiam prison in South Lebanon and in Israel. The official Israeli view on this has been that those detained in its prisons are not hostages, but terrorists, who should be treated accordingly.

Israel has not ceased pressing for information on another missing soldier, the navigator Ron Arad. On 16 October 1986, Amal militiamen shot down an Israeli warplane just after it had carried out an air raid on Lebanon. The pilot managed to eject and was later rescued by an Israeli helicopter, but his air force navigator, Ron Arad, was captured by the group's fighters patrolling the area. Arad was held by Amal's head of security, Mustapha al-Dirani, also known as Abu Ali Dirani. He was expelled from the party the following year because of his affiliations with Iran and his differences with Amal's secular line.

In retaliation, Dirani, who was personally responsible for Arad, took the prisoner with him and later started the splinter group Believers Resistance Front. Dirani is affiliated to the Party of God, but has maintained autonomy through his direct links with Iran. Israel has relentlessly accused Hezbollah of holding Arad. The Party of God has openly admitted its possession of the bodies of the two dead infantrymen, but has vehemently denied holding the navigator. Reports on his possible location periodically appear in the press, but Arad's whereabouts have remained a mystery. Israel has not abandoned its quest and Arad has almost become a symbol of its military loss in Lebanon.

By mid-1986, the Islamic Resistance realised its war against Israel was not going too successfully when it suffered twenty-four fatalities in one attack. The group took a respite to reassess their situation. In addition to its military losses, Hezbollah had also begun to alienate itself from the people whose support it needed most: the residents of South Lebanon. It was not that the southerners were averse to the concept of resistance itself: they had, after all, grown to live with it and had participated in its activities. The problem was that they were angered at having to bear the brunt of the reprisals, as well as taking huge losses in operations that were more often than not doomed. They were also outraged by the extreme transformation which was taking place in the South as it came under the influence of Hezbollah's religious militancy.

Shortly after its arrival in the South, the group banned the sale of alcohol in shops and restaurants and prohibited parties, dancing and loud music. They also closed down coffee shops. The old men who used to frequent the coffee shops in the afternoons and early evenings were deprived of their simple pastime of playing cards and backgammon. A strict code of Islamic behaviour was imposed on the towns and villages bringing with it some extreme interpretations of what was considered permissible behaviour. Although there were those who were happy to abide by the new regulations and restrictions, many others rejected them.

Hezbollah's hard-line restrictions only served to isolate the area and further undermine the already battered economy. Popular weekend retreats on the coast became ghost towns. The Lebanese boycotted the restaurants and went in search of places without restrictions, where alcohol could be served without fear of harassment from the Islamic militants. Mixed bathing was banned and women were forbidden to wear swimming costumes. Tyre, which used to pride itself on having one of the best stretches of beach in Lebanon, spent many summer months empty of clients. Those who wanted to enjoy Lebanon's long season of sunshine simply stopped going south, while the residents of southern villages travelled north to the beaches around Sidon and Beirut.

South Lebanon was suffocating. The region had become a war-like state severed from the rest of the country. The Islamic Resistance carried out seven or eight assaults a day against the occupying force and the southerners lived under the constant threat of Israeli reprisals. Timur Goksel summarised Hezbollah's attitude and mistakes in those days:

> Until 1988, they were paranoid, very unkind to foreigners, too suspicious and secretive, impossible to talk to and communicate with and extremely, unrealistically, fundamentalist. This was as far as the UN was concerned. When they tried to take over people's lives, Hezbollah lost their support. They disregarded the one thing that the Lebanese, and in particular the southerners, are renowned for – the high level of importance they place on their individuality.

It was a measure of their frustration that Hezbollah had accused the UN of deliberately obstructing the Islamic Resistance in an attempt to protect the security of Israel. It had also charged them with being accessories to a conspiracy against it and threatened to launch attacks against their troops in the South.

The group which had so cleverly won the support of the population in the Bekaa and Beirut was failing in the one place that mattered most to them: South Lebanon. While reassessing the situation, the Islamic Resistance noticeably decreased its operations.

By the late Eighties, Hezbollah was facing opposition on another front which posed a serious threat to its future. Hezbollah's rapid growth had brought the group into conflict with Amal and its sponsor Syria. Assad's involvement with the Shiites of Lebanon dated back to his friendship with Musa Sadr and, as a Shiite himself, he identified with their cause.* Sadr's movement, Amal, had become a Syrian protégé and Assad was not prepared to let his ally lose ground to the new, Iranian-backed movement of Hezbollah. Syria had permitted Iran to send the Iranian Revolutionary Guards to Baalbeck in 1982 and it had not stood in the way of the Iranian embassy in Damascus when it became extensively involved in founding Hezbollah.

At the time, Syria was isolated: it had taken a severe military battering following Israel's invasion of Lebanon and had been side-lined while America became a mediator in the civil war. Syria therefore needed Iran's support: the Islamic Republic sent 500 volunteers to fight alongside Syrian troops in the Bekaa Valley.** However, when the Iranian-Hezbollah strength in Lebanon looked likely to threaten Syria's ally, Amal, Assad faced a crisis. Iran was pleased at its initial success in exporting its revolution and sought to further its enterprise. Its aim was to promote Hezbollah so that it became the sole Shiite Islamic force in the country, as a prelude to Iran's final phase of replacing the Lebanese political system with an Islamic order. Syria, meanwhile, was set on continuing its traditional role of playing the different Lebanese political parties off against each other and keeping Lebanon within its orbit. The local rivalry which had developed between Amal and Hezbollah therefore became

---

* See *Asad*, Patrick Seale, p. 351f
** Ibid., pp. 394–5

a reflection of a power struggle between Tehran and Damascus for domination in Lebanon.

In February 1987, Syrian troops in West Beirut clashed directly with Hezbollah fighters and killed more than twenty of the Muslim militiamen, who had refused to allow them on their turf. It was the first confrontation between the two and a clear message from the Syrian government that it would not hesitate to use force to impose its will and curtail Hezbollah's political aspirations in Lebanon. Hezbollah's call for an Islamic state in Lebanon, dictated by the Iranians, posed a serious threat to the future and stability of Assad's Alawite Syrian regime, the first sectarian minority to rule the country's Sunni majority. If the Shiite extremists in Lebanon were successful they could trigger an uprising among Sunni fundamentalists in Lebanon and Syria. If aided by the dominant Sunni sect of the Middle East, such a movement could ultimately challenge Assad's legitimacy as the power base of the Syrian Baath Party.

Amal and Hezbollah's differences had first come into the open when Israel withdrew its troops from most of the South and retreated to the 'security zone' in June 1985. Amal's more moderate policy differed sharply from Hezbollah's determination to fight the occupation under the banners of Islam and Iran until all Lebanese soil was liberated. The two factions had also begun to clash over another issue that year. Palestinian guerrillas had begun returning to the refugee camps in Lebanon, and Amal was determined not to allow them to regain their hold on the country. With Syria's blessing, Amal began to attack the camps. Hezbollah strongly objected to Amal's actions and came to the aid of the Palestinians. The fuse was finally lit between Hezbollah and Amal in South Lebanon on 17 February 1988, with the kidnap of the American Lieutenant-Colonel William Richard Higgins just outside the coastal town of Tyre. Higgins, commander of the Lebanon unit of the United Nations Truce Supervisory Organisation (UNTSO), was driving back to Naqoura, UNIFIL'S headquarters, having conducted a routine meeting with Amal officials in Tyre. A group of UNTSO officers was travelling ahead of Higgins's Jeep Wagoneer, which was marked as a UN vehicle. Six kilometres south of Tyre, in Ras el-Ain, the leading officers noticed that Higgins was no longer with them. They turned back only to discover his empty Jeep.

His abduction was obviously well planned and carried out in a matter of seconds with military precision. A long bend in the road had allowed the leading vehicle to lose sight of Higgins's Jeep for a short, but clearly critical, period. A vast search, the biggest ever conducted in Lebanon for any hostage, was mounted for Higgins. Higgins's UN status and US nationality ensured the participation of both the UN and Israel in the search. Amal's leadership ordered its militiamen to help, especially since its rival, Hezbollah, was assumed to be behind the kidnapping. Hundreds of Amal militiamen and UN troops sealed off a 300-square-mile area. They set up roadblocks, searched cars and trucks, and brought in police-trained German Shepherd dogs to help. Even UN helicopters were employed in the search. The main objective was to prevent Higgins from being smuggled out of the area to Hezbollah strongholds in Beirut or the Bekaa Valley.

Amal leaders in Tyre rounded up scores of Hezbollah followers and even raided and searched houses of the group's sympathisers. The move reflected the growing tension between the two rivals and triggered fears that an all-out war for control of the South was only a matter of time. Two days after Higgins's abduction, on 19 February, a statement issued by the Organisation of the Oppressed on Earth was delivered to a Western news agency in Beirut. The communiqué claimed responsibility for his abduction and was accompanied by a photocopy of Higgins's two identity cards to authenticate the group's claim. The statement accused Higgins of using his work with the UN as a 'cover for his dangerous espionage work with the CIA' and said it would put him on trial.

The group made three demands in return for Higgins's freedom: an Israeli withdrawal from South Lebanon, an end to American 'interference' in the Middle East, and freedom for all Lebanese and Palestinian prisoners held by Israel. The

Organisation of the Oppressed on Earth was one of a number of shadowy groups which had emerged during the eighties and which took foreigners hostage in a campaign against the West. It was part of a covert apparatus which had its own channels to Iran and was considered to be affiliated to Hezbollah.

On 22 February 1988, a seventy-second videotape of Higgins was issued by the kidnappers. Looking gloomy, unshaven and wearing the same dark green UN jumper in which he was abducted, he reiterated the kidnappers' demands. The tape was accompanied by a brief communiqué in which the group insisted that Amal terminate its search and threatened to carry on seizing 'suspect' Americans. In order to defuse the mounting tension with Hezbollah, Amal declared that it would not use military means to secure the release of Higgins, although it insisted that its decision was motivated out of concern for the safety of the hostage.

War finally erupted between Hezbollah and Amal in May 1988. It became known as the 'War for Supremacy of South Lebanon'. Amal, with military support from Syria, instigated the war on the basis that it was foiling Hezbollah's attempts to take over its territory in South Lebanon and transform the area into an Islamic state. Hezbollah fighters were often caught sandwiched between Amal militiamen on the one side and Israeli fire on the other. The Party of God was expelled from the South and its fighters banned from carrying out attacks against Israeli or South Lebanon Army targets. The battle spread to the southern suburbs of Beirut where Hezbollah defeated Amal. Only the intervention of Iran stopped the militant group from liquidating Amal altogether in its few remaining strongholds in Beirut.

The inter-Shiite fighting literally pitted brother against brother, splitting families whose sons belonged to each of the rival factions. In one particular incident, a father visited his two sons in hospital each having been injured by the other side. At the end of 1988, Hezbollah recuperated from its earlier defeat and launched an offensive against Amal in South Lebanon.

Syria ultimately played a trump card: Damascus gave signals

that it was entertaining a possible move towards *rapprochement* with Iraq, and Iran finally conceded to Syria's dominance in Lebanon and accepted the reality of its own limited leverage in the country. The conflict was resolved in an Iranian-brokered agreement in January 1989, signed in Syria under the auspices of President Assad and known as the Damascus Agreement. The pact allowed Hezbollah an initially limited return to the South and stipulated the formation of a joint Amal–Hezbollah military operations room. In return for the resumption of Hezbollah operations in the South, Tehran paved the way for the deployment of Syrian troops in Hezbollah's bastion, the southern suburbs.

Syria was perfectly capable of wiping out Hezbollah as a military force. Hezbollah admits that it was well aware of Syria's strength, but it also knew that Damascus had no wish to ruin its relationship with Tehran. Syria's alliance with Iran had been a shrewd political move in the wake of Egypt's peace treaty with Israel at Camp David and Assad was aware that the emergence of Hezbollah formed an effective force against Israel and the United States. Even when Damascus laid its heavy hand on the group, it continued to tolerate and encourage its anti-Israeli activities in South Lebanon.

The Syrian-backed Amal war with Hezbollah was a strong demonstration of Assad's determination and power in Lebanon. The clashes also brought home to Hezbollah the fact that Damascus was the ultimate authority in Lebanon and that its survival and political continuity depended upon Syria's approval. If Hezbollah had harboured any notions of replacing Amal it was forced to realise that the secular movement was Syria's political arm in Lebanon.

The Damascus Agreement marked a watershed for Hezbollah. For the first time, the group had the chance to convince Assad, during a high-level meeting with the Syrian leader in Latakia, that its prime goal and mission was to fight the Israeli occupation. It assured both Syria and Amal's leadership that, contrary to their belief, it had no interest in forming Islamic cantons in the South and was not interested in taking over as the Shiites' political leader. With the ground-rules finally established, Hezbollah was allowed to continue its war of liberation with Israel.

It was Israel, however, which struck the next blow. On 28 July 1989, an airborne unit of Israeli commandos swooped on Jibsheet, Hezbollah bastion and home of the murdered Sheikh Harb. The commandos abducted Harb's replacement Sheikh Abdul Karim Obeid and two of his aides, a cousin, Ahmed Obeid, and Majid Fahes. A neighbour who tried to intervene was shot dead. In his mid-thirties, Obeid was Imam of the militant village. His name had previously been associated with the kidnap of Higgins. Israel also maintained that the clergyman had been involved in the capture of the two Israeli soldiers near Qounin.

Although international reaction was swift, it fell short of taking any real action against Israel. US President George Bush said that he could not condone the abduction and both the UN secretary-general and the British Foreign Office deplored it, asking Israel to free Obeid and his two aides.

Obeid's abduction sparked anger in Lebanon and both Hezbollah and Amal's leadership called for a one-day strike to be observed in protest at the kidnapping. The day after the incident, the Organisation of the Oppressed on Earth, which had seized Higgins a year earlier, issued a statement threatening to execute him if the Muslim clergyman was not freed. The threat, which was made on 30 July, gave a twenty-four-hour deadline which expired at 1200 GMT (1500 local time). None of the three Lebanese captives was released: Israel continued to insist that Obeid was behind major attacks against their country as well as being heavily involved in the kidnap of the American UN officer.

Nearly two hours after the deadline expired, an international news agency received a statement from the group claiming to have hanged Higgins. The communiqué was accompanied by a chilling video-tape showing him dangling from a makeshift scaffold. The tape provided no proof of his time of death and forensic tests and studies would later confirm the theory that

Higgins did not die of hanging, but possibly of torture. The hanging was merely staged for publicity purposes.

Twenty minutes after the deadline expired, the Israeli prime minister offered to exchange all the Shiite Muslim prisoners whom Israel was holding in exchange for the freedom of the three Israeli servicemen and foreign captives. Later that day, and in what appeared to be attempts by Israel to deflect criticism for its behaviour, Israel said Obeid had confirmed all the charges which it had made against him. But it refused to allow any visits to Obeid, including representatives of the International Committee of the Red Cross, so there has been no corroboration of their claims.

Hezbollah continued to deny its involvement in hostage-taking and issued a statement on 5 August in which it said that the seizure of Obeid had halted all possibilities of an exchange of prisoners with Israel. On 19 August the Islamic Resistance retaliated for Obeid's abduction with a human bomb attack against an Israeli military convoy killing five soldiers and several SLA militiamen.

Hezbollah ultimately emerged from the crises of the late eighties as a stronger force. Its military performance dramatically improved and helped the group to regain the respect of the population in South Lebanon.

'The real change came in 1991,' Timur Goksel recalled. 'First of all I think they mainly improved their field security. They had realised that they had allowed themselves in the past to become oversized, and if a guerrilla organisation is too big then it is easy to track. The military tactics used were of a professional calibre. They included intelligence and reconnaissance. Their attacks had all the elements and ingredients of military operations.'

By 1991, the Islamic Resistance was adopting bolder measures. It had begun to take the initiative and was no longer restricting its warfare to the old tactics of planting roadside bombs and booby traps. Its fighters were now launching raids and assaults against Israeli positions and strongholds in Lebanon as well as threatening the security of Israel's northern border whenever the lives of Lebanese civilians were endangered. It was also reducing the number of its fatalities, by securing the safe return of the guerrillas after their missions.

Timur Goksel attributes the improvement in the Islamic Resistance's performance to a change in the structure of command. Hezbollah gave the Islamic Resistance the status of an autonomous body, able to deal with the day-to-day attacks on Israeli targets without having to refer to the leadership in Beirut. This has allowed the Islamic Resistance a free hand in making military decisions based on the circumstances in South Lebanon, which they are in a better position to judge than their leaders in Beirut. The new body of command is known as the 'Rear Support Headquarters in South Lebanon'. Most attacks are planned by a military leadership which also includes local political figures. According to Timur Goksel, a few hundred expert guerrilla fighters form the core of the enterprise. The entire armed forces of the Islamic Resistance is estimated at 5,000. 'Since the changes in the military style, the Islamic Resistance is in full control over the initiative,' said Goksel. 'The trend lately has been in a gradual increase in the number of operations launched from South Lebanon. They are averaging at least three operations a day in some months and that is a lot. They are using every kind of attack in the book.'

Sheikh Nabil Qaouq, Hezbollah's main military leader in South Lebanon, claims that the Islamic Resistance is in some respects more advanced than the Israelis:

> We have acquired a level of technology which, for example, prevents even their state-of-the-art technology from locating and diffusing our roadside bombs. They cannot even block or interfere with our communication systems. There are various ways of blowing up roadside bombs, but there are certain occasions whereby we have to do so electronically from a distance, for security reasons. In the past we had problems because Israel sends in daily reconnaissance flights over the area before the movement

of their ground convoys. These flights used to cause us problems because they would instigate static interference that would automatically detonate the bombs, rendering our traps and missions inactive. So we have acquired certain kinds of bombs that cannot be jammed or detonated by the enemy's high-tech facilities. They are so unique and different to those available on the market that the Speaker of Parliament Nabih Berri asked us to give him some for his Amal fighters. We gave him ten pieces.

A tall, thin man, Qaouq is fair-skinned with a heavy black beard. He is not dressed in military fatigues, as one might expect, but in the turban and cloak of a cleric. He continues:

You see Hezbollah, on the military level, has taken massive steps forward from when it first started. When the invasion first took place we did not have the experts nor the experience that we do now. The Resistance today can boast of having specialised regiments each with its own particular weaponry. We now have an infantry, an engineering division, an artillery force, a general staff, a signals body and the financial backing required to carry on. In other words we have all the ingredients of a regular army. Of course this took a lot of time to arrive at and we benefited a lot from our experiences. The Resistance is on a different psychological level than it ever was before. A main factor which has played a vital role in our positive attitudes and performance is that we are strengthened by the people's support for us and their adoption of our cause. This is something very significant.

The Islamic Resistance's major operations have to be cleared by Hezbollah's leader Sayyed Hassan Nasrallah and the group's council. On these occasions, operators from the Bekaa and Beirut come south to organise the logistics. In Goksel's words:

If there is a major operation they do not announce it to

39

the other fighters in South Lebanon for their own security. They are very careful for fear of being found out. Usually, the first signals we get of a pending operation is when there is a sudden increase in the number of motorcycle drivers in South Lebanon. Big ones of the Yamaha type. These guys, with helmets, are not armed. They are dressed in civilian clothes and most of them don't even have beards [the common identifying religious feature of Hezbollah's adherents].

These motorcycle guys come into the area at very short notice before the actual attack is to take place, because they have already got the weapons in position. They come in with their own plan and gather their followers from the villages concerned. The local fighters until that moment don't even know about the attack, let alone where it is scheduled. Suddenly we hear the bangs and half an hour later, depending on the length of the operation, we see the motorcycles going away. Mission accomplished. These guys come from other areas and are the elite force.

This new tactic, however, caused resentment amongst the Islamic Resistance's fighters in South Lebanon, who felt they were being left out of the planning and decision-making of such operations. On several occasions, Goksel recalled, the locals' reactions on hearing of the elite force's attacks have created problems. 'The local youngsters are all dying to become like these men and so sometimes they launch an operation locally without telling their superiors. They would fire a couple of rocket-propelled grenades themselves and this has on some occasions nearly got the elite forces in trouble because it immediately attracted Israeli anti-fire which got them cut off when they were withdrawing.'

Other military experts in the area who have observed the group's progress over the years, and who spoke on condition they remain anonymous, attributed the changes in the Islamic Resistance's performance to its success in combining the art of guerrilla warfare with the tactics of a conventional war:

> The main characteristics of a guerrilla-type war are usually a fixed target, the light-calibre weapons used, the element of surprise, the limited duration of the attack and the small geographical area in which the scene of the attack usually takes place. In contrast, a classical war usually involves an open and defined army using heavy weapons over a large geographical area for as long as is required to achieve their goals.

> Hezbollah has reached a level where it is combining both strategies. They have taken the Israeli troops by surprise by no longer restricting their attacks to the front line, but by sometimes taking them to the depths of the 'security zone'. Having done so the group has not only laid the usual roadside bomb, but has initiated attacks against Israeli positions using heavy-calibre weapons ranging from artillery tank fire to surface-to-air missiles and heavy machine-gun fire. Furthermore they have succeeded in engaging in several hours of fighting in an area ranging between ten and fifteen kilometres, at the end of which they have successfully slipped out of the zone taking their heavy weapons with them without being caught. This is a big change in the Resistance's performance.

> In the past a few fighters would have placed a roadside bomb and then withdrawn. These days they set the trap and wait around for the arrival of the enemy's back-up to launch another attack or engage in a fight with them. Although on many occasions they do not succeed in getting the target one hundred per cent, and even though they still take casualties, the fact remains that they have started to take steps not associated with normal guerrilla warfare. It is these bolder, but effective measures of fighting which have taken the Israeli forces by surprise and caused concern amongst their generals.

Sheikh Nabil Qaouq proudly explained the thinking behind the Islamic Resistance's new strength:

> The Resistance was always trying to gain new experience as well as improve and update its military tactics to a level that would guarantee it success. It has always competed with the enemy on the methods used in the conflict. From the beginning, the Resistance's experts spent much time concentrating on studying and analysing the ways and means of changing the calibre of the fight. They scrutinised the types of weapons used by the enemy, how they used them and what their effects were, as well as studying the psychological effects of our operations against the Israeli soldiers and the psychological state in which the soldiers returned to Lebanon to fight. When the Resistance was launched it was primarily triggered by our religious obligation as well as our national duty. But the national duty could never overtake the fervour of our religious responsibility.

Alongside its growing military initiative, Hezbollah was also making use of a newly discovered power – the media. Its weekly newspaper, *Al-Ahed*, (The Pledge), was launched on 13 June 1984. Hezbollah's radio station, 'Al-Nour', (The Light), was born during the Amal–Hezbollah war, when a group of young Hezbollah followers spontaneously began to broadcast news of the conflict. Hezbollah's television station, 'Al-Manar', The Beacon, soon followed: its first broadcast was Ayatollah Khomeini's funeral in 1989. In the past few years, 'Al-Manar' has begun to broadcast the Islamic Resistance's activities. When the militant guerrillas launch their raids and attacks, a hidden cameraman films them from a distance. The video-tapes are then shown by 'Al-Manar', which is broadcast to most areas of Lebanon. Hezbollah was determined to prove the effectiveness of its Resistance against the Israeli occupation and with each broadcast the Party of God gained new momentum and a new influx of recruits.

Hezbollah has realised that its years of self-imposed

underground existence have hurt its image, which has always been associated with terrorism and fanaticism. UNIFIL, Arab governments and even European countries, including Britain, have described Hezbollah's war with Israel as a justified fight for the liberation of occupied territories. Yet by the time Hezbollah came into the open, it felt that its war with Israel was being falsely portrayed. As a result, in the past few years, Hezbollah has engaged in a propaganda war with Israel. It has concentrated a large section of its campaign on proving that, contrary to the portrayal of its guerrillas as a bunch of fanatics, the Islamic Resistance's members are fighting for a just cause, as Sheikh Nabil Qaouq says:

> While it is important for Israel to portray the battle as a fight between Israel and Hezbollah, it is more important for us to show it in its true form – a war, not just between Hezbollah and the Israeli soldiers but one in which the whole of Lebanon and its people are in danger. In this we can say that Hezbollah has largely succeeded in transforming the outlook of people towards its Resistance. We can now honestly say that we have reached a stage where we have raised popular awareness as well as gaining the people's support for the Resistance – both Christians and Muslims alike.
>
> This has really disturbed Israelis, whose politicians and prime minister have publicly stated on several occasions that no matter how much they have threatened Hezbollah they have only succeeded in rallying further support for it – even when they have used the policy of purposely attacking civilians in a bid to turn them against the group.

This was no exaggeration. On at least two significant occasions, Israeli efforts to distance the Lebanese public from the Islamic Resistance and Hezbollah have failed. On 16 February 1992, Israeli helicopter gunships carried out an air attack against Hezbollah's secretary-general, Sayyed Abbas Musawi, killing him, his wife and one-year-old baby as well as the escorts and bodyguards driving in his motorcade. Musawi had been attending the anniversary of Ragheb Harb's murder, which also coincides with the launching of the Islamic Resistance.

Musawi was one of Hezbollah's main founders and a major player in the Islamic Resistance's development. A fierce fighter himself, he had personally inspired, planned and led many attacks against Israel's forces in Lebanon when he was the Islamic Resistance's leader in South Lebanon. He had then moved to Beirut and the Bekaa and was elected secretary-general in 1991. Israel, which for years had rightly blamed most attacks and the Islamic Resistance's progress on Musawi, believed that by assassinating him it would remove the head of the dragon and weaken the military wing of Hezbollah.

The attack on Musawi coincided with a period when Hezbollah's influence had begun to stagnate. The group was preparing itself, under Musawi's leadership, to participate in Lebanon's elections and was discarding its shroud of extremism. Lebanon had just ended its civil war and most of the militias in the country had been disarmed. The Lebanese, weary after sixteen years of strife, were taking a respite while reassessing their political affiliations. Following the end of the Gulf War, there was talk of peace with Israel. The political scenario in the region was geared towards halting military action against Israel, especially in South Lebanon, and Hezbollah was facing the possibility of being asked to cool down its *jihad* against the occupation.

Although the loss of Musawi was the most severe direct blow to Hezbollah in its ten years of existence, some analysts claim that the assassination also acted as a positive catalyst for the group's re-emergence. Musawi's murder along with those of his wife and baby incensed a large sector of the Muslim community and triggered a new surge of mass sympathy and support for the Party of God.

On 17 February, tens of thousands of Shiites flocked to Beirut's southern suburbs to pay their respects to Musawi, whose coffin was carried through the streets of Hezbollah's bastion before being driven to his hometown in the Bekaa for the funeral. A similar turnout, led by religious clerics, Lebanese politicians and even government representatives, lined the roads of the Bekaa Valley all the way to Musawi's village, Nabi Sheet, where he was buried. Men and women wailed and sobbed. They raised clenched fists in the air in a sign of defiance and chanted slogans against Israel and America.

Sayyed Hassan Nasrallah was immediately elected secretary-general. In an emergency meeting of Hezbollah's higher council, hours after the assassination of Nasrallah's old-time friend and former religious tutor, he pledged to continue with Musawi's legacy and vowed to raise the heat of the battle and avenge the murder. In a passionate speech he charged Israel with 'committing its worst folly yet'.

The situation in South Lebanon deteriorated after that; Hezbollah and the Israeli forces became locked in a chain of tit-for-tat attacks. The Islamic Resistance increased its attacks on Israeli forces in the 'security zone'. It heightened its barrage of Katyusha rockets against settlements along Israel's northern borders, sparking further retaliation in the form of air raids. The chain of violence had entered a phase of no return. Even reports from Israel suggested that the assassination of Musawi might have been a misjudgement on their behalf. For instead of destroying the conceived brains behind the Islamic Resistance, the murder seemed to have launched a deadlier, more dangerous force that would cause serious aggravation to Israel's occupying forces in Lebanon. Between 1992 and 1993 the Islamic Resistance undertook more daring attacks against Israeli troops. For Israel, South Lebanon became a quagmire from which its army never returned in glory.

During a popular television debate in 1996, broadcast by the Lebanese Broadcasting Company (LBC), a leading station founded and controlled by the Christian Lebanese Forces, Hezbollah's leader Sayyed Hassan Nasrallah proudly summarised his group's achievements to thousands of viewers, who had tuned in to hear him participate in an open debate on the ideology and policies of his group with his Christian host:

The Resistance is our right as much as it is yours. It is our duty and your duty. We are fighting on behalf of a people, a nation and a government.

Let us look at our experiences. Between 1982 and 1985, Israel withdrew from a large sector of the land which it occupied. Who do you think forced it to withdraw to its current 'security zone'? [Former President] Amin Gemayel? Negotiations? The Americans? The United Nations Security Council? The Arab League? Only the Resistance forced it to withdraw.

If [Lebanon] has or wields any power in the peace process, it is solely because of its Resistance. Our conviction is that negotiations do not liberate land and the greatest example of this is what is currently going on between the Palestinians and the Israelis. Where has it got them? We believe and consider the Resistance to be the only way.

2

The Party of God

Surely the party of God [Hezbollah] *are they that shall be triumphant.*

Surat al-Ma'idah, 55, The Quran

When Israel launched its invasion in June 1982, Lebanon's leading Shia Muslim clerics were in Tehran, attending the annual Islamic Conference. The timing was fateful: Iran immediately volunteered to help its Lebanese brethren and the Iranian Revolutionary Guards were swiftly dispatched to Baalbeck in the Bekaa Valley. Sheikh Subhi Tufeili and Sheikh Ragheb Harb had both attended the conference and were to be central figures in realising Iran's initiative: Tufeili became the first leader of the new Islamic movement and Harb was to die fighting for its cause. Hezbollah had been conceived.

Those were heady days in Lebanon. At least twenty-five different groups and militias were locked in a continuous round of fighting. The emergence of yet another entity did not spark great enthusiasm amongst the war-weary people nor attract much attention. The West's intelligence services, who boasted about their close monitoring of Iran's movements at the time, failed to recognise the shoots of the new group. It was an oversight in those first, highly sensitive months that would eventually exact a high cost.

In the long, hot summer days and stifling nights of 1982, Baalbeck hosted scores of feverish, secret meetings in the homes of young Shiite men and revolutionary clerics. All were still inspired by the success of the Iranian Revolution and they spent months discussing the nature of the emerging party. They were devout Muslims, disillusioned by the established parties' political ideology and intent on going back to basics by creating an entity which would conform to Islamic *sharia*, Islamic law, and the word of the Almighty Allah.

The model of Iran's Islamic Republic had rekindled their own revolutionary spirit. They pledged their theological allegiance to Khomeini and harboured the dream of instigating a similar revolt in Lebanon in the hope of transforming the multi-confessional state into an Iranian-style Islamic country. Sheikh Naiim Qassem, who had been a cleric in Amal and became Hezbollah's deputy secretary-general, summarised the feelings amongst those who strove to form Hezbollah at the time. Qassem is a gentle, handsome man and an eloquent spokesman. His green eyes are framed by thick, dark lashes and he has long elegant hands. Beneath the customary black cloak worn by Hezbollah's clerics, it is surprising to see his Western footwear: socks and moccasins.

> The common denominator among those people was the strong feeling that what was present in the arena in the form of parties and organisations did not express their [political] proposals nor the structural format they sought. What contributed also was the breaking of the Iranian Revolution in 1979. This inspired these men to establish relations with the Revolution and to benefit from its experiences. So, from 1979 until 1982, there was only a general desire to create something that would translate the interests of our Islamic proposals. There was a need to develop a force which would also enjoy a popular political extension, something that was not available from any of

the organisations and personalities on the ground.

But having a desire to start something could only be achieved if the right circumstances prevailed. That only came about when Israel invaded Lebanon. That provided the conditions to realise the already present desire. With the willingness of the Islamic Republic to support the motives of this alliance, Hezbollah's take-off occurred.

The group of clerics began to form the backbone of Hezbollah, making frequent visits to their Iranian mentors, both in Tehran and Damascus where Iran has one of its largest embassies. The Party of God's current leader, Sayyed Hassan Nasrallah, was among the clerics. He had been a member of Amal's politburo and it was disillusionment with Amal's secular course under Nabih Berri that caused him to leave the group. At the age of sixteen, Nasrallah had travelled to Najaf, Iraq, to pursue his theological studies and he became one of several protégés of his predecessor Sheikh Abbas Musawi. Following Musawi's murder, Nasrallah was elected as Hezbollah's secretary-general at the age of thirty-two and became the youngest leader ever to run the Party of God. He described the group's priorities and activities in its first months of formation in an interview with the newspaper *Al-Safir*:

The main effort at the time went into mustering and attracting young men and setting up military camps where they could be trained and organised into small groups capable of carrying out resistance attacks against the occupying force. There were no institutions like now, no large organisation or specialised departments. There was only a group effort concentrating on two main issues. The first being the banding together of young men, training and organising them into small groups and then dispatching them to the occupied areas from where they were instructed to carry out attacks.

The second effort was spreading the word among the people, first, in a bid to raise their morale, and second to instil in them a sense of animosity towards the enemy, coupled with a spirit of resistance in the face of the occupying forces. This required us to use a language of indoctrination rather than realpolitik. People then were not in need of political analysis, they were in need of being incited and goaded. They did not need to be lectured, they needed to be freed.

The Party of God had quickly registered the tolerance of many Shiite Muslims towards the Israeli army and immediately sought to bring its influence to bear. To assert that the soldiers were occupiers and not their saviours was imperative, not only for the Party of God's initial recruitment programme, but for the success and continuity of the struggle.

Amal's leader Nabih Berri meanwhile came close to losing his hold over the Shiite movement. In the eyes of many Shiites, he had made the unforgivable error of participating in the National Salvation Committee, an emergency executive which brokered the 17 May 1983 accord between Lebanon and Israel. The accord was sponsored by the United States, which was keen to push through a second Arab–Israeli peace treaty following Camp David. Muslims and Druze considered it to be a vehicle for securing Israel's dominance in Lebanon. Its terms allowed Israel's proxy Christian militia to control a 30-mile area in South Lebanon and permitted its army to conduct patrols with the Lebanese army as far as the Awali River, north of Sidon.* When Berri refused to join the National Salvation Front, which had been instigated by Syria to sabotage the 17 May accord, it was the last straw. His stance was considered by the Muslim extremists to be an acceptance of US mediation in Lebanon.

Hezbollah had few arms at the beginning and it lacked the means for mass communication. It did, however, have important elements necessary for a *jihad*: Iranian money at its disposal

---

* See *The Fateful Triangle*, Noam Chomsky, pp. 425–6

and, on its doorstep, Iranian Revolutionary Guards expert in the art of warfare. The Iranian Revolutionary Guards took charge of Hezbollah's security and resistance operations. Iran's backing, combined with the presence of a core of dedicated men and an increasing number of warriors graduating from the Iranian Revolutionary Guards' military training programmes, set the group forth on its long, deadly and often chilling journey. The clerics used every opportunity to spread their word and ideology. They preached tirelessly in mosques, Husseiniyahs, at funerals and anywhere a crowd could be found. Their style was simple, but direct. They fed on Israel's mistakes, the Lebanese government's impotence and the West's blunders. Over the next two years, Hezbollah continued to operate underground from its main base, Baalbeck, in the eastern Bekaa Valley. Baalbeck was not under Israeli occupation and provided the group and the Iranian Revolutionary Guards with a safe haven from which to work and organise the movement. It was also close to Syria, giving Hezbollah the freedom of movement to travel to Iran. Its fighters worked under the banner of the Lebanese National Resistance and did not claim credit for any of the new, daring attacks that had started to make an impact among the Israeli soldiers. They concealed their joy when operations went well and hid their anguish when they failed.

From the very beginning, the United States and Israel searched in vain for the individuals within the new movement who were responsible for the group's attacks. They assassinated and kidnapped the group's officials in the belief that they had captured the ringleaders. To date, they have failed to grasp that the Party of God's chain of command has a structure which ensures that, even if its head is eradicated, the group can successfully continue. The group's decision-making policy is run in a manner whereby no single individual is ever solely responsible for making key decisions. Its history has proved that the killing of its leader does not necessarily warrant a change in its policies nor guarantee a moderate replacement. On the contrary, such events have, if anything, usually brought forth a more radical commander and an increase in militant tactics.

While theWest searched for answers, Hezbollah's cadres grew secretly. Between 1982 and 1985, the Party of God was training hundreds of young men, spreading the word amongst the population and working on creating a political agenda of its own. It had also established several social services for the inhabitants of its main base in the Bekaa Valley and in the city of Baalbeck.

In early 1983, Hezbollah formed a central leadership which incorporated three members. They became Hezbollah's first *shoura*, council, and were responsible for the Bekaa, Beirut and the South. The *shoura*'s job was to initiate and decide on all military, political and social issues. It also delegated the task of recruitment to other officials, leaving itself more able to concentrate on setting up its political and social agenda. Shortly after Israel's withdrawal to the Awali River in 1983, the *shoura* sent three of the group's top men, who had largely participated in founding the party, to Beirut's southern suburbs. The suburbs were an Amal stronghold and became a vital centre for Hezbollah's expansion. Beirut also brought the group closer to the South. The majority of the suburb's Muslims were Shiite refugees from South Lebanon and Hezbollah was now ready to plant its seeds amongst them.

By the end of 1983, it was becoming more noticeable that a new force was in town. Few Lebanese had yet comprehended the nature of the force, but late that year and in early 1984, West Beirut was turning into a bleak and frightening city. The face of the once famously cosmopolitan capital was undergoing a swift transformation. With the Shiite takeover of West Beirut, heavily bearded Hezbollah militiamen became increasingly visible in the city's battered streets. They wore green bands around their heads bearing inscriptions such as '*Allahu Akbar*', 'God is Greater', and '*Qaaidouna Khomeini*', 'Our leader is Khomeini'. The Ayatollah became a prominent image on many of the city's streets; posters of the Iranian leader were plastered on the walls of shops, boutiques, banks and even hospitals. Schoolgirls, some as young as seven, replaced their jeans and T-shirts with long-sleeved shirts and skirts and wore their hair concealed under tightly knotted black or white scarves. Women who were considered to be dressed in an improper manner were often harassed by the radical newcomers and rumours circulated that acid had been thrown at girls dressed in an 'un-Islamic' way as a lesson to others. These stories were never verified, but for a long time afterwards many felt uneasy walking the streets of West Beirut.

Shops selling alcohol were sometimes sent a warning in the form of a few sticks of dynamite hurled at their front doors. On other occasions they were raided by unknown militiamen who took to smashing the bottles of alcohol on display after lecturing the owners on the vices of their commodities. The attacks were intended to be messages and they usually occurred late at night and after closing hours. Those who continued to sell alcohol did so secretly and customers disguised their heavily wrapped purchases in inconspicuous carrier bags. The few popular restaurants which remained open hung signs on their entrances with the words 'Family restaurants only' insinuating that they were 'dry' premises. Even the famous Commodore Hotel, home to most of the hard-drinking foreign press corps, had to play the game. During the Muslims' holy month of Ramadan the bar was emptied of all its stock apart from soft drinks. The remaining 'prohibited' drinks were transferred to a suite on another floor.

By late 1984, Hezbollah's militiamen were out in the open, but very little was known about its leaders and hierarchy. The group had by then become an umbrella for most of the Muslim factions around, ranging from Islamic Amal to the al-Dawa party and the Islamic Students' Union. Islamic Amal had been started by Hussein Musawi in 1982, following Musawi's objections to Nabih Berri's political stance towards the Israeli invasion. Musawi was one of the few visible radicals in the early eighties. He was one of the many militants who held America responsible for encouraging and allowing Israel to invade and occupy Lebanon. His continuous denunciation of the West and his close relations with Iranian radicals made him a prime suspect during the West's desperate search for the names behind the new, invisible Islamic phenomenon.

The al-Dawa party had originally been an Islamic Iraqi party which was crushed by Saddam Hussein in the seventies and early eighties. Its ideology sprang from Ayatollah Khomeini's circle in Najaf.* According to Subhi Tufeili, who describes himself as the godfather of Hezbollah in its early stages, the al-Dawa party's members were the first to volunteer for the fight against Israel. 'The Dawa party was a clandestine presence which incorporated the main religious cadres of Amal and those outside Amal. Hezbollah is in essence the Dawa party from which we removed the title of Dawa and entered it into military rounds in order for it to start the resistance.' Those Hezbollah sympathisers who remained within the ranks of Amal were encouraged not to defect by the Party of God and were urged to work on transforming the Shiite movement from within.

On 16 February 1985, Hezbollah made its public debut to the world. The group's manifesto was declared by Hezbollah's spokesman, Sheikh Ibrahim al-Amin, who was one of the three official clerics who had been dispatched to Beirut to spread the Party of God's agenda to the people of the suburbs. The publication of the manifesto coincided with the anniversary of Ragheb Harb's death and his face appeared on the cover. Ayatollah Khomeini appeared on the back of the manifesto.

The contents of the booklet came under twenty-five headings which explained the Party of God's message in detail and set forth its Iranian orientation:

> We, the sons of Hezbollah's nation in Lebanon, whose vanguard God has given victory in Iran and which has established the nucleus of the world's central Islamic state, abide by the orders of a single wise and just command currently embodied in the supreme exemplar of Ayatollah Khomeini.
>
> From this basis, we in Lebanon are not a closed organisa-

---

* See *Islam in Revolution*, R. Hrair Dekmeijan, pp. 166–8.

tional structural party, nor are we a narrow political framework, but we are a nation interconnecting with all Muslims of the world. We are linked by a strong ideological and political connection – Islam.

From here, what befalls the Muslims in Afghanistan, Iraq, the Philippines or anywhere else verily afflicts the body of our Islamic nation of which we are an inseparable part, and we move to confront it on the basis of our main legal obligation and in the light of a political view decided by our leader the *Wilayat al-Faqih* [Ayatollah Khomeini].

As for our learning, this is primarily derived from the Holy Quran, and the infallible Sunnah [model of the ways of the Prophet], as well as the laws and edicts emanating from the Faqih.

No one can begin to imagine the scope of our military strength and capability. No one can even fathom its size. For we do not have a separate military wing which is independent from the parts of our bodies. Everyone of us is a fighting soldier when a call for *jihad* arises and each one of us carries out his mission in battle on the basis of his legal obligations. For Allah is behind us supporting and protecting us while instilling fear in the hearts of our enemies.

The manifesto described the West as the 'tyrannical world set on fighting us'. It accused the West of collaborating with the Soviet Union and waging war against the Muslims, charging that they had purposely defamed Hezbollah's reputation by labelling it as terrorist to 'stunt and deform our great achievements with regard to confrontations with the United States'. Hezbollah regards the West, and particularly the United States, as its staunchest enemy after Israel.

Hezbollah associates the West with European imperialism and the struggle for independence from colonial rule. It traces the antagonism between Christendom and Islam back to the Crusades: Hezbollah believes that the West's opposition to its vision springs from this ancient religious rivalry. Although it recognises that there are political differences between Western countries, it none the less considers that they unite collectively in their hostility towards Islam and that Muslims must therefore similarly unite to confront them.

The militant group has modified its definition of confrontation with the West since the publication of the manifesto. In its early years, Hezbollah aimed at removing the Western presence from Lebanon and the group incited war against Western targets, both locally and abroad. The Party of God currently speaks of resisting the West on 'cultural and political levels'. From his modest office in Hezbollah's heavily guarded headquarters in the midst of the teeming southern suburbs of Beirut, Naiim Qassem, Hezbollah's deputy secretary-general, explained the source of confrontation with the West.

'In our region we have a problem with the West which at one time placed us under the French mandate, at other times under the British mandate and over certain periods we were politically governed by the whims of the United States.' Hezbollah regards itself as occupying the opposite end of the spectrum to the West's concept of capitalism. 'There are contradictions between capitalism and Islam, there is a mental conflict between them,' Qassem argued, and went on:

When the West moves into a region, it does so with the intention of marketing its principles. It establishes schools, its own educational curriculum, Western cultural institutions, its own media, practically its own way of life and thinking. All of this, in a bid to impose its own ideologies in our region.

So when the West, for example, speaks of women in our areas it wants them to be prototypes of theirs in the way they think and behave. When they speak of economic markets, they do so according to their outlook on things. In other words, they seek to impose their own Western principles, not taking ours into consideration, in an attempt to suck us into their own agenda. From here we consider that there is a cultural conflict between us and the West and it is our job to invalidate their concepts here, to prove their evil and to spread our vision instead. If we succeed we will have obstructed their political agenda and this is our first kind of confrontation.

Hezbollah argues that the West's intentions in the Middle East are primarily based on self-interest. It perceives its presence in the region as an attempt to control the area's economic infrastructure and it condemns the Arab world, especially Saudi Arabia and the oil-rich Gulf states, for having fallen under Western influence. The Party of God regards the United States as the main player in the region and lays much of the blame at its doorstep. America, it claims, is expanding exclusively in the Middle East and imposing its political might and economic policies on Arab countries, while blocking other Western countries from having any influence in the area.

In its manifesto, Hezbollah blames the United States for all the region's catastrophes, describing it as the foremost enemy of all the Muslims of the world. 'We shall proceed to fight the vice at its very roots . . . the first roots of such vice being the United States.' The manifesto calls on its people to remember that 'the leader Imam Khomeini emphasised on many occasions that America is the cause of all our calamities and that she is the mother of all malice. If we fight her we will in effect only be exercising our just rights in defending our Islam and the honour of our nation.'

Hezbollah's grievances against the United States are largely based on the US's support of Israel during the 1982 invasion. The American administration's behaviour confirmed Hezbollah's belief that Israel exists to execute American policy and that US foreign policy in the Middle East is often undertaken with Israel's prime interests in mind.

For many Lebanese, resentment towards the American administration reached its height during the 1982 invasion when it failed to denounce the Israeli bombardment and the killing of thousands of innocent civilians. The bombs that flattened whole residential neighbourhoods and the war planes which blitzed Beirut were made in America. 'They [Israel] attacked our country, destroyed our villages, slaughtered our children and dishonoured our sanctity,' stated the manifesto. 'They unleashed criminals who practised massacres against us and still they [the US] continue to support Israel and prevent us from deciding our destiny,' complained Hezbollah in its manifesto. 'Their [Israel's] bombs used to drop on our people like rain during the Israeli invasion of our country and the siege of Beirut, while their planes carried out continuous day and night raids against us . . . We called out and appealed to the conscience of the world, but heard no sound from it.'

Over the years, the United States has attacked Hezbollah's Islamic Resistance for carrying out raids against Israel's occupying forces in Lebanon, while failing to call on Israel to adhere to the United Nations Resolution 425, which calls for Israel's unconditional withdrawal from the country. While many in Lebanon have misgivings about Hezbollah's ideology and extremism, most politicians and Lebanese unite in regarding the Resistance as the right of a country under occupation.

The Gulf War in 1991 drove more people to join the ranks of the Party of God. America's defence of Kuwait against Saddam Hussein's invasion stood out in stark contrast to its policy towards Israel's occupation in Lebanon and confirmed the militants' suspicion that US policy in the Middle East was based on self-interest. Hezbollah sees itself as a party which has been left with no choice but to confront its enemies.

'Freedom is not freely given or granted, but it is retrieved through the exertion of souls and blood,' declared the manifesto, adding, 'We can no longer be patient for we have been patient for tens of years.'

Hezbollah is unyielding in its hatred towards Israel, which it sees as a Western conspiracy planted in the Middle East to ensure instability in the region. Its manifesto describes Israel as 'America's spearhead in our Islamic world'. While Hezbollah sees itself as capable of having relations with the West in the future, it cannot envisage such a possibility with Israel. The manifesto stated:

Our struggle with Israel stems from an ideological and historic understanding to the effect that this Zionist entity is an aggressor in its development and formation and is existing on a land usurped at the cost of the rights of the Muslim people. And so our confrontation with this entity should end only when and after it has totally been eliminated from existence. Based on this we do not admit to nor abide by any cease-fire decisions against it nor do we adhere to any peace treaty with it.

Hezbollah believes that Israel has expansionist plans in the Middle East, claiming that it dreams of creating a Greater State of Israel from the Euphrates to the Nile. Hezbollah's belief may spring from a biblical verse, in which God promises Abraham the land from the Nile to the Euphrates (Genesis 15; verses 18–21). While right-wing groups in Israel have based their claim to the West Bank on biblical history, any grandiose ideas of territorial expansion in the Middle East are confined to the ravings of Israeli fringe extremists. Hezbollah, however, declares that the occupation of Palestine was only the beginning and that Israel will not settle until it has regained what it regards as its Promised Land. Naiim Qassem explained:

The main basic background for this conflict with Israel is because Israel is an occupier of land. We consider the occupation of the Palestinian land as an occupation of an Islamic land. Agreeing with or remaining silent over this occupation of Islamic territory also encourages Israel to take a dominating role in the region.

From reading and analysing their history and politics we conclude that these people, despite their talk of peace and security, which is only aimed at making us feel safe, strive to occupy much more than they already have and are willing to admit.

With the prevailing international mood which is sup-portive of Israel, we consider ourselves not to have any other choice, but to confront and fight Israel until such a day when they leave our land. Only if and when they leave the occupied land will the problem finally be over, and by occupied, we mean everything that is occupied, not just Lebanon.

Ultimately, Hezbollah envisages reclaiming Palestine and al-Quds, Jerusalem, the third holiest city of Islam.

Many officials within Hezbollah even refuse to utter the name Israel when referring to the country. Officials specifically ask journalists to use their exact terminology when quoting them. While a few will go as far as calling it the 'Zionist entity' when discussing it, most others insist on describing it as Palestine. To refer to it as Israel is seen by Hezbollah as an admission of its legal status, which Hezbollah refuses to recognise. In an interview with Hezbollah's weekly newspaper, *Al-Ahed*, on 6 December 1985, Sayyed Mohammed Hussein Fadlallah, a leading cleric, outlined the argument: 'Israel cannot be viewed as a state with the right to security and peace just like any other state in the region. We cannot see Israel as a legal presence, considering that it is a conglomeration of people who came from all parts of the world to live in Palestine on the ruins of another people.'

As far as Hezbollah is concerned, fighting Israel's occupation is not just a national duty. It is a religious obligation that falls within their concept of *jihad* and they are determined to continue the fight until Lebanese soil is liberated and every Israeli soldier has withdrawn from the country. They consider that the animosity between Muslims and Jews goes back to the early days of the rise of Islam in the Holy Land. A verse from the Quran is often quoted in Hezbollah's propaganda campaign against the occupation:

Certainly you will find the most violent of people in enmity for those who believe are the Jews and those who are polytheists, and you will certainly find the nearest in friendship to those who believe are those who say: 'We are Christians'. This is because there are priests and monks among them and because they do not behave proudly. (*Surat al -Ma'idah, verse 82.*)

The lines are broadcast regularly on Hezbollah's television channel 'Al-Manar'.

Hezbollah's manifesto also declared its political agenda. The group vowed never to participate in any of the government's institutions, so long as the 'current decaying sectarian system' exists, emphasising that no measure of reform would be considered sufficient to remedy Lebanon's political establishment. The manifesto demanded that the Lebanese be granted the opportunity to decide on the political system they wish to follow and invited the population to adopt its proposal of introducing an Islamic system:

> We do not seek to impose Islam on anyone as we hate those who impose their beliefs and regimes on us and we do not want Islam to reign Lebanon by force . . . But we confirm that we are convinced by Islam as an ideology and a system and call on everyone to make its acquaintance and to follow its *sharia* [law] as we call upon them to adopt it as a religion and to abide by its teachings whether on the personal, political or community level.

Even after the publication of its manifesto, very little was yet known or revealed about the group. Hezbollah continued to conceal the identities of its leaders. There was no press office to visit, no obvious official to interview and no listing in the telephone directory. The only noticeable move on the ground that the Party of God did take at the time of its public debut was to declare the birth of its military wing, the Islamic Resistance, *al-Muqawama al-Islamiyah*. The move indicated that Hezbollah's fighters had broken away from the Lebanese National Resistance and was suggestive of Hezbollah's dispute with Amal regarding the two groups' differing tactics towards Israel's occupation.

Naiim Qassem, deputy secretary-general, described the group's reasons for remaining underground in its early stages and its hesitation in announcing itself to the world:

> Up until 1985, Hezbollah was not yet a single entity that could stand up and speak for itself. We used to work without anyone knowing who we were or who was related to whom. We were still weak and had we been discovered we would have certainly been struck down. So, naturally, we remained closed within ourselves and kept a distance. We worked on forming a line of continuation amongst us, so that if one of us was hit, there was always another able person to carry on from where the first left off.
>
> The nature of our formation required clandestine behaviour. In 1985 we made an announcement. This announcement made public some of our figures, but others remained unknown. Since then there have been many serious schemes made against us. There were strong attempts made to prevent us from interacting with the people. What people have not been able to do, is to visualise us beyond anything but fighters.
>
> You see, Hezbollah is here to stay. It is not just a political or military trend that will pass away when those circumstances [war with Israel] end. Instead, it is a carrier of an Islamic principle which is impossible to eradicate.

Hezbollah's hierarchy is based on its *Majlis al-Shoura*, council, led by clerics, who arc considered to have the authority to speak in the name of God, as Naiim Qassem went on to explain:

> We are working to create a trend, not to create an idol to worship. We are an Islamic current which derives its origins from our beliefs and principles. We do not allow anyone to reach a certain position within the group if he lacks the principles that we carry. Our strategy works on the promotion of principles as the basis for uniting the forces, unlike other parties who, due to the lack of common, basic

beliefs, ended up suffering from corruption in the ranks of their leadership and working for their self-interest by exploiting the needs of their people.

Following Hezbollah's success in attracting the existing Lebanese Muslim groups, which agreed to dissolve their organisations and unite as one under its banner, Hezbollah moved to its next stage – devising a formula that would best suit its needs. Its followers spent many a night holding heated discussions about the final format of the structure of their new creation. The dilemma which they faced was whether Hezbollah should have a rigid structure, like most other political parties in Lebanon and the West, or maintain a more loose and fluid structure similar to Iran's, which revolved around the personal appeal of its religious leaders. Hezbollah opted for the second choice, but had to improvise with its structure since it was not possible to copy the Iranian model completely.

When Khomeini had returned to Tehran he argued that an Islamic government not only meant the implementation of Islamic *sharia*, law, but also required the rule of the clerics. He based his theory on the belief that the clerics were morally superior to the masses and that they should therefore have the right to govern. According to Shiite doctrine, only the Prophet and his descendants, the Twelve Imams, had the right to lead and guide the Muslim people, because they were seen as infallible. The *mujtahids*, religious scholars, were deemed capable of taking over the responsibility of commanding the Muslim masses, by virtue of their faultless religious knowledge and scholarship. Some even went as far as believing that these scholars had inherited the infallibility of the Imams and possessed a unique insight into the truth.

Khomeini argued that the clerics should rule under the guardianship of a sole Shiite exemplar or jurisprudent, *Wilayat al-Faqih*. The position of supreme guide, he concluded, should be extended only to the most knowledgeable and morally upright *mujtahid*, in this case himself. With that, Khomeini became the ultimate guardian of Shiite Muslims both in Iran and abroad and his dictum was enshrined in the Islamic Republic's constitution.

The Iranian structure therefore rotated largely around Khomeini, the constitutional leader of Iran. Khomeini's job was to supervise and provide guidance to the country's government when the need arose or when the higher interests of the Muslims were in question. He was also the supreme theological authority on all religious matters and he would make his orders and edicts known through a publicised statement, which in turn would be adopted by the *ulama*, religious class, of the country and communicated to the people and worshippers through mosques, Husseiniyahs and any other religious centres. Khomeini, as the supreme exemplar, would issue guidance only on general matters which he regarded of importance to the Muslims and he would do so in broad terms, leaving the interpretation of his statements to the *ulama*. Khomeini, for example, set the agenda regarding Israel when he made the infamous declaration that Israel was an evil and called on all Muslims around the world to 'fight the Jewish state until its eradication'. Such a directive is taken to heart by most pious Muslims, such as Hezbollah, who regard his guidelines as second to God's word.

The Party of God's founders were drawn to this style because of its popular characteristics and the absence of a fixed chain of command. Critics of the Iranian model observed that Hezbollah would have to find a symbolic leader who had the necessary requirements to act as Lebanon's Khomeini and they doubted whether such a figure existed; a structured organisation also appeared to be a necessary requirement for a group to function in Lebanon's multi-confessional society.

'We concluded at the end that we needed a structural organisation which was in some aspects rigid enough to be able to prevent infiltration by the enemy and at the same time flexible enough to embrace the maximum sector of people without having to go through a long bureaucratic process of red tape,' explained Naiim Qassem.

By implementing this formula, Hezbollah succeeded in

creating an entity which, while loosely structured in some respects, was also clearly defined in others. Its result was a group with two parts. The first part incorporates the officials who hold positions of office in the hierarchy of the group: they are regarded as the 'subscribers' of the Party of God. The second part revolves around the masses, the group's followers. Hezbollah does not have members: it considers itself to be a pan-Islamic movement, whose ideology spreads beyond the domestic confines of a conventional political party. When the Party of God calls for a rally, thousands of people rise to its call. Only a very small fraction of the numbers who respond to the call consists of representatives and officials of the group. The majority who attend the rally are, perhaps, like supporters of a football club: they identify with the cause, and consider themselves to be affiliated to Hezbollah, but they cannot actually become a member of the team. As in Iran, Hezbollah revolves around the clergymen and *ulama* who provide the masses with both spiritual and political guidance. It is through these men, their preaching and power of persuasion, that the public receives Hezbollah's line on major political issues and even their justifications for violence. Each cleric has his own particular mosque, like a parish, in which he preaches to the population.

Hezbollah's *shoura* is headed by the secretary-general. The size of the *shoura* is not fixed but there are at present seven members. Most decisions are taken jointly by the *shoura* members and the secretary-general is not permitted to make any decisions alone, as Sheikh Subhi Tufeili explained:

There is no such hurry whereby one is forced to make a decision without waiting for a certain period of time. Also, seeing as Lebanon is such a small country, and Beirut is relatively tiny in size, the *shoura* members are always capable of meeting or contacting one another. Having said so, I must explain that there is a system for dealing with emergencies if one arises and, say, not all the *shoura* members are in town. Then, so long as a certain forum is present, a decision can be made. But there are no such things as solitary decisions.

The secretary-general is looked upon as the co-ordinator. He co-ordinates the political relationships, but requires the collective decision of his fellow members to take or carry out any decisions or laws.

Each member of the *shoura* has a specific portfolio and is expected to implement the council's decisions in his particular field. The *shoura* itself is divided into two parts: *shoura qarrar*, the decision-making council and *shoura tanfeed*, the executive council. The first body represents the leadership of Hezbollah which makes the decisions and the second is the body that executes its directives. The executive body, whose numbers vary according to the portfolios, has a limited scope of jurisdiction, which allows it and its members to be able to act on minor issues without having to refer to the higher council. If, in the process of performing its job, it comes across an issue which requires clarification or action, it can raise the matter to the higher council.

The secretary-general must be a member of the higher *shoura*. He is elected by the members of his council from among their number. They in turn are elected every two years by a special secret committee of prominent clerics and devout senior Muslims. Hezbollah also has a politburo of twelve members which includes all the party's deputies in parliament. Subhi Tufeili claims that Iran does not dictate the identity of the group's secretary-general, although he admits that if the Islamic Republic favours one candidate over another it might rally support among the remaining members to elect that person. He adds that the group has not yet faced a situation where the Iranian Republic has had to instruct the *shoura* on its appointment of the secretary-general.

In its earlier years, Hezbollah kept a tight lid on the identity of its *shoura* members. It is only since 1989 that the Party of God has begun a gradual process of publicising its internal affairs. While to this day it never discloses the exact dates and location of its elections, the group has recently got into the habit of revealing the results to the media and the public, usually a few days after finalising the affair.

For a few years after the group's inception, the West focused its attention on Ayatollah Sayyed Mohammed Hussein Fadlallah, whom it believed to be the Party of God's leader. Fadlallah denied this, although he took pleasure in pointing out that many of the group's adherents, such as Ragheb Harb, were his former disciples. Journalists sought him for interviews and Western intelligence lapped up his statements and rhetoric. A grandfatherly man, Fadlallah was born in Najaf, in 1935, to a Lebanese father who was a student and teacher there. He lived and studied in Iraq until 1966 when he returned to Lebanon and quickly established his reputation as a leading religious authority.

From an intellectual point of view, Fadlallah owes little to Iran or Khomeini, even though he preaches a similar message. He had preached the doctrine of an Islamic state in Lebanon since he returned to the country in the sixties, long before the Iranian Revolution. He is without doubt the most eloquent speaker and defender of the Islamic cause in Lebanon. He has on many occasions openly identified with Hezbollah, but he has also opposed their position.

Although it has become more widely accepted that Fadlallah is not Hezbollah's leader, he is still referred to as Hezbollah's sole 'spiritual leader'. Both Fadlallah and the Party of God have consistently denied the description. Despite his influence upon the group, he can best be described as a strong source of inspiration rather than its spiritual mentor. Fadlallah considers himself the spiritual guide of *al-Halat al-Islamiyah al-Shiiyah*, the Islamic Shiites' situation. He has a strong following within the Shiite community which is independent of Hezbollah and he is not the Party of God's prime source of guidance. For this reason his views cannot always be deemed as typical of Hezbollah's perspectives. It has also been suggested that Fadlallah, who had links with the al-Dawa party, has preserved his independence both to command a wide audience and also to protect himself. He had perhaps learnt from the tragic fate of Mohammed Baqir al-Sadr, Iraq's most important Shiite leader, who was executed by Saddam Hussein in 1980.*

While Hezbollah does not always adhere to Fadlallah's reasoning and ideas, the group respects him highly. No other religious authority in Lebanon has quite the same impact as Fadlallah and Iran knows that he is of great importance to Hezbollah. 'All the Islamic views and principles that Hezbollah embraces are shared by Fadlallah,' says Naiim Qassem. 'The political stance with regard to common Islamic issues is also similar between the two. It is natural for us to have many common views so that the outside observer will find it difficult to distinguish between us, because our Islam is one.'

When Hezbollah was forming it attempted to bring Fadlallah into its circle. In Subhi Tufeili's words:

> Sayyed Fadlallah did not have a direct role. In other words, he was not involved nor did he join in the meetings and the initial work carried out during Hezbollah's formation. He is a respected theologian and one sanctified by every-one. His presence in Beirut was greatly benefited from. Because he was in harmony with the proposals of the Islamic Republic and those of our men, he was consulted on many issues. We can say that he was consulted on most major political issues and that he was a cardinal stopping point for us.
>
> Having said that I must stress, as regards the issue of consulting him, that Sayyed Fadlallah's opinions were not always binding or obligatory. He never expected them to be and our brothers never regarded them as such. I have to add here, that had he wanted to have a larger role [in Hezbollah] he could have achieved that. He alone defined the limit and the size of his role despite helping us greatly in those days. Even I tried on several occasions to suggest, and persistently for that matter, that he should have a larger

---

* See *Shi'i Thought from the South of Lebanon*, Chibli Mallat, pp. 27–9

role or a specific position within the group, but the Sayyed preferred not to. He wanted to be [there] for everyone.

The United States believed that Fadlallah occupied a key role in Hezbollah and considered him responsible for the bombing of the multinational forces in Beirut in 1983, in which the US Marines and French Paratroopers suffered devastating losses. Most of the evidence in Lebanon suggests that the Lebanese Forces, an alliance of Christian militias, leaked Fadlallah's name to Western intelligence and Israel. Fadlallah instantly became an international celebrity and a prime target for assassination. Many analysts say that the Lebanese Forces' decision to point the finger at Fadlallah was aimed at punishing the Shiite cleric: Fadlallah had called for war against Israel's occupation and had been one of the leading Muslim clergymen to lead a strike on the day that the 17 May treaty between Israel and Lebanon was signed in 1983.

In early 1985, a massive car bomb, meant for Fadlallah, exploded at a building near the cleric's house in Bir al-Abed. It killed eighty-five people, including children and pregnant women and maimed nearly two hundred. The *Washington Post* reported that the failed assassination attempt was carried out by CIA-trained Lebanese agents. The CIA denied this, but that did little to ease the outrage of the clergyman's supporters, who called for American blood beneath a banner covering the demolished building which said: 'Made in the USA'. In his book about the CIA, *Veil*, Bob Woodward reported that the assassination attempt was a joint US–Saudi operation organised by a British mercenary. Woodward draws from the memoirs of William Casey, the head of the CIA agency, reporting that Saudi Arabia's ambassador to Washington at the time, Prince Bandar Bin Sultan Abdel Aziz, financed the American agency with the sum of three million dollars to carry out the attack. Following the failure of the attempt, Woodward relates that the Saudis paid Fadlallah two million dollars in humanitarian aid for Shiite refugees in an apparent bid to halt any retaliatory attacks against the US and Saudi Arabia.

The CIA denied the charges vehemently as did President Reagan, who said that he did not order or sanction such an attack. The Saudi government also flatly denied any involvement, while Fadlallah denied having accepted any money for his silence, challenging people to prove the contrary. Following the Bir al-Abed bombing, Hezbollah's security apparatus engaged in a long investigation and arrested twelve people who confessed to being hired and trained as surrogates to carry out the assassination by the CIA's counter-terrorist department. One of the twelve who had been arrested and had apparently played a major role in the attack was the daughter of an acquaintance of Fadlallah. Close aides recalled that the girl's father pleaded with the cleric not to permit her execution and to accept the offer of blood money. Fadlallah, however, could not intervene: the agents were sentenced by an Islamic court and in accordance with Islamic law.

Hezbollah and Fadlallah each follow a different religious exemplar, known as the *Wali al-Faqih*. The *faqih* is chosen for his ability to master and fathom the word of God. While Hezbollah subscribes to this principle of rule by a supreme guardian, it elected to follow Ayatollah Khomeini as its *faqih*. Fadlallah, however, took Sayyed Al-Khouii of Iraq as his theological reference and recognised Khomeini as a political leader.

Entrusting religious authority to someone in Shiite Islam entails giving that person the power to determine every religious aspect of life, from details as basic as how to pray, to contemporary moral issues such as test-tube babies. The *faqih* usually writes a thesis of about three hundred pages on all aspects concerning a Muslim's way of life. The thesis should in effect explain and interpret all the complex aspects of Islam as well as answer the Shiite population's main questions. There are occasions when slight differences of interpretation can occur between past and present authorities. This variance is known as the jurisprudence, in other words, the capacity of interpretation which Islam enjoys.

In a lecture on the subject published in Hezbollah's newspaper

Al-Ahed, Hezbollah's leader Sayyed Hassan Nasrallah described the central role of the *faqih* in Shia Islam:

> The *faqih* is the guardian during the absence of the Twelfth Imam, and the extent of his authority is wider than that of any other person . . . We must obey the *Wali al-Faqih*, disagreement with him is not permitted. The guardianship of the *faqih* is like the guardianship of the Prophet Mohammed and of the infallible Imam. Just as the guardianship of the Prophet and the infallible Imam is obligatory, so too is the guardianship of the *faqih* . . . His wisdom derives from God and the family of the Prophet, and he approaches the divine . . . When the *Wali al-Faqih* orders someone to obey and that person disobeys, that is insubordination against the Imam. When the *faqih* orders someone to be obeyed, such obedience is obligatory.

After the deaths of Khomeini and Khouii both Hezbollah and Fadlallah decided on the same man, Ayatollah al-Ozma Sayyed Reza Mohammed Golpayegani, for both leadership and religious guidance. When he died, the two camps once again split and each followed a separate exemplar once again. Hezbollah chose to follow Ayatollah al-Ozma Sheikh Mohammed Ali Araki while Fadlallah followed Ayatollah al-Ozma Sayyed Ali Hossein Sistani. Hezbollah currently follows Ayatollah Khameini as both its religious and political leader.

Very little has changed in Hezbollah's ideology since it first announced its manifesto in 1985. The group has, however, shown an ability to learn from its past experiences and to adapt to the political climate. Hezbollah was initially opposed to the changes which ushered in the end of the civil war. The Taif Accord of 1989 proposed to address the political imbalance in Lebanon. Under the Accord, the political system was to be reformed: the number of Christian and Muslim deputies in parliament was made equal and the executive power of the president was transferred to a council of ministers. Hezbollah considered it to be no more than continuation of the status quo. Syria, however, was fully behind the measures, which also recognised its military presence in the country. Assad further consolidated his position in Lebanon in the Treaty of Brotherhood, Co-operation and Co-ordination two years later. Israel had to watch bitterly from the sidelines as Syria tightened its hold on Lebanon.* At the end of Lebanon's civil war in 1990 Hezbollah astutely realised that, unless it participated in the rapidly changing political scene in Lebanon, it could end up being isolated and lose its official backing and representation. Encouraged by both Syria and its Iranian mentors, the Party of God dropped its earlier objections to participating in Lebanon's political system and entered the country's 1992 parliamentary elections, the first to take place for twenty years. Hezbollah won with a landslide in the areas where it had candidates and secured eight members in parliament. Along with four other allied deputies, who ran on the same list as Hezbollah, the group commanded the largest single political bloc in the house until 1996. It was also the first Islamic bloc in the Lebanese parliament.

Sheikh Subhi Tufeili had misgivings about the move. He had served as the Party of God's secretary-general in the group's most critical years, when it believed that extreme radicalism and total secrecy were vital for its survival. As a result of his hard-line position, Tufeili was isolated and he is no longer a member of the *shoura*. Hezbollah did not, however, air its internal differences in public. Unlike other parties in Lebanon the group is always careful to maintain a united front; from the secretary-general to the bodyguards at the doors of Hezbollah's offices, its officials all keep to the party line. Tufeili also kept his criticisms to himself despite many attempts by journalists at the time to discover why the group which he had worked so hard to create had sidelined him. Tufeili has an intimidating air and he does not mince his words. He expresses his opinions on Hezbollah in a hoarse, loud voice and speaks in the raw, unpolished dialect

---

* See *Lebanon Fire and Embers*, Dilip Hiro, pp. 162–3, 166

of the Bekaa Valley. He has thick, rugged hands and a dark, heavy beard. Tragedy struck his family in the summer of 1995 when his wife and one of his children were run over in an accident. A second child was paralysed.

Hezbollah rationalised its decision to enter Lebanon's parliament by arguing that its members had been elected by the people and had not been appointed by the government, which it opposes. Hezbollah now argues that working from the inside allows it to influence change and monitor events. While there is some truth in this, the initiative for Hezbollah's entry into political participation sprang from the negotiated settlement between Tehran and Syria.

By the end of the Gulf War, the general mood in the Middle East was changing. The Americans were playing a major role in mediating peace between the Palestinians and Israel, while Syria was keen to improve its relations with the West having lost its Soviet sponsor. As a reward for its role in joining the allies against Saddam Hussein, Syria was granted by the United States the one thing it had fought to establish – the role of sole political guardian of Lebanon. This also guaranteed its desire to maintain troops in Lebanon until such a time when the Lebanese government and army reached a position where they would be able to extend their power over the country.

Hezbollah, however, was in grave danger of being destroyed if it did not legalise itself and play politics. With the end of the civil war in 1990 the reign of the militias was drawing to a close. Assad knew that if Hezbollah was persuaded to participate in Lebanon's parliament and abandon its shroud of terror, the group would gain official political cover. It would also allow Syria to argue legitimately when it needed to defend the group that Hezbollah was an official party with members in parliament and not an outcast terrorist organisation.

Hafez al-Assad, one of the shrewdest politicians to come to power in the Middle East, has been under constant American pressure to take action regarding Hezbollah since Syria established its position of influence. The group, however, remains an important tool for Syria to use against Israel and

Washington. Israel seized Syria's Golan Heights during the Six Day War in 1967 and annexed them in 1981. Syria has not been willing to compromise on its demand for the full withdrawal of Israeli troops from both the Golan Heights and from South Lebanon in return for peace. Furthermore, like his Iranian counterpart, Assad is one of the few leaders in the Arab world who is against relinquishing the concept of resistance against Israel. He has backed Hezbollah's Islamic Resistance consistently, even when Syria's relations with Hezbollah were at their worst. By entering the Lebanese political arena and turning down its extremism, Hezbollah did in effect secure the endorsement it needed to legitimise its Islamic Resistance. It is the only group to have remained armed since the militias were disarmed at the end of the civil war. There is not a single politician in Lebanon currently, from the extreme Christian camp to the Muslims and Druze, who does not defend the activities of the group's fighters. Despite the fact that many do not agree with Hezbollah's ideology and political vision for Lebanon and may merely be paying lip-service in the name of political correctness, they have all come to recognise and respect its combatants' opposition to the occupation.

3

Human Bombs

And do not speak of those who are slain in Allah's way as dead nay [they are] *alive, but you do not perceive them.*
Surat al-Baqarah, 154, The Quran

On 11 November 1982, a new style of warfare made its shocking debut when a young man drove a white Mercedes, filled with explosives, into Israel's military headquarters in Tyre. The blast destroyed the eight-storey building and killed 141 people. It was the first human bomb.

Witnesses in the area saw the car approach the headquarters and then, from a distance of 20 metres, furiously accelerate towards its target. The guard at the perimeter gate had no chance to fire. When news of the attack reached Beirut there was widespread jubilation and rounds of gunfire echoed in the streets. At the assailant's own request, his identity was only revealed two and a half years later: he had believed that South Lebanon would be liberated from Israeli occupation by then and had wanted to protect his family from reprisals. His name was Ahmad Qassir and he was seventeen years old. Hezbollah did not formally exist in 1982, but it claims the attack as one of its own. Ahmad was a member of the Lebanese National Resistance

(LNR), whose ranks included Hezbollah's fighters until the birth of the Islamic Resistance in 1985.

Ahmad succeeded in setting a lethal trend. Between 1982 and 1985 there were at least thirty similar attacks. Bombs were dispatched in cars, suitcases and even, on one occasion, by donkey. The inspiration for the new strategy came from Iran. During the Iran–Iraq war, Khomeini justified the practice of sending children across the minefields by extolling the martyrdom of Shiite youth. Young boys, some no older than nine, sacrificed their lives as human minesweepers by running through the Iraqi minefields to clear the way for the Iranian troops.* Whether deliberately or not, the Iranian leader succeeded in giving new meaning to the act of martyrdom and self-sacrifice.

During Lebanon's civil war, human bombs were used to devastating political effect. The Israelis' headquarters were attacked for a second time a year later, but they were not the only target. On 18 April 1983 the American embassy on Beirut's seafront was destroyed in a massive explosion and sixty-three people were killed. At the time of the attack, members of the Beirut CIA were holding a meeting with the agency's leading Middle East experts. US Under-Secretary of State Lawrence Eagleburger told a congressional investigating committee that the attack was 'virtually impossible to defend against if the driver was prepared to commit suicide'. Nevertheless, Washington reasserted its commitment to Lebanon and President Reagan declared: 'This criminal attack against our diplomatic mission will not deter us from continuing with our goal to achieve peace in the area and we shall carry on with what we know to be right.' The question was – right for whom?

Not all Americans shared Reagan's determination and confidence. Republican Senator Barry Goldwater demanded that it was time to pull out the Marines and voiced his concern when he warned, 'We are heading for trouble.' He could not have been more accurate. Six months after the bombing of the

---

* See *Sacred Rage*, Robin Wright, p. 37

embassy, 241 US Marines died in the single largest non-nuclear explosion since the Second World War. The US had not suffered this level of loss of life in a single incident throughout the war in Vietnam. At least 18,000 pounds of explosives were used in the attack on the Marine barracks near Beirut's airport, leaving a crater more than four metres deep. There was another blast twenty seconds later, which killed fifty-eight French paratroopers four miles away, in France's worst military loss since the Algerian war.

The multinational forces (MNF) had come to Lebanon as peace-keepers to oversee the evacuation of the PLO from Beirut in August 1982, but they had ended up taking sides in the conflict. Arafat had insisted that a multinational force be sent to Beirut to supervise and provide cover for the safe departure of his fighters. Israel's Minister of Defence Ariel Sharon, who had planned and commanded the invasion, refused to accept a European force without American troops. The MNF unit they sent comprised Americans, French and Italians.

In the same month, Bashir Gemayel was elected president. His election had been backed by the Israelis and it marked the fulfilment of one of their aims when they invaded Lebanon: installing a Christian president who would be friendly to Israel. Israeli tanks had even personally delivered deputies to the election post to ensure a forum for Gemayel's election, but their efforts to shape Lebanon's political future were to be in vain: Gemayel was assassinated less than a month after the elections in an explosion which blew up the Lebanese Forces' headquarters in East Beirut. Israel then invaded West Beirut, breaking its promise to the United States that it would stay out of the district, and took Bashir Gemayel's Phalangist militia in with them. The Phalangists took their revenge in a brutal massacre of Palestinian refugees in the camps of Sabra and Chatila which lasted for two days. Thousands of women, children and old men were shot dead on sight. Among the victims were Lebanese Shiites who were refugees from the south and had taken shelter in the Palestinians' refugee camps.

The militiamen buried many of their victims below earth

mounds and would have continued to hide all traces of the massacre had journalists not discovered the atrocity by the second day. The carnage enraged the PLO leader Yasser Arafat and the Muslim leaders, who had accepted the US's pledges that Israel would not enter the Western sector after the evacuation of the PLO and that the remaining families of the exiled Palestinian guerrillas would not be harmed.

President Ronald Reagan was horrified by the incident. The multinational forces, which had left after the evacuation of the PLO, were dispatched to Beirut once again. In a letter to Congress, Reagan declared: '[The Marines'] mission is to provide an interposition force at agreed locations and thereby provide the multinational presence requested by the Lebanese Government to assist it and the Lebanese Armed Forces. Our agreement with the Government of Lebanon expressly rules out any combat responsibilities for the US forces.' The new Lebanese government, however, was headed by Bashir's brother, Amin. It was a strongly Phalangist administration which soon alienated the Muslim population. Amin Gemayel used the army to intimidate the Muslims of West Beirut: he had thousands of Muslims arrested and many disappeared in his bid to crush the leftist and Muslim militias and any sympathisers with the Palestinian cause. He also used the army to drive the southern Shiite refugees from the shantytowns in which they were squatting. Nabih Berri, the leader of Amal, and his Muslim allies urged Amin Gemayel to tackle the question of political reform. Gemayel invited his Muslim opponents to a national reconciliation conference, but insisted that all foreign troops would have to leave Lebanon before the Muslims' demands could be addressed. Gemayel wanted to see the Syrians leave the country along with the Israelis.

While the multinational forces supported the administration, the US did not make itself any more popular by sponsoring the Lebanese–Israeli peace agreement in May 1983, which sought to turn Israel's military gains in Lebanon into political profit. The US hoped to bring about the withdrawal of Syrian and Israeli troops from Lebanon as part of a comprehensive peace initiative, but neither the Syrians nor the Lebanese wished to see Israel rewarded for its invasion.

America's attempts to remedy the Lebanese crisis as a neutral mediator collapsed that autumn, when fierce fighting broke out in the Chouf, a Druze fiefdom. Israel had occupied the Chouf and installed Christian militias in the region. In September, Israel abruptly withdrew from the area and full-scale battles erupted between the Druze and the Christians. The US Marines intervened and began shelling Druze targets. Reagan justified the move by claiming that the Soviets were arming the Syrians and the Muslims in an attempt to destroy US interests in the Middle East. More fuel was thrown upon the flames when the Lebanese army's Commander Brigadier Ibrahim Tannous claimed that his units were being attacked by Iranians and Palestinians and warned that the government was in danger of collapsing. Robert McFarlane, Reagan's Middle East envoy, believed that the future of American policy in Lebanon depended on the survival of Amin Gemayel's administration and responded swiftly to Tannous's alarm: the US Defense Department launched a huge operation to bring supplies to the Lebanese army. On 19 September, US warships fired 300 shells against Druze and Syrian targets to save the Lebanese army and President Gemayel. It was the last straw: the multinational forces had entered the civil war and violated their status as peace-keepers. The US Marines and the French paratroopers were bombed the following month. 'The image of the US multinational force, in the eyes of the factional militias, had become pro-Israeli, pro-Phalange and anti-Muslim,' declared the Long Commission's investigation into the bombings.*

An unknown organisation named Islamic Jihad claimed responsibility for the attacks in telephone calls to the news agency Agence France Presse. They identified themselves as Lebanese Muslims and 'soldiers of God who yearn for martyr-

---

* See *Beirut Outtakes*, Larry Pintack

dom'. Their aim was to expel the Israelis from Lebanon and to establish an Islamic republic. 'Violence will remain our only way,' declared the caller. It did not take long for the United States to come to the conclusion that Hezbollah was behind the attacks and that Islamic Jihad was merely a name or a wing of the group, dedicated to killing Americans and threatening Western interests in Lebanon. The United States pointed the finger at Hussein Musawi, who had broken away from Amal to form Islamic Amal in 1982. Mohammed Hussein Fadlallah, the spiritual leader, was another suspect.

While Hezbollah has consistently denied responsibility, it has nevertheless exalted the deeds and the perpetrators. In its manifesto, Hezbollah calls the attack on the American Embassy 'the first punishment' and it lists the MNF bombings as further punishments. At the time, Hezbollah was not yet properly formed. It did not have the fully fledged structure or the leaders and officials which it now possesses and was therefore not in a position to plan and execute such operations alone. There were powerful figures operating behind the scenes.

Iran was outraged by the Israeli invasion of Lebanon and had resolved to help the Lebanese Muslims.* Nor were the Iranians happy about the support which America had given to Israel's actions. Iranian hostility towards the American and Western presence in Lebanon was a continuation of its own struggle against the United States, which was an integral part of its revolution. Extending this conflict to Lebanon allowed it to continue its fight, while providing the Islamic Republic with a base for activism outside its boundaries.

Syria, meanwhile, had its own agenda. Its foremost priority was to drive the Israelis out of Lebanon: their presence in the South and the Bekaa Valley threatened Syria's heartland and jeopardised its national security. Damascus was also gravely

---

* The author has based the following account on talks with Arab and Western analysts and intelligence sources as well as discussions with Lebanese Muslim officials who were on the ground at the time of these events.

concerned about the outcome of a pro-Western, pro-Israeli regime in Lebanon.

Both countries therefore found common ground for an alliance in Lebanon to protect their interests. The two would embark on a counter-offensive, using their Lebanese Muslim proxies, that would eventually lead to the withdrawal of the Israeli forces into their self-declared 'security zone' in the spring of 1985 and the abrogation of the US-sponsored Israeli–Lebanon peace accord. The plan would also culminate in the US decision to withdraw the multinational forces from Lebanon in February 1984, thus allowing Syria to regain its authority in Lebanon.

Syria encouraged its allies in Amal to fight on the political front, while the Iranians inspired their own Lebanese surrogates to intensify a military campaign against both the Israelis in South Lebanon and the Western forces in Beirut. The Syrians had been tipped off by intelligence from their regional backers, the Soviet Union, of the CIA's scheduled top-level meeting at the US embassy in Beirut on 23 October. The Soviet embassy in Beirut had always been the largest and best equipped of all the foreign embassies in Lebanon and constantly monitored everyone else's movements and activities. At the time, the Soviets were still in the grip of the Cold War and had been angered by America's moves to weaken Syria, their strongest ally in the Middle East, and by Israel's attack on Syrian targets in Lebanon.

Damascus shared the Soviet intelligence with the Iranians and the decision was made to attack the US embassy in Lebanon. One point on which they were both in total agreement was that they would not carry out the attack themselves: the job had to be done by their Lebanese surrogates. They would plan and provide the logistics and intelligence, as well as the political cover needed to see them through.

The Lebanese Shiites did not need much encouragement. In their eyes, the United States was largely responsible for the Israeli invasion in not having taken a tougher stance against the Jewish State. Nor had the United States taken any action when Israel stormed into West Beirut, the Muslims' sanctuary and capital. Worse still were the massacres of defenceless Palestinian women and children, in the refugee camps, whose safety America had guaranteed.

Imad Mughniyeh and Mustapha Badredeen took charge of the Syrian–Iranian-backed operation. Mughniyeh had been a highly trained security man with the PLO's Force 17, Arafat's elite personal security apparatus, and Badredeen had been a fierce member of the al-Dawa party's military wing. Their mission was to gather information and details about the American embassy and draw up a plan that would guarantee the maximum impact and leave no trace of the perpetrator. A human bomb was the ultimate method of attack. Not only would it bring large-scale destruction, but it would incur minimum losses and ensure that no clues were left behind.

Meetings were held at the Iranian embassy in Damascus. They were usually chaired by the ambassador, Hojjatoleslam Ali Akbar Mohtashemi, who played an instrumental role in founding Hezbollah. In consultation with several senior Syrian intelligence officers, the final plan was set in motion. The vehicle and explosives were prepared in the Bekaa Valley which was under Syrian control. A few days before the attack, the vehicle was transported across the Syrian checkpoints and into Beirut's teeming southern suburbs.

When the multinational forces were attacked in October, Syria and Iran did not in fact specify a target. The militants were told that pressure on the Westerners had to be kept up and it was left to them to decide on how to deal the second blow against the Americans. All Syria and Iran had to do was go over the plans and provide the logistics once more. The Americans had just confirmed the Shiites' belief that they harboured bad intentions towards the Muslim population when they had ordered ships from their flotilla, off the shores of Lebanon's Mediterranean coast, to open fire. The security experts needed no help in determining their target. The MNF barracks were their ideal choice: the Marines were military men and, in their view, should therefore pay the price for their country's mistaken military actions in Lebanon.

Once again the vehicles were driven from the Bekaa Valley across Syrian checkpoints and into the suburbs, which overlooked the Marines' barracks. At about 5.07 a.m., the suicide bomber prepared himself for his journey. Having performed the dawn prayers and drunk a few cups of sweet, strong tea, he went through the details of his attack for the last time with his leaders, received the blessings from a senior cleric and positioned himself in the truck.

He was all set to go and meet his awaited martyrdom. He knew from all the preaching and talks he had received that the instant he died he would be met by Hour al-Ayn, a nymph of unimaginable beauty and serenity. She would tend his wounds, wipe away the blood and escort him to heaven. He would die the most sublime death of martyrdom and paradise was certainly his reward.

The Marine barracks had been under surveillance for months. The planners knew that the soldiers slept late on Sunday. They knew what time the vegetable and provision trucks arrived in the area, which was near a huge market, and delivered goods to the American base. They had memorised practically every detail down to the colour of the trucks used. Not far away from the scene of the explosion, on the roof top of a nearby building, Mughniyeh and Badredeen smiled with satisfaction as they calmly watched the execution of their plan through binoculars. Mughniyeh was later to kidnap most of the Americans who were held hostage, as well as the British envoy Terry Waite.

Ten days later a carbon copy of the attack was launched against the Israelis in the second attack on their headquarters, in a different location, in the southern coastal city of Tyre. According to Israeli sources, the blast killed twenty-nine Israeli troops and wounded more than thirty. Lebanese sources, however, said the final toll was higher as the Amal militia announced that it had lost thirty-five prisoners being held inside the two-storey yellow building at the time. Islamic Jihad declared that it was willing to send 2,000 fighters to martyrdom to expel the Israelis and that it was preparing for attacks all over the world. Moshe Arens, Israel's defence minister, vowed to strike against

Lebanon which he described as one big nest of murderers: 'We are fighting a cruel and oppressive enemy who does not work with logical methods at least with regards to the general basis and principles acknowledged in the civilised world.' True to his word, Israeli warplanes wasted no time in bombarding Palestinian strongholds and pro-Iranian Shiite bases in the eastern Bekaa Valley, despite the lack of hard evidence at that stage of the identity or affiliations of the attackers.* The French soon followed suit and launched more reprisal air raids against targets in Baalbeck.

America initially had little means with which to trace those responsible, since the core of its intelligence had been killed when the embassy was bombed. It was clear, however, that a new movement was making its presence felt in Lebanon. Furthermore, the unfriendly force was continuously and openly broadcasting its hatred of the United States and threatening its interests there. It was also doing so in the name of Islam and under the banner of religion.

Hezbollah's leaders like to boast of having a long list of young Shiites eager to lay down their lives in martyr attacks, *al-Amaliya al-istishhaadiya*, as they call it. They passionately defend the practice and dislike the term suicide attacks. Although many Islamic scholars argue that the Quran prohibits suicide, the Shiites of the Party of God consider it the ultimate sacrifice in the course of defending their faith and existence. Their promotion of self-sacrifice is inspired by the fate of their Imam, Hussein, who died contesting his right to lead the Muslim people.

Following the death of the Prophet Mohammed, two schools of thought emerged over the question of his successor. It was a dispute that would lead, thirty years later, to the emergence of Islam's two main branches – Sunni and Shia. The majority of his followers believed that since the Prophet had not named a

---

* See *Sacred Rage*, Robin Wright

successor, his close companions should select one to lead the community. The other school of thought, however, argued that Mohammed had designated Ali, his cousin and son-in-law, to lead the community both as the Caliph, the political leader, and as the Imam, the spiritual leader. His followers became known as the Shiites or partisans of Ali. After the Prophet's death, Muslims who favoured other candidates repeatedly blocked the accession of Ali to the Caliphate. When he finally did come to rule, they withheld their allegiance.

Ali was murdered in 661 and the dominant Sunnis again chose a leader from outside his family. The Shiites, however, designated his son, Hussein, as his successor. In 680, Hussein, together with 100 followers and family members, set off to defend his right to the role of Caliph. They were massacred at the Iraqi town of Karbala by the Sunni Caliph of the Ummayad dynasty, Yazid, who had an army of thousands.

According to the dominant tradition in Shia Islam, Ali, Hussein and their successors are known as the Twelve Imams. The Twelfth Imam, or Mehdi, is believed to have disappeared in 874 and gone into occultation until the time comes for him to return and end tyranny, bringing the full and final revelation of God's word. Until this date, Shiites believe they are living in the *ghayba* era, concealment period.

The anniversary of Hussein's death is commemorated each year in the month of Muharram on the day of Ashura. The Shiites hold a public re-enactment of the events at Karbala. Processions are held in which recitations of Hussein's death from religious texts are read to wailing women and weeping men. The crowd usually works itself up into a state of frenzy. In the southern village of Nabatiyeh, men cut their heads open with razors and systematically beat their wounds to the rhythm of the recitations until the blood flows. Not all Shiites agree on the ritual of self-flagellation: while the secular party Amal condones it, Hezbollah actually frowns on the practice and has issued an edict, *fatwa*, against the custom.

Hussein's self-sacrifice in the face of tyranny has become a symbol for the Shia, particularly in Iran and Lebanon. He is known as the Prince of Martyrs. Given Hussein's symbolic stature, the Shiites were bound to be severely provoked by the Israelis' interruption of the Ashura festival in Nabatiyeh in October 1983. The incident was an appalling blunder and a decisive factor in the emergence of the Shiites' resistance against Israeli occupation.

Hussein's martyrdom served as a potent metaphor for the Iranian revolution and the festival of Ashura became an expression of revolutionary spirit. 'Fight through martyrdom,' instructed Khomeini, 'because the martyr is the essence of history.'* Hezbollah's human bombs have taken the same message to heart. Before Salah Ghandour drove his car into an Israeli convoy in 1995, the final message he taped on video showed that he did not see his deed merely as an act of war, but as a link in the chain of Shia martyrs, from Hussein onwards, until the final apocalyptic *jihad*, when the vanished Imam will return:

> I, Salah Mohammed Ghandour, known by my alias Malak, angel, ask God to grant me success in meeting the master of martyrdom Imam Hussein, this great Imam who taught all the free people how to avenge themselves on their oppressors.
>
> I shall, *inshaallah* [God willing], shortly after saying these words, be meeting my God with pride, dignity and having avenged my religion and all the martyrs who preceded me on this route. In a short while I shall avenge all the martyrs and oppressed of Jabal Amel, South Lebanon, as well as the children and sons of the Intifada in ravished Palestine. I shall avenge all those suffering in the tortured security zone. Oh sons of Ali and Hussein and sons of the great Imam Khomeini, God bless his soul. Yea sons of the leaders Khameini and sons of the martyr Abbas Musawi and Sheikh Ragheb Harb [Hezbollah martyrs], your *jihad*, *inshaallah*, is the preparatory *jihad* for the anticipated Imam, so let us continue until we achieve our desired target

---

* See *Islamic Fundamentalism*, Dilip Hiro, pp. 167–8

and the Godly gratification and thus arrive at our Godly promise. We belong to God and to God we shall return.

The literal definition of *jihad* is 'effort directed towards a goal'. In Islamic tradition, the goal is to spread Islam throughout the world by means of military force, if necessary, and it is every Muslim's duty to take part in the enterprise. Modern Islam has since come to rely on pacific forms of proselytism for its expansion, while the conditions for waging a *jihad* are now limited to cases of self-defence. In Shia Islam, only the Twelfth Imam is permitted to lead an offensive *jihad* and the practice has therefore long been in abeyance. Hezbollah's *jihad* is defined as a defensive *jihad*: Islamic law dictates that when land has been confiscated or occupied by an outside force, Muslims are obliged to participate in an armed struggle until the land is retrieved. In carrying out a *jihad*, Hezbollah is also relieving other Muslims of the responsibility to join in the fight. It is every Muslim's individual duty, *fard ayn,* to participate in a *jihad* unless a group like Hezbollah undertakes the struggle on their behalf as a collective duty, *fard kefaya.*

From his office in the southern suburbs of Beirut, Hezbollah's Deputy Secretary-General Naiim Qassem explained the terms of the *jihad*:

If the nation is not brought up on the principles of being prepared and willing to struggle or wage a *jihad*, then it cannot ever win against its enemies. We cannot rely on having rights alone. It sometimes takes power and force to attain those rights. Sadly, we live in a world where the law of the jungle applies – that is the stronger will always try to dominate the weaker. We see ourselves as a people whose rights have been taken away and so we need to have a force to help us. It is impossible for us to relinquish this. *Jihad* is a fundamental basis for us. We do not use it as a means of imposing our views on others, but consider ourselves in a state of *jihad* to defend our rights.

The use of human bombs has been an integral part of the *jihad*. To Hezbollah, it is not just a means of guerrilla warfare. Qassem explained that when a Muslim dies in a defensive *jihad* he fulfils two important objectives – his religious duty of waging a holy war as well as gratifying God by making the ultimate sacrifice. 'We are convinced and have faith that the moment of death of each person is in God's hand and is determined by God. We believe such dates are known to God and are recorded with the angels.' Qassem backed his explanation with a Quranic verse: 'And if their time of death arrives they cannot delay nor bring it forward.'

> Since we believe that our moment of death is recorded and determined by God, it follows that whether one hides in a shelter, is crossing the road or is fighting the enemy, he will die when his time arrives. Having established this it follows that when a fighter goes to fight in a *jihad* we do not consider him to be taking any more risks than the next man nor do we think he is bringing his moment of death closer. So, all he has done is to choose the manner or method in which he will die, if he is doomed to die at all on that particular day. If you understand Islam, you will undoubtedly be able to comprehend that this person is not being killed prior to his time. From here we regard martyrdom as a Muslim's choice of the manner in which he seeks to die.

Some Muslims, however, who lost their lives in human bomb attacks had not chosen to die in such a manner: when the Israeli military headquarters was attacked in Tyre, Palestinian and Lebanese prisoners in the building were killed in the blasts alongside Israelis. When the Shiite radicals met at the time to discuss the bombings of the two IDF bases, they were faced with an acute moral dilemma. Torn between their desire to attack Israel at the heart of its operations in Lebanon and their Islamic teaching and upbringing which condemned the killing of their fellow Muslims, the fighters realised that what they needed was not just a military decision, but a religious edict, *fatwa*, from a scholar. Edicts are widely used by Muslims for issues which are not clearly defined in the Quran and require further clarification.

While the Quran abhors and strongly prohibits the killing of Muslims by fellow Muslims and warns of harsh punishments to those who commit such acts, Hezbollah defend their case by saying that certain areas in the Quran allow for interpretation and thus provide their fighters with scope for action that can be justified religiously. Hezbollah's justification was that 'any action which constrains the enemy and foils their schemes is permissible in Islam, but also requires sanctioning by a scholar for it to fall within the Islamic laws'. Religious scholars have, according to Hezbollah, deduced that if the enemy uses Muslims as human shields, then Muslim fighters can kill them in their quest to annihilate the enemy. Although in these incidents the prisoners were not actually being used as human shields, the Muslim scholars decreed that the end justified the means. Such a doctrine, however, is only permitted if the enemy's toll of casualties exceeds the number of Muslim victims. An edict was duly passed which allowed the fighters to carry out the attacks despite the presence of the Muslim prisoners.

Hezbollah admits that in its early years, when the group was scarcely formed, some young men were allowed to sacrifice their lives as human bombs, even though, with hindsight, they might not have been of the right age or level of maturity. Today, although Hezbollah enrols fighters as young as seventeen for the continuing war of occupation with Israel, it selects only men of what it describes as a certain age-group, maturity and understanding, to go on its special missions and attacks.

Children are drilled in the merits of self-sacrifice from an early age, even though Hezbollah admits that the philosophy of martyrdom might be beyond their comprehension. Islamic religious studies, which are obligatory in all the curricula of Hezbollah schools, start introducing the tenet to the young by teaching them that paradise is their reward for death in battle. 'Al-Manar', Hezbollah's television station which currently transmits to most areas of Lebanon, is dominated by religious programmes. Pictures and names of martyrs are screened, supported by verses from the Quran which glorify such deaths: 'Therefore let those fight in the way of Allah, who sell this world's life for the hereafter, and whoever fights in the way of Allah, then be he slain or be he victorious, we shall grant him a mighty reward.' (Surat al-Nisaa, 74, The Quran). The aim is simple: to indoctrinate the minds of young and old with the idea that those who seek martyrdom will be rewarded with more pleasure than can ever be achieved during this earthly lifetime.

Hezbollah's technique has won success amongst its viewers. Contrary to the general belief that the group's military branch attracts only the minds and souls of the troubled, impoverished and uneducated, the Islamic Resistance delights in listing the range of its membership – from the unemployed to doctors and engineers. Even Shiite women have been caught up in the Hezbollah fever. Although not permitted to take part in the physical aspect of the *jihad*, most of the group's womenfolk pray that, should their fighting husbands die, they do so on the battlefield. To lose one's husband in a *jihad* brings a certain standing to a widow in society.

Rima Fakhri, a graduate in agriculture from the American University in Beirut, is planning to table a proposal for Hezbollah to recant a decree which prevents women from becoming human bombs. She is a member of Hezbollah's 'Women's Association'. She began to support Hezbollah at university, to the displeasure of her family. Her four brothers have since all become supporters. She believes that it is not possible to understand the concept of martyrdom without faith. She grew up in a devout Muslim family and has learnt and read all there is to know about the meaning of self-sacrifice. To her, it is as normal as being taught in childhood that stealing is a sin:

In our belief, a martyr is a human who has reached the pinnacle of humanity. We believe that such a person has transferred himself from this temporary world to what we regard as the everlasting and eternal world.

I know a woman whose husband was one of Hezbollah's cadre and who had volunteered himself as a martyr. Her husband died in a car crash and this woman was devastated more because he had not achieved martyrdom. You see, martyrdom is the objective of love and the route to victory. It is the topmost status of a lover.

In the early eighties, there were at least three female human bombs. A seventeen-year-old Sunni girl, Sanaa Muhaidily, became the first symbol of women's participation in the battle against Israel when she drove her white Peugeot car at an Israeli target, killing herself and two Israeli soldiers. Prior to the attack, she had disappeared for a year and her family had assumed that she had run away with a man. In fact she had joined the Syrian Social Nationalist Party (SSNP), one of the oldest parties in Lebanon, which calls for the creation of a Greater Syria including Lebanon. Like Salah Ghandour, Sanaa recorded a message on video which was broadcast around the Arab world. The beauty and youth of the young woman made a particular impact on the Lebanese public. President Assad of Syria praised her action and some of the region's best poets, including the Egyptian Khaled Mohammed Khaled, dedicated verses in her memory. Sanaa made her farewell in highly charged, romantic terms. She asked her mother to treat her death as if it were her wedding day and asked to be remembered as the Bride of the South:

> I have witnessed the calamity of my people under occupation. With total calmness I shall carry out an attack of my choice hoping to kill the largest number possible of the Israeli enemy. I hope my soul will join the souls of the other martyrs.
>
> I have not died, but am moving alive among you. I sing, I dance, and I am fulfilling all my dreams. How happy and joyful I am with this heroic martyrdom that I give. I plead with you, I kiss your hands one by one, do not cry for me, do not be sad for me, but be happy and smile. I

am now planted in the earth of the South irrigating and quenching her with my blood and my love for her. If only you knew the extent of my joy, you would then certainly encourage all those marching along the path of liberation to stand against the terrorist Zionists.

Few who have seen the video have forgotten the gentle face and voice of the girl. While the glory of martyrdom clearly played an important role in her act, her poetic valediction sprang from a fanatical sense of nationalism rather than from the religious principles which inspire Hezbollah's human bombs. The SSNP claim that Sanaa volunteered to make the attack; she was not the party's only human bomb, but in the past seven years Hezbollah alone has continued to keep up the practice of sending their fighters off to martyrdom.

Hezbollah has no shortage of intelligent and well-educated supporters who can justify the use of human bombs. Hassan, a young civil engineer, is one such case. He would not hesitate to go on such a mission himself, given the chance:

You look at it with a Western mentality. You regard it as barbaric and unjustified. We, on the other hand, see it as another means of war, but one which is also harmonious with our religion and beliefs. Take, for example, an Israeli warplane or, better still, the American and British air power in the Gulf War. They dropped tons of bombs on their targets. The goal of their mission and the outcome of their deeds was to kill and damage enemy positions just like us, except our enemy is Israel. The only difference is that they had at their disposal state-of-the-art and top-of-the-range means and weaponry to achieve their aims. We have the minimum basics, but that does not bother us because we know that if and when required we also have ourselves to sacrifice. They get medals and titles for their feats of bravery and victories. We, on the other hand, do not seek material rewards, but heavenly ones in the hereafter.

But in truth there is no difference between their attacks

and ours. Both of us have one thing in common – to annihilate the enemy. The rest is mere logistics and differences in techniques. Whether one attacks by planes or by car bombs the objective is the same. Who is to say that they are better or more civilised just because they use twentieth-century equipment? Who decides that it is more right or correct or even more acceptable to kill one's enemy by warplanes rather than by car bombs?

His sentiments echo those of Japan's kamikaze fighters in the Second World War. In his book *Suicide Squads*, Richard O' Neill recounts the US Strategic Bombing Survey's (USSBS) interrogation of a Japanese Lieutenant General, who explained the kamikaze soldiers' motivation:

> We believed that our spiritual convictions and moral strength could balance your material and scientific advantages. We did not consider our attacks to be suicide . . . [the pilot] looked upon himself as a human bomb which would destroy a certain part of the enemy fleet . . . [and] died happy in the conviction that his death was a step towards final victory.

The USSBS's report on kamikaze missions could be contemporary: 'Macabre, effective, supremely practical under the circumstances, supported and stimulated by a powerful propaganda campaign.'

Hassan is thirty-two. He graduated as a civil engineer in the United States and returned home to Lebanon a few years ago. He was one of the more fortunate, whose family could afford to send him to America for further education. On his return, he could have worked for any company in Lebanon, yet he decided to join the ranks of Hezbollah, putting his degree and knowledge to use with one of the group's construction organisations. Hassan spends three months a year with Hezbollah's hard-core resistance fighters. After that, provided he does not get killed, he returns to civilian life in the city, where he continues to construct buildings and maintain a normal existence. Israeli citizens lead a similar double life, spending part of each year in the army reserves:

> I joined the group because, contrary to what many believe or say, Hezbollah is very sincere in its motives and goals. I found that my political views and beliefs are most harmonious with those of Hezbollah. To me, this is the group. It continues to make sacrifices and fight against the enemy when all others have forsaken us. The world today complains about Hezbollah, yet it has not lifted a finger to end our people's suffering. It calls us terrorists. Imagine! Israel occupies our land and we, the occupied people, are branded terrorists.

Hassan was speaking from one of the front lines of South Lebanon. A teacher, an engineer and a doctor gathered round to listen and all agreed with his views. While Hassan fiddled with his M16 rifle, Israeli warplanes flew over the hills and the men scattered to take up their combat positions. Fortunately, it was not an air raid, but one of Israel's daily reconnaissance flights. Once the planes had flown over, the fighters relaxed. Hassan's earlier friendly look had become a steely glare and he continued with an icy voice:

> The West demands that we halt all attacks and end our war with Israel. How can we listen to, or even obey, such a world when it so blatantly defends the side which is committing the wrongdoing and condemns those with a cause? Why should we listen to such a world order? You tell me! How come every country in the world rallied its support against Saddam for invading Kuwait, and the United States, the so-called defender of human rights and freedom, instigated a war against him to free Kuwait. Why wasn't the same done for Lebanon? How come Israel's occupation of Lebanon has been allowed to go on for more than fifteen years?

Don't you see, we have wised up to the fact that it's all a charade. We know that nothing any more is about human rights and freedom. Everything these days is about self-interest. The world is not bothered with Lebanon because, unlike Kuwait, we are not an oil-rich country. There are no gains to be made here and so it does not matter much to them whether Israel continues to occupy South Lebanon or not. That may be so in their view, but for us, Lebanon matters. It is our home, it is our country and above all it is our children's future. That, to us, is worth all the oil in the world. So our choice is to fight on and liberate it ourselves. That will be our legacy to our future generation.

4

Export of a Revolution

He was blindfolded and taken away at the dead of night on more than one occasion. Each time, Giandomenico Picco could never be sure that they would let him go. But in order to negotiate with the ringleaders of the hostage crisis Picco, deputy to the UN secretary-general, had to put his life in the hands of their henchmen and be virtually taken captive himself. They would collect Picco in West Beirut and change cars about four times, depending on the length of the journey. When he was finally brought into the presence of the kidnappers, they never revealed their faces: they sat opposite him in balaclavas, while their associates hovered in the background.

It was a dangerous odyssey, but Picco succeeded where many others had failed and secured the freedom of all the remaining hostages in Lebanon, including John McCarthy, Terry Waite and Terry Anderson. Sometimes he would leave the meetings with one of the hostages. At other times, the kidnappers would release a hostage while the negotiations were taking place. Finally, on 17 June 1992, Picco escorted the last two hostages home from captivity: the German aid workers Heinrich Struebig and Thomas Kemptner.

A suave and handsome man, Picco had credibility. Without it, he claims, he would not have accomplished his mission. Thanks to his extensive experience in Iran, he knew whom to approach in Lebanon. Picco had won the trust of the Iranians: in 1988, he had negotiated the cease-fire of the Iran–Iraq war which had lasted for eight years and cost the lives of more than a million Iranians and Iraqis. 'The end of the war with Iraq, which had a lot to do with this story as far as I am concerned, was very handy for the Iranians who were losing the war at the time, although there were still those who did not want the war to come to an end. All these things created a very interesting chemistry. What I did [for the Iranians], and what the Iranians thought the world would think of them, gave me very good credit,' he smiled.

When he first tried to broach the subject of the hostages, the Iranians rebuffed him. Officials told Picco that the time to solve the hostage crisis was not yet ripe. Then, in January 1989, President Bush made overtures to Iran in his inauguration speech, 'Goodwill begets goodwill,' and the Iranians responded. 'It was the first opening for this issue in theory, but a very important one,' Picco recalled. During a meeting with Picco, a senior Iranian raised the question of the hostages and said that, while Iran did not control the situation, it could perhaps wield some influence over the Lebanese. Even though he was reiterating Iran's official line, Picco instantly knew that the wheels had been set in motion. The mere fact that a senior Iranian official had personally brought up the subject indicated that the Islamic Republic was finally ready to play. 'That was their position and it was fine by me. I decided to take their "influence" as enough for me and thought, "Let's see what we can do with that basis." That was at least the rationale behind it.'

So Picco began his odyssey. It would take him on endless trips and on a trail of covert meetings and discussions that would lead to Lebanon, a country where civil war and ethnic cleansing, foreign invasions and assassinations, car bombs and kidnappings all appeared to have become a way of life. Ultimately, it took Picco to the southern suburbs of Beirut, bastion of the Islamic militants. The shadowy groups which had held the Western world to ransom for nearly a decade were born in the grinding poverty of this neighbourhood. The dark maze of narrow alleyways sheltered the perpetrators of the kidnappings and became the prison of the Western hostages. It was the heart of Hezbollah's operations and Hezbollah was alleged to be the mastermind of the hostage crisis. 'Hezbollah was the political force behind the whole crisis, no doubt in my mind,' claimed Picco. 'But whether that carries the responsibilities all the way down is open to discussion. Does Sinn Fein control the IRA? I don't know if we have the same story here.'

Many clues pointed to Hezbollah's involvement. Hezbollah had never hidden its animosity towards the West, and in particular the US and Israel. It had also exalted some of the acts of terrorism committed against Western targets. During the course of the hostage crisis, a security source known as 'the Baron' claimed that Islamic Jihad, one of the leading, faceless groups which took Westerners hostage, was simply a covert name. He insisted that they were all one and the same – Hezbollah. He explained that the groups were part of Hezbollah's 'secret security apparatus' and that their sole mission was to penalise the West by whatever means available: they were the Party of God's hidden hand of terrorism. The source appeared to be reliable: he was a senior member of an intelligence apparatus which headed Beirut security operations for a Muslim militia. He had also revealed that Terry Waite had been kidnapped at a time when journalists still believed that Waite was conducting negotiations with the kidnappers of the American hostages. Yet Hezbollah itself has continuously and vehemently denied involvement in the kidnappings. There is no doubt that Hezbollah shared a common ideology with the kidnappers and allowed them to operate in the areas under its control. It is not so certain, however, that Hezbollah was the prime mover; there were other players with stakes in the game, whose influence spread beyond the boundaries of Lebanon.

The hostage crisis began in 1984, but the gambit was played during the pivotal summer of 1982 when Hezbollah was in its infancy. In July, the Christian militia of the Lebanese Forces kidnapped three Iranian officials and their driver at the Barbara checkpoint, 25 miles north of Beirut, on the edge of the Christian enclave. They were important men: Ahmad Motevaselian, commander of the Iranian Revolutionary Guards in the Bekaa, Mohsen Musavi, Iran's chargé d'affaires in Lebanon and Kazem Akhavan Allaf, a journalist for Iran's official news agency. Their driver's name was Mohammed Taghi Rastegar Moqadani. Two weeks later, on 19 July 1982, gunmen abducted David Dodge, an American, from the campus of the American University in Beirut (AUB) in broad daylight. Dodge was the acting president of the AUB. He knew Lebanon well: he had lived there since the late fifties and had worked on the oil pipelines. He had left the country briefly after civil war broke out and then returned to be an administrator at the university.

It was the first abduction of a foreign national in Lebanon. At the time, the kidnappings did not appear to be related. The four Iranians' abduction had not attracted much attention in the Lebanese and foreign press. In fact, many had even missed the incident completely. The West's intelligence services in Beirut later revealed that not only had they misjudged the episode and failed to anticipate the possible repercussions, but that they had also gravely misinterpreted the significance of the Iranian Revolutionary Guards' arrival in Lebanon. Information regarding the fate of the Iranians was to become one of Iran's main conditions in return for its help in securing the release of the Western hostages. In December 1988, Hashemi Rafsanjani publicly addressed the Americans just before he was elected president of Iran: 'If you are interested in having your people [who are] held hostage in Lebanon released, then tell the Phalangists [Christian militia] to release our people who have been in their hands for years.'

Dodge was abducted initially by the Lebanese. He then became a pawn in the hands of their more powerful sponsors: the Iranians and the Palestinians. All were involved in his abduction at different stages and all hoped to use him to fulfil their different demands. The episode not only presaged things to come, it reflected a momentous change which was taking place on the ground. The Palestinians were on their way out of Lebanon and the Iranians were making their entrance. Their involvement in the kidnap heralded Iran's debut and marked the swansong of the PLO.

The details of Dodge's abduction emerged many years later in unlikely circumstances – during preparations for a picnic in the BekaaValley in August 1994.The host, who will be identified as Farid for the purposes of this book, played a key role in the kidnap. Farid is related to a notorious clan in the area, and his brother-in-law was directly linked to the kidnap of Terry Waite, John McCarthy and Brian Keenan.The family also includes a cousin who was involved in the abduction of the Korean hostage Do Chae-Sung. He was arrested by the Syrian authorities shortly after exchanging the captive for a ransom of 1,150,000 dollars.

Farid is a professor of literature and a graduate of the Lebanese University of Beirut. He is a handsome man with piercing blue eyes. Like hundreds of other Lebanese young men, including many university students, he joined the ranks of the PLO guerrillas in his youth to fight with his brethren for the Palestinian cause. Many such men, who would later break ranks with the PLO, had also been members of the PLO's Force 17. His explanation was revealing:

> When we kidnapped Dodge we chose him first because of his nationality and his status as the administrator of the American University of Beirut.We believed that we could use him as a means of pressuring the Americans to do something about the Israeli invasion of Lebanon and to warn them against trying to impose their political agenda regarding Israel in Lebanon's political scenario.
>
> We knew that Arafat and Abu Jihad [chief of PLO's military forces] had opened channels with the Americans and were beginning to soften their approach after the Israeli invasion with regards to the cause.We were getting disappointed with the Palestinians, mainly Arafat and Abu Jihad, and we felt they had betrayed us and the cause to which we had been dedicated. At the time there was no such thing as Hezbollah or Islamic militants, we were a group of young Muslim Lebanese *shabaabs* [guys] fighting with the Palestinians and Force 17. We knew it was time to

split from the PLO and to develop our own force if we were to carry on with our war against Israel's occupation. Dodge was only a means for us to make our political grievances known and to try and achieve something from the Americans.

Farid spoke without regret or remorse as he recounted the details. Even years after the event he still stood by the beliefs which had motivated him in 1982. Lebanon was a small, defenceless country and the Lebanese were caught in the middle of Israel's war against the PLO. Farid and his comrades believed that the world had abandoned them at the time. They felt that they had to strike back if only to make themselves heard. As one analyst put it:

The whole process was never about what people would think of them. That did not matter. What mattered most to these men was to draw attention to their cause and to do so they would undertake the worst and most extreme acts to make their point heard. That the world would call them terrorists or threaten them was of little significance to these men. It was the least of their worries. You see, in their minds they totally believed in what they were doing, regardless of what the rest of the world thought and that was their driving force.

While his wife prepared the picnic, Farid went to a closet in the bedroom and took out an old shoebox filled with papers, letters and old snapshots. After flicking through its contents for a few minutes he selected two pictures; they were photographs of Dodge's family, 'These were sent to [Dodge] while he was a captive,' said Farid, 'but he never got them.'

For more than ten years, these photographs of Dodge's son and daughter in their graduation gowns had been sitting in the old shoebox on the top shelf of Farid's wardrobe, in this remote village in the Bekaa Valley. The pictures had been sent to Dodge by his family as a reminder of his loved ones during his year in captivity and had instead been kept by one of his captors as a memento of Lebanon's first foreign hostage. Many other homes may hold similar souvenirs. Letters written by the captives that were never sent, unpublished photographs of the hostages in their wretched circumstances, daily journals of their lives in captivity in which some exposed their rawest emotions, as well as some of the personal items taken from these men at the start of their bondage.

About three weeks or so after Dodge was first kidnapped, his guards told him they would be taking him on a trip that would lead to his release. The Israeli army was blockading Beirut and the kidnappers had sensed that the army was about to invade the capital. They needed to move Dodge to the safety of the Bekaa where the Israeli troops had no jurisdiction. The area was still under Syrian control and not far off were the new arrivals, the Iranian Revolutionary Guards.

'It was crazy,' recalled Farid, revealing for the first time how the kidnappers managed to remove Dodge from Beirut under the noses of the Israelis:

> There was no way for us to move him without him being discovered by the Israeli troops surrounding the city. Finally we thought of building a compartment in one of the sofas and putting him in the compartment below the cushions and pretending that we were a family moving out of Beirut. The sofa would be placed with other pieces of furniture in a station wagon and it would look like someone was moving house rather than smuggling a hostage out. We had to give him several drug injections, though, just to make sure that he would not wake up in the middle of the trip and cause us problems.

Dodge became a joint hostage of the Lebanese kidnappers and the Iranians in the Bekaa, who also saw him as a means of getting information about their four abducted compatriots. One of the guards told Dodge that his release depended upon the fate of their 'four friends'; another guard remarked to him, after

Israeli war planes renewed their attacks on Beirut, that war planes from Dodge's country were bombing the city. These were the only indications which Dodge received of the kidnappers' motives in holding him hostage.*

With Dodge safely tucked away in the Bekaa and far away from the reach of the Israelis and Palestinians, his kidnappers set about making their demands. Dodge's kidnapping had forced the Americans to seek the influence of the PLO for the first time. The PLO had established a large and effective intelligence apparatus in Lebanon, which was more likely to be able to trace Dodge than the Lebanese authorities. In Farid's words:

> We let Abu Jihad know that we had Dodge and asked him to send our demands to the Americans. They were simple. We wanted an end to the Israeli invasion and an end to the Israeli–US-backed efforts to impose a pro-Israeli government in Lebanon. We knew the Americans were seeking information about the hostage through Abu Jihad so we decided to use the Palestinians as well. We would give Abu Jihad information on his well-being and progress to pass on to the Americans in return for arms and money from the PLO that we needed in order to reorganise ourselves and prepare ourselves for carrying on with the struggle against the Israelis after the PLO's withdrawal.

Abu Jihad knew that it would only be a matter of time before Israel finished off his guerrillas. They had been pushed out of the South and were now trapped in West Beirut. The Mediterranean was on one side and Christian East Beirut, bastion of the PLO's enemies, on the other. He had to save the situation and maintain what was left of his army. Abu Jihad thought fast and decided to act as a middleman between the kidnappers and the Americans. In his desperation he too took advantage of Dodge's abduction to win US concessions for his

---

* See *Hostage*, Con Coughlin, p. 29

men's survival. He needed guarantees for the PLO's evacuation and future safety. Abu Jihad provided the Lebanese kidnappers with arms and ammunition, as well as dozens of forged passports, and talked the Americans into securing a safe way out for the PLO guerrillas. The passports were later to be used by some of the men wanted for abducting hostages and for making attacks against Western targets. Abu Jihad also supplied the Lebanese with the TNT which blew up the Israeli military headquarters in Tyre later that year. It was his legacy to the Lebanese who had fought side by side with the Palestinians.

While Abu Jihad secured the safe departure of the PLO, Dodge remained in the hands of his kidnappers. The Iranians had taken charge of him and prepared to move him to another location. Again Dodge was told he would have to be drugged before being transported. His kidnappers told him that they were moving him back to Beirut as a prelude to his release, but Dodge regained consciousness to find himself in a wooden crate. He had been taken to Tehran and spent the next three months in the infamous Evin jail, where the Iranian Revolutionary Guards had executed hundreds of the Shah's followers in the wake of Khomeini's Islamic Revolution. Whenever he was interrogated, he was asked for information about the missing Iranians.

On the first anniversary of his abduction, Dodge was taken out of his cell, given back the clothes he had worn on the day of his abduction, and driven back to the airport by an official of the Iranian Revolutionary Guards. From there, he flew first class to Syria. His distinguished travelling companions included Syria's Foreign Minister Farouq al-Sharaa and a company of Iranian Revolutionary Guards on their way to Lebanon. At Damascus airport his escort handed him over to a waiting car and from there he was taken to the home of President Assad's brother. The following morning he was handed over to the American embassy.

President Assad had been enraged by Iran's role in the abduction. The Iranians had, in effect, engineered a second kidnap. He was also displeased with the Iranians for abusing their diplomatic privileges and smuggling Dodge into Iran via Syria. He was not prepared to let Tehran embarrass him further with the West by undertaking terrorist acts that would rebound on Syria. Assad therefore secured Dodge's release as a signal to his Iranian allies that there were limits to their activities in Lebanon.*

Dodge's kidnapping proved to be something of a dry run for the Lebanese and Iranian kidnappers. One of the most important lessons learnt by the Lebanese abductors during the Dodge affair was that they could only wield influence if they maintained physical control of their captives. By allowing the Iranian Revolutionary Guards to take over and ship Dodge to Tehran, the Lebanese kidnappers gave up any command over his fate and lost their bargaining power.

Farid explained that the error was due to their lack of organisation at the time. 'We had no central structure and were still very much in our infancy. It was a learning process for us. We were told that the Americans were not interested in our demands and that Dodge had become a losing card which was better set free,' he explained in embarrassment, as if he had realised their naïvety for the first time. 'We would do better with the future hostages. At least in the French mediation we managed to get what we wanted.' Farid, in later years, was one of the Lebanese intermediaries in the negotiations conducted with French officials for the release of their nationals.

The Iranians, meanwhile, were only too happy to adopt a distant participation in future episodes of hostage-taking. They had learnt the hard way that harbouring hostages in their country would not be to their political advantage, even if it was on behalf of their staunchest allies. The Islamic Republic was determined never again to be caught in a position where the West held proof of its involvement in such acts of terrorism. It could fend off accusations that it was encouraging its Shiite disciples to carry out abductions, so long as there was no hard evidence of

---

* See *Hostage*, Con Coughlin, pp. 36–6

its physical involvement. To be seen to be holding the captives in Iran, it had learnt from the Dodge affair, would deprive it of the argument which it used in later years and reiterated to Picco: that it was not in control of the kidnappers, but that it could exert some influence.

Dodge's kidnap marked the end of an era and ushered in a new order. The PLO's influence was waning. They had trained and armed Lebanese militants for years. The men like Farid who kidnapped Dodge were graduates of the PLO's military camps and they had turned to the PLO for help during the abduction. But the operation had been hijacked by the new-comers on the Lebanese scene, the Iranian Revolutionary Guards. Even as Arafat was packing up and leaving Beirut that summer, the Guards were already making their presence felt. In future, they would provide the training to the Lebanese radicals. The enemy, Israel, had not changed, but the agenda was altogether different.

The arrival of the Guards in Baalbeck in the Bekaa Valley during the summer of 1982 did not attract much attention or arouse the curiosity of the buzzing local journalists and Western media who had converged on Beirut to cover Israel's invasion. Most were too engrossed in the Israelis' activities to pay much heed to what the Iranians were doing. Certainly no one remembered Khomeini's declarations of exporting the Revolution. Iran was thousands of miles away and the Lebanese, the Shiites included, were known for their secular way of life and their co-existence in a multi-confessional system, despite the ongoing civil war. Baalbeck, the capital of Lebanon's Bekaa Valley, had once drawn crowds to its festivals in the fifties and sixties. The celebrated Lebanese singer Fairuz had performed there alongside other international stars. Baalbeck's ancient Roman temples of Jupiter and Bacchus were also major tourist attractions. Everything changed with the arrival of the Iranian Revolutionary Guards and the birth of Islamic militancy; the neighbourhood became off-limits to foreigners and Lebanese alike.

The Guards set up training camps in the Bekaa and attracted

scores of young men to their military training programmes. Furthermore, they had organised special teams to rove the region and the remote villages scattered around the Bekaa Valley to preach the tenets of Islam and the teachings and doctrines of Khomeini to the villagers. They were proving popular with the locals: along with the religious rhetoric which they spread, they were also advising the community on issues as diverse as martyrdom and harvesting.

Lebanon's preoccupation with the civil war and Israel's invasion gave the Guards the freedom to operate. The Lebanese government was not equipped to stop their activities and the country's internal security system had almost ceased to function. Much of the country had been divided into fiefdoms under the control of the country's confessional sects. Baalbeck and its surrounding vicinity became a no-man's-land, cut off from the rest of the country. It had turned into a miniature Iranian republic, where the doctrine of the Guards, Khomeini and the Shiite clerics of Hezbollah reigned.

Even the Lebanese army, based in the notorious Sheikh Abdullah Barracks in Baalbeck, was evicted shortly after the arrival of the Guards in the Bekaa. In November a demonstration instigated by the Guards and Lebanese radicals brought thousands of men and women to the barracks to demand the eviction of the Lebanese army which they accused of being a tool in the hands of Bashir Gemayel, and party to Israeli–American scheming against the Muslims. In the ensuing fracas, hundreds of women, dressed in *chador*, forced their way into the barracks. It was the last time that the Lebanese army would have any presence in the town until 1992, when Hezbollah formally handed back the barracks to the government. Until then, however, the Sheikh Abdullah Barracks served as a fortress and base for the Iranian Revolutionary Guards. Many of the hostages are said to have been kept there at some point in their captivity. It was also conveniently close to Damascus, where the Iranian embassy, led by Mohtashemi, served as a base for the export of the Revolution to Lebanon and the Middle East. Free from official Lebanese control in the area, the Guards' contingent turned Baalbeck into a base for launching its extreme anti-American ideological campaign.

Following the success of Iran's Revolution, Khomeini had embarked on an agenda known as *Mashru al-Thawra al-Iraniyah*, the Project of the Iranian Revolution. This aimed at furthering Islam by reviving the Islamic *Ummah*, the worldwide Islamic Nation, which was to be based in Iran and led by Khomeini as the *Amir al-Muminun*, Commander of the Faithful. In Khomeini's view, the revolution marked the second advent of the true Islam and his goal was to spread its influence beyond the boundaries of Iran. Khomeini stressed that in exporting the revolution he did not seek to invade neighbouring states and did not harbour expansionist plans: the goal was to be achieved by means of an 'invisible force' and the route to success lay through cultivating the populace.

'If we wish to export the revolution, we should do something so that the people hold the reign of affairs and the so-called third class have the upper hand,' declared Khomeini on 14 October 1981. 'It is only through non-official trips that you can have contact with ordinary people in the streets and awaken them. Being among the people without official decorations is more effective and better for propaganda.'

The Islamic Revolutionary Guards Corps became an integral part of the programme.* They were initially set up in 1979 as an internal security apparatus to consolidate Khomeini's grip on Iran and grew to become one of the strongest institutions ever produced by the revolution and a primary tool for promoting Khomeini's doctrines. Ayatollah Montazeri, one of Khomeini's closest aides and his heir apparent, laid down the guidelines for the Guards' mission abroad. A staunch supporter of the concept of exporting the revolution, he took every opportunity to explain the programme to the Iranians as well as to foreign delegates and Muslims overseas, and, he declared:

---

* See *The Warriors of Islam*, Kenneth Katzman, p. 7

Had the aim of the Islamic Revolution of Iran been merely to overthrow the Shah of Iran, it would have been confined within the borders of Iran. If it had intended only to fight the US, it would possibly have penetrated the countries dominated by the US. But as the Islamic Revolution of Iran is an unswerving process which intends to eradicate falsehood, it will advance in any land where falsehood exists.*

The Guards Corps included 'cultural units' to spread the word of the Revolution and rescue the deprived of the world from the domination of the superpowers. The importance of their task placed them above the law, said Montazeri:

> The essential responsibility of the Guards of the Islamic Revolution, as stated in the constitution, is to protect the revolution from internal and external plots, and it is natural that if the revolution cannot export its universal message, its spiritual and ideological dimensions to other lands it will stagnate at home and so eventually be destroyed.
>
> Therefore the Guards Corps is duty bound, especially the institution's units, to act with more power and freedom, disregarding all obstructive officials and bureaucratic delays, and utilising the guidance of religious guardians and the leader of the revolution. They should be inspired directly by the thoughts of the *ulama* [religious class] in order to be able to perform their great responsibility.

The Guards set off to realise Khomeini's dream. This was to be carried out through flagrant military intervention, as was the case in Lebanon, and through covert political interference. The Guards did not create a separate division to export the revolution; they trained and armed militant surrogates and

---

* Montazeri's quotes cited in *Extracts from Speeches of Ayatollah Montazeri*, ed: Mustafa Izadi

agents at many camps and locations throughout Iran. These agents then personally recruited Shiite militants overseas to carry out operations both in the Middle East and Europe. The Guards supported revolutionary activists outside Iran and built a network of die-hard extremists. The Guards operated in Arab states, in particular the Gulf region, and in countries which had allied themselves with Iraq during the Iran–Iraq war. In Saudi Arabia they have been heavily involved in planning and instigating rioting during the annual Islamic Hajj pilgrimage season. The apparatus ran under the national command of the Guards in Tehran, but the agents, units and cells also had the assistance, financial backing and logistical support of a running network of hard-liners placed both within the Iranian hierarchy inside the Islamic Republic and outside Iran. This included Mohtashemi and Hossein Sheikh-Ol-Eslam, Iran's deputy foreign minister for Arab affairs. He was a key leader of the 'students' who seized the US embassy in Tehran and held its staff hostage in 1979.*

The Guards' agents occupy positions at Iranian embassies across Europe, Africa and Asia. Under diplomatic cover, they have recruited proxies and cells for operations worldwide, including the assassination of Tehran's opponents abroad. In 1992, a group of Iranian Kurdish activists was murdered in a restaurant in Berlin by a hit-squad. German police arrested five suspects: four Lebanese and an Iranian agent. Their trial began in 1993 and had still not reached a conclusion in 1996. Iran's embassy in Bonn is considered to be the headquarters of Iran's operations in Europe. The State Department and the CIA claims that Iran has been behind 1,000 deaths in 200 terrorist strikes since 1979.**

French targets were being attacked from as early as 1980 by the Guards' apparatus. Not only had France offered sanctuary to members of the Shah's administration, it had also armed

---

* See *The Warriors of Islam*, Kenneth Katzman, pp. 95–101
** 'Iran's State of Terror', *Time Magazine*, 11 November 1996

Iraq in its war against Iran and had frozen Iranian assets. On 18 July 1980, Annis Naccache was arrested for the attempted assassination of the former Iranian Premier Shapour Bakhtiar. Naccache was a Christian Lebanese who had converted to Islam and pledged allegiance to Khomeini following the success of the revolution. A *gendarme* and a bystander were killed in the subsequent battle with the police. Naccache and three others were given life sentences, while the fifth participant received a twenty-year sentence. Naccache's release later became a condition for freeing the Western hostages in Lebanon.

On 4 September 1981 the French ambassador to Lebanon, Louis Delamare, was shot dead. While France blamed Syria for the attack, officials and Lebanese intelligence claim that the murder was carried out by Shiite extremists belonging to the al-Dawa organisation. In March 1982, three months before Israel's invasion, the French embassy in Beirut was bombed. Nine people were killed and twenty-seven wounded. Shiite extremists, belonging to the al-Dawa party and sponsored by the Guards, were considered to be behind the bombing too.

When Israel invaded Lebanon, Montazeri told the Lebanese clerics who were visiting Iran in August 1982 that they should draw inspiration from the Islamic Revolution. The following month he declared, 'It is disgraceful for Muslims to keep silent and let Zionists ruthlessly transgress their territory causing so much damage, ruin and loss of life . . . it is the duty of all Muslims to react and deal a blow upon the enemy.'

With each such declaration, Montazeri was issuing a licence to kill and instigate violence. Militants both in Tehran and abroad considered that Montazeri's orders emanated from Khomeini himself. The Guards duly embarked on their campaign in Lebanon to carry out Khomeini's orders of punishing the 'crimes and oppression of the enemies of Islam especially America and Israel'.

Hezbollah was just one of the Guards' protégés in Lebanon. The Guards had also come with a covert mission to recruit agents and set up an apparatus, beyond Hezbollah, for its hard-line Islamic Revolution. The agents would undertake military

Remains of barroom graffiti from the bombed American Marines barracks.

This house at Qaaqaiyet, near Jibsheet, was raided by Amal militiamen cooperating in the search for American hostages Lt Colonel Higgins and CIA chief William Buckley whose bodies were later returned to the US government at the end of the hostage crisis. In a garage at the rear the Amal men found a false wall which, when revolved, revealed several small cells where it is thought Higgins and Buckley were both held after their capture in Southern Lebanon and before they were moved to Hezbollah strongholds. The men shown are Amal members.

Abbas Musawi, leader of Hezbollah until his murder (along with that of his wife and youngest child) by an Israeli helicopter gunship attack on his motorcade in 1992.

Hezbollah leader in 1996, Sayyed Hassan Nasrallah: 'We are fighting on behalf of a people, a nation and a government.'

The first foreign national to be kidnapped in Lebanon was the president of the American University in Beirut, David Dodge. The photograph is of Dodge's son and daughter in 1982 (the year of the kidnap) never reached Dodge and are retained to this day by his kidnapper as a commemoration of the event.

Hezbollah fighters on the edge of the security zone in South Lebanon, equipped with Sam-7 missiles and mortar.

Sayyed Mohammed Hussein Fadlallah, Shiite cleric, and though not
formally a member of Hezbollah, a guide to many of Hezbollah's members
– here with bodyguards.

Sheikh Subhi Tufeili, Hezbollah 'godfather' and founder, in the courtyard outside his home in the Bekaa, with bodyguards.

The author with Sheikh Naiim Qassem, Hezbollah's deputy general secretary.

**The Israeli Khiam prison, where many Lebanese Shiites have been held
without trial.**

'Hostage Hilton' in the Southern suburbs of Beirut. One of several prisons where Terry Waite, John McCarthy and the other Western hostages were held, it is an unfinished school that was subsequently used as a barracks.

One of John McCarthy's prisons: he was held for some months in the basement of this building in the Southern suburbs of Beirut.

The shelling of Nabatiyeh, April 1996. Immediately behind the villa shown is the home of a Lebanese minister critical of Israel's occupation of the security zone.

The youngest victim of Operation Grapes of Wrath: four-day-old Nour, smaller at her death than the 155mm howitzer shell that killed her in Nabatiyeh.

Abbas and his surviving family with pictures of his wife and daughters who were killed as they fled the South of Lebanon in an ambulance which was attacked by a helicopter gunship. Abbas had taken no part in the conflict in the Lebanon, returning there from Germany only in 1995.

General Antoine Lahad, commander of the Israel-sponsored South Lebanon Army, sentenced to death with eighty-seven others in autumn 1996 by the Lebanese government for collaboration with Israel.

The massacre at Qana, 18 April 1996, a UN compound shelled by 155mm howitzers. The troops in the photographs are Fijian UN forces, clearing the carnage over which they had no control; 109 Lebanese refugees were killed.

The mourning at Qana. This, more than any other single factor, has sustained Hezbollah's resistance.

The body of a child killed at Qana.

operations on its behalf against Arab, Western and American targets in the name of cleansing the region from foreign dominion as a preliminary step to the ultimate dream of establishing Islamic Republics similar to that in Iran.

Lebanon's Islamic Jihad and its shadowy sister groups were part of this operation. Islamic Jihad threatened, terrorised and claimed responsibility for a chain of horrendous attacks. Yet it had no distinct public figures, no one particular leader or chieftain to arrest, no offices and worse still no specific address against which counter-attacks or retaliations could be launched. Its name was deliberately contrived by the Guards and their recruits to cast confusion. With the exception of the extremist Palestinian Islamic Jihad, which currently exists in the West Bank and Gaza Strip and whose name was inspired by the Lebanese example, Lebanon's entity was more of a phantom than a fully fledged organisation. It existed only when it was committing an atrocity against its targets: rather like a phoney company which rents office space for a month and then vanishes.

Until the early eighties, the practice of kidnapping was confined to the local population in Lebanon and thousands of Lebanese were abducted. During the hostage crisis, at least eighty-seven foreigners were kidnapped, including seventeen Americans, fourteen Britons, fifteen French, seven Swiss and seven West Germans. At least ten hostages perished in captivity: some were murdered and others died from illnesses which did not receive adequate medical attention. The first foreign hostage to be murdered was the Dutch Catholic priest Nicholas Kluiters. A total of seventeen different phantoms claimed responsibility for the abductions. Some were related to Islamic Jihad. These included Organisation of the Islamic Dawn, Islamic Jihad for the Liberation of Palestine, the Revolutionary Justice Organisation, Holy Warriors for Freedom, Khaibar Brigade, Organisation of the Oppressed on Earth and Revolutionary Cells. Islamic Jihad for the Liberation of Palestine abducted four professors at Beirut University: Alann Steen, Jesse Turner, Robert Polhill and Mitheleshwar Singh. The kidnappers brazenly posed as members of Lebanon's Internal Security Forces and visited the university campus on the pretext that they had come to advise the professors on security. They then kidnapped them.

Western intelligence plunged into a long, frustrating and fruitless quest for Islamic Jihad. The US Department of State continued to place advertisements in European and Arabic newspapers for a year after the release of all the hostages, offering rewards of between one and two million US dollars to anyone with information leading to the identity of the captors. The advertisements also promised immunity, new identities and the right to abode in the US. But they brought the US no closer to catching the phantom.

In its early days, Islamic Jihad would publicise its deeds to Western news agencies by delivering prepared statements over the telephone. In a macabre turn of events, news agencies began to receive hoax phone calls from individuals claiming to be members of Islamic Jihad. This placed journalists in the surreal predicament of having to distinguish between the authentic callers of a faceless organisation and the pranksters. News agencies which failed to make the distinction would receive threats from Islamic Jihad's spokesmen who were not happy to find their name being used in vain. A frustrated journalist ultimately managed to persuade an Islamic Jihad caller to provide news agencies with written statements and evidence to authenticate their claims of holding hostages. Islamic Jihad obediently adopted the practice of delivering pictures of the hostages whom they were holding to the news agencies. Since the postal service in Lebanon during those days of the civil war was almost non-existent, mail would generally arrive at the news agencies from a number of different sources, so it was not possible to distinguish Islamic Jihad's messengers from others. On one occasion, however, a news agency took delivery of only one piece of mail all night and it turned out to be a message from Islamic Jihad. When the porter was asked to describe the messenger, he related that a man had walked into the agency in a hurry, holding an envelope wrapped in tissue paper. Such were the niceties of one of the most feared groups in Lebanon: they did not mind delivering a message personally, but they were concerned about leaving fingerprints.

Islamic Jihad's most notorious figure was Imad Mughniyeh. He had been a member of the PLO's Islamic wing, which was known as 'Khomeini's Fatah Islamites'. A hardened militant Muslim member of the PLO's elite Force 17, he had specialised in their explosives department and had excelled in his field. He was resolute in his hostility towards the Israeli occupiers and the Western presence in Lebanon. In the summer of 1982, Mughniyeh had seen his village occupied by the Israeli troops, his Palestinian comrades killed and evicted from Lebanon and their families later massacred in cold blood while the Arab leaders watched from a distance and the Western world and the US issued lame condemnations.

According to the security source 'the Baron', who believed Hezbollah to be behind the kidnappings, Mughniyeh was the invisible head of Hezbollah's security service. Like most in Lebanon, 'the Baron' was aware of Mughniyeh's affiliations with the Islamic trend but he lacked intimate knowledge of the hierarchy behind Mughniyeh. In the early years of the crusade, the phantom was at its most secret and no one was privy to such information aside from perhaps the leadership of Hezbollah and the Iranian Revolutionary Guards themselves. Although much is still unknown and the exact details may never come to light, some well-placed sources are currently more willing to testify than previously. It is from such experts that it is possible to come closer to the course of events.

'The Baron's claim was circulated by journalists, but Mughniyeh was no politician and he had no interest in joining the ranks of Hezbollah's founders. His ambitions went further. Shortly after the PLO's eviction from Beirut in August 1982, Mughniyeh was injured when the Israeli-backed Christians unleashed an artillery offensive against the Muslim population of the southern suburbs in full view of the multinational peace-keeping forces and with the support of America's warships. Like thousands of other Shiite Muslims, he and his family had taken refuge in the southern suburbs after being forced out of their village in South Lebanon. Disillusioned by the failure of the PLO and further radicalised by the events of the summer, Mughniyeh turned to the newly arrived Iranian Revolutionary Guards. He was obsessed with the goal of making war against the Israeli occupiers and intent on organising a movement of resistance. A source claimed:

> When Mughniyeh joined the Guards he did so on the basis of first conforming with the declared agenda of establishing a resistance movement. The scheme was based on the concept that the resistance would be more ideological and faithful to its cause than the PLO was. There was a general obsession at the time, of which he was part, that while this resistance would be of Lebanese nationality, it would also be of Iranian affiliation.

When the bombing of the American embassy and the multinational forces was discussed by the Iranians, Syrians and their Lebanese proxies, Mughniyeh was given the chance for which he had been waiting. He was assigned the task of tendering a selection of targets as well as putting together a plan for the attack. The MNF soldiers' barracks overlooked the impoverished southern suburbs of Beirut where Mughniyeh's family and people lived. The soldiers had witnessed the siege of the area and the artillery offensives unleashed against its inhabitants by the Christians, but had done little to alleviate their plight. Instead, the US government had ordered its forces to open fire against the Muslim population and, in Mughniyeh's view, the soldiers deserved to be punished.

The success of the bombings immediately set Mughniyeh apart and confirmed to the Guards that he was a man worth cultivating. Mughniyeh simply fitted the criteria which the Guards sought in their recruits and they would never regret their decision to take him under their wing. The Lebanese militant would become a bonus member of their special security apparatus and one of their loyal adherents in their international network. According to an analyst with close contacts to the Iranians, 'One must regard Mughniyeh as someone who is on the margins. In other words, he believes in Hezbollah's ideology and Iranian-styled goals, but he is not their agent. In fact, Mughniyeh does not report to Hezbollah, but to the Iranians. He is what would be described in the West as the hit man.'

Mughniyeh was not the only Lebanese hard-liner to join the Guards' apparatus. Other clan members, whose names are not as well known as Mughniyeh, were also deeply involved in the Iranian mechanism. They included members of the Hamiyeh clan from the Bekaa, the Musawis, the Aqeels, Shehadehs and the Ezzedeens. The Iranians rewarded their new recruits with diplomatic passports and immunity, a privilege which was not bestowed on Hezbollah's leadership. These men were in a class of their own. The Guards allowed them to pursue their own agenda, but always saw that Iran's own interests were served in the process. Islamic Jihad's operations usually bore the hallmarks of the Guards' training: their attacks and abductions were obviously well researched and conducted with precision.

The Iranians also provided intelligence to the kidnappers. According to a security source, the information which led to the kidnap of William Buckley, the CIA station chief in Beirut, in March 1984, was gathered during the take-over of the US embassy in Tehran on 4 November 1979. Militant students stormed the embassy and held fifty-two diplomats and other personnel hostages for 444 days. The seizure of the embassy had the blessing of Khomeini himself. It brought the downfall of the liberal government headed by Mehdi Bazargan, who was trying to normalise relations between the newly established Islamic Republic and the United States, and was a triumph for the Iranian hard-liners.

According to highly placed sources in Lebanon, with close contacts to both Hezbollah and Iran, a special committee was set up whose sole task was to paste together the hundreds of documents which the embassy staff had shredded in the last hours before the take-over. 'This was the extent that the Iranians went to and it is from these pasted documents that they got hold of the identity and status of William Buckley,' claimed a source.

Buckley was kidnapped by Islamic Jihad and was the fourth American hostage to be abducted. He was kidnapped as he stepped out of the elevator on his way to the car park of his apartment block. He was tortured by his Lebanese and Iranian interrogators and died in captivity. Islamic Jihad announced that it had executed him on 4 October 1985 in retaliation for America's alleged assistance in Israel's air raid on the PLO head-quarters outside Tunis four days previously. Fellow hostages, however, claimed on their release that Buckley had died several months earlier from lack of medical attention after his torture.

Buckley had been assigned to Beirut in 1983 following the attack on the US embassy, which had decimated the CIA's operatives in Lebanon. The agency is said to have mounted a massive crusade to locate their missing agent and gain his freedom. US officials considered his capture a disaster for the agency, since he carried a considerable amount of sensitive information. Islamic Jihad claimed that it had obtained 'volumes of information' on his CIA activities. The same sources who revealed that Buckley's name and position in the agency were first discovered during the Iranian siege of the embassy in Tehran disclosed that while 'volumes' of details were indeed elicited, Buckley's confessions were never made public as the CIA managed to save their intelligence by purchasing his disclosures from the Iranians with the help of mediators.

The affair confirms the direct involvement of the Guards' special security apparatus in the kidnapping of Western hostages and suggests that Buckley's abduction was not a spontaneous local act but a pre-planned operation. By using their Lebanese proxies, the Guards were careful to avoid being held accountable themselves. Some of the hostages reported after their release that Iranians had made appearances during their captivity. Iranian Revolutionary Guards, in full uniform, delivered food to the hostages Benjamin Weir and Martin Jenco. An expert explained:

The whole plan was designed in such a way that it would not be possible to recognise, identify or actually prove who the real brains behind such attacks were. It was beyond any intelligence services. This was not an individual group or an organisation, which they could search for and eventually find. This was counter-intelligence at its best, and a mammoth institution at work. It was designed so that years later one might be able to correctly conclude that Mughniyeh, for example, was responsible for this or that particular act, but not to be able to pinpoint it beyond that. He was only one of the players, the front man if you want: the rest were untraceable. The beauty of the design, if one can describe it as that, is that nearly a decade later the intelligence services are still blaming Hezbollah as if it was one individual person. This is because no one yet has been able to come up with an accurate list of names or a break down as to who was behind what and how the chain of command actually worked, and no one will ever be able to.

Mughniyeh now has Iranian citizenship. When his identity was revealed as a key player in the hostage crisis and in the bombings of the multinational forces, he moved to Iran with his family as a safety measure to escape the West's intelligence services. The Lebanese militant continues to live there and his visits to Lebanon are never publicised or announced.

In the early days of the hostage crisis, 'the Baron' often met with Mughniyeh. During their meetings, he would let Mughniyeh know that he was aware of his abductions and would try to reason with him. 'The mood was always charged in these meetings and, whilst Mughniyeh would know that we were aware of his movements, he was also content in the knowledge that we could not do much about the situation. He knew that any intervention on our part could instigate massive fighting between factions and further disrupt the country's unstable security situation.'

People who have met Mughniyeh describe his appearance

as unexceptional: short and chubby with a babyish face – someone you would pass in the street without even noticing or giving a second glance. Despite his notoriety, very little information has ever been available on him. He has never made public statements and he has certainly never given any interviews, be they to local or foreign journalists. To this day only one photograph, taken years ago when he was much younger, has ever been published. Those who know him keep a tight lid on his secrets.

In December of 1994, a car bomb was placed outside a shop owned by Mughniyeh's brother. The blast killed him, but Imad was not on the scene. Hezbollah's security apparatus was involved in the ensuing investigation and arrested several Lebanese, including a woman, who admitted that she had been trained and hired by Mossad to carry out the attack. Hezbollah's leadership handed the assassins over to the Lebanese government to be tried for murder as well as treason.

Some of the kidnappers were independent of Islamic Jihad and pursued their own agenda. They were offshoots of Abu Nidal's Fatah Revolutionary Council and were pro-Libyan, Palestinian factions largely based in South Lebanon. One group, Arab Commando Cells, executed three hostages, Philip Padfield, Leigh Douglas, both British, and Peter Kilburn, an American, in retaliation for the US bombing raids on Libya in April 1986. It is thought that they were kidnapped by freelance agents and bought by Libya. Another Briton, Dennis Hill, had died the previous year at the hands of kidnappers. It is not clear who abducted him. Another group in this category, the Revolutionary Organisation of Socialist Muslims, kidnapped and executed the British journalist Alec Collett. His murder was also alleged to have been in revenge for the bombing of Libya. During the course of researching this book, an interview was conducted with one of Abu Nidal's officials. He claimed that a faction within the Fatah Revolutionary Council still had possession of Collett's body and that the faction could be persuaded to give up Collett if letters were secured from his widow and daughter.

However the Fatah Revolutionary Council (FRC) then denied having any knowledge of either the faction or the fate of Collett and, in a menacing and highly unnerving interview, forbade any further research into the subject. It later transpired that the Fatah Revolutionary Council had just seen an article in the British press in which John Major was quoted as saying that the British government was determined to bring the kidnappers of British nationals to justice. The FRC had assumed that the research into Collett was an intelligence ruse. The accusation was nothing new: most journalists working in Lebanon had encountered the 'Mukhabarat Syndrome', intelligence syndrome, as it came to be called, and had been accused of being intelligence agents at some point. Abu Nidal's officials, however, were ruthless men and their animosity was palpable.

Collett, like Padfield, Douglas and Kilburn, had originally been kidnapped by a freelancer. His name was Ahmad Shouker, a Shiite Muslim from the village of Nabi Sheet in the Bekaa Valley, where his father was mayor. Hussein Musawi, the leader of Islamic Amal, also came from Nabi Sheet and was implicated in the kidnapping of the four professors at Beirut University College. According to 'the Baron', Shouker admitted to selling Collett for 25,000 dollars to the pro-Libyan group. He also confessed to belonging to the Organisation of the Oppressed on Earth (OOE). It is unclear whether Shouker was acting on behalf of the OOE or independently, but the network was clearly widespread and extended beyond the influence and programme of the Iranian Revolutionary Guards.

The Italian Alberto Molinari also appears to have been abducted by freelancers. The sixty-four-year-old businessman had lived and worked in Lebanon for nearly thirty years and was kidnapped in Beirut on 11 September 1985. Nothing has been heard of Molinari since and his fate remains a mystery. Most believe that Molinari was mistaken for a Lebanese and was kidnapped while crossing from the eastern sector in a tit-for-tat kidnapping operation between rival militias.

While no one else has been able to verify the story, Farid claims that freelance kidnappers intended to sell Molinari to one of the groups and that he had a heart attack as he was being driven to his cell. Farid reports that the men responsible for Molinari's abduction would always refer to him as the hostage 'who never made it to captivity because of his heart attack'. Farid says that the abductors then went on in panic to bury Molinari's body somewhere in the Bekkaa and that his corpse remains there in an unidentified grave.

The emergence of the freelance kidnappers was a particularly sinister side-effect of an already terrorising phenomenon. The network of freelancers was supplying the demand for a continuous flow of Western hostages and, ironically, they wanted the 'Great Satan's dollar currency in return. Hostages had become valuable and the Iran–Contra affair added further to their worth. America's secret arms-for-hostages deal was revealed by the Syrian magazine *Ash-Shira* in November 1986. Congress had banned the sale of American arms to countries which sponsored terrorism, but Robert McFarlane, head of the National Security Council, had hatched the plan of trading arms to Iran in exchange for the hostages. Oliver North then channelled the profits of the sales to the Contras in Nicaragua. The plan was to make deals with the moderate camp in Iran and ultimately cultivate relations between Iran and the US. The first consignment of arms was 100 anti-tank TOW missiles, provided by Israel. The missiles were delivered in August 1985 and another 408 were sent the following month. As a result of the deal, the American hostage, Benjamin Weir, was freed in Beirut after being held for 495 days. Encouraged by the first result, the US president authorised McFarlane to make a secret trip to Iran to negotiate. McFarlane duly arrived in Iran on 25 May 1985 with a small consignment of HAWK spare parts. Only two more hostages were released as a result of the scheme: Jenco and David Jacobsen. Nor did it bring the kidnappings to a halt. 'These Western governments, led by the United States, ended up contributing in transforming a bunch of otherwise local terrorists into international players,' commented 'the Baron'.

Terry Anderson, who was held hostage for almost seven years, longer than any other captive, speaks with great anger about the affair. An American, he was the bureau chief of Associated Press in Beirut and was abducted on 16 March 1985 by Islamic Jihad. He was dropping off a colleague, Don Mell, after a game of tennis when the kidnappers seized him. They held Mell up at gunpoint and dragged Anderson into their car. He was still wearing his tennis shorts. His daughter, Sulome, was born while he was in captivity. He did not set eyes on her until she was six years old. 'I am convinced that Ollie North kept me in there a couple of years longer. Sure, they secured the release of their hostages, but they paid. And in doing so they also convinced our captors that they could continue to do this and that people were willing to pay for it. Really it only ended when our captors became convinced that there was nothing further they could gain from us.'

As a journalist, Terry Anderson had vividly reported on the ruthlessness of the Israeli invasion and had put his life on the line for the sake of pursuing the truth. Militiamen had not bothered the foreign press corps in the past and had never attacked its members intentionally even at the height of the civil war. Even the largely illiterate gun-toting fighters understood the importance of having journalists like Anderson in Lebanon. Without them, the invasion of Israel in Lebanon might have passed as an acceptable and necessary Israeli military exercise.

Journalists were not able to change the course of events, but they brought the Israeli blitz of Beirut and the suffering of its people to the attention of the world. For aside from Lebanon's local newspapers, known to be the best and most open in the Arab world, none of the Arab states' writers or photographers had dared come to the country during the civil war. Most had stayed in the safety of their own countries, replicating from afar the stories of journalists like Anderson. The foreign press corps had stayed behind when, with hindsight, all signals had bidden them to depart. They had continued their reporting of Lebanon in the hope and belief that they would finally witness the recovery of the country which they had seen disintegrate.

But most of all they had stayed behind because of the faith their presence gave to the people they had come to love and know and whom they had seen deprived of every shred of hope as the country plunged further into the abyss.

Sheikh Subhi Tufeili was Hezbollah's secretary-general during the hostage crisis. He maintains that Hezbollah was not involved and that the group actually attempted to intervene and end the crisis. Since Tufeili has a reputation as a radical and was allied with an extreme wing in Iran, his claims were unexpected. 'We stated our view at the time that the hostage issue was actually a process that harms Lebanon,' he recalled. 'It damaged our reputation worldwide. It was not in our interests and was contrary to our beliefs and our issues.' Tufeili recounted that Hezbollah brought its influence to bear and received word from the kidnappers that they were prepared to release the hostages. He claimed that contacts were made with European representatives and Syria. Iranian officials, said Tufeili, then appeared on the scene in Lebanon:

> Here I would like to stress that the Americans were informed by the Syrians that the hostage issue was about to be resolved and they [the Americans] aborted it instead. They [the Americans] came into the picture and through some intermediaries contacted the kidnappers and actually sabotaged the release. I do not want to go into names and details, but they ruined the whole issue. It then became clear to us that the Americans had their own agenda – that of McFarlane [Iran–Contra] – and they had started their own bazaar in dealing with the hostage issue which was related to their own agenda.

Tufeili carried on to say that when the releases did not take place as promised, the Syrians threatened Hezbollah:

> They were furious and [Ghazi] Kanaan [Syria's Military Intelligence Chief in Lebanon] gave us an ultimatum, either to solve the issue or that he had orders to hurt us. They

were still unaware of the American intervention and it took them a while to understand what had occurred and to believe that we had nothing to do with this incident.

Terry Waite also recalls that, before he embarked on his sole-church mission to seek freedom for the foreign hostages of Lebanon, he had initially sought the Iranians' aid over the issue.

Waite said he visited the Iranian embassy in London in a bid to arrange for a visit to Iran itself, where he had previously ensured the release of British hostages shortly after the Iranian Revolution. He met with little enthusiasm from the Iranian side who appeared uninterested and unwilling to help him with his mission.

'I could not understand why at the time, but now I know,' Waite said with a wry smile. 'It was because they [the Iranians] were already in touch with [Oliver] North. It is clear now. They were following their political objective for the Iran–Iraq war and that objective was with America. At the same time they were playing off their Lebanese [allies]. So it is clear now. But I did try to get into Iran and I had been advised that Iran was the key and I recognised that. You have to take the entry point that you are given and the only entry point that I was given was that entry point [Lebanon], but that doesn't mean to say that I did not try.'

Sheikh Subhi Tufeili also alleges that the French approached him when Jacques Chirac was running against François Mitterrand in the elections of 1988:

There were many hands involved at the time with the issue of resolving the hostage crisis and every now and then rumours or talk would suggest that the French hostages were about to be released. At that time, it was also obvious that the Syrian and French authorities were working in earnest to secure release for the hostages before the elections, so that Mitterrand could use their freedom as a trump card in his public campaign.

Through some mediators of Chirac's, however, I

remember receiving a contact who came to speak with me personally on the basis and assumption that Hezbollah was involved in the hostage crisis and that, since I was its secretary-general, I was thus responsible and the man to contact. He then asked me if I could delay any release prospects of the hostages [until after the elections] in order to prevent Mitterrand from benefiting during the election campaign.

I could not help but be amused by the request and thought to myself that things like this just did not happen in our part of the world.

France had suffered the repercussions of the hostage crisis on its own soil. In 1986, six years after Annis Naccache was imprisoned for the attempted assassination of Shapour Bakhtiar, a wave of bombings in France killed eleven people and injured more than 150. The Committee for Solidarity with Arab and Middle East Prisoners claimed responsibility and demanded the freedom of Naccache. The group was another phantom created for yet another specific task – in this case to pressure the French into freeing Naccache.

Mughniyeh had not forgotten Naccache either and demanded his freedom in exchange for the Western hostages held in Lebanon. Mughniyeh blatantly visited France in the late eighties, at the height of the hostage crisis, when the US secret services were hot on his trail. Despite the Americans' request for his arrest, the French authorities permitted the Lebanese radical, who was travelling under a false identity, to leave France freely. They had been warned that, if Mughniyeh came to any harm, the French hostages held by Islamic Jihad would suffer.

On 5 March 1986 Islamic Jihad claimed it had executed the French hostage Michel Seurat. His fellow hostages revealed on their release that Seurat had died of hepatitis. He was thirty-eight years old. Seurat was an Arabist and sociologist and was married to a Syrian Christian. Thanks to the mediation of an Amal official, Ali Hamdan, Seurat was allowed to visit his family during his captivity on his daughter's birthday. It was a rare display of clemency on the part of the kidnappers. Seurat was treated during his illness by a Lebanese Jewish doctor, Ellie Hallak. He was also a hostage, but was never blindfolded. He told the French hostages that he knew that the kidnappers were going to kill him and so they did not bother to conceal their identities from him. The French nicknamed him 'Dr Death'.★ His grim story throws light on the fate of the Lebanese Jews during the civil war and the destruction of their community in the Jewish quarter of Beirut, Wadi Abu Jamil. Those who were not kidnapped or killed fled the country.

Although the French denied reports that the deal which was ultimately struck with the kidnappers of the French hostages included Naccache's freedom, he was freed on 27 July 1990, together with four accomplices, after being pardoned by President François Mitterrand. All five men were put on a plane bound for Tehran. The deal also brought political, military and financial benefits to Iran itself: the release of its frozen assets and desperately needed spare parts for their armaments. The French also kicked out most of the Iranian opposition leaders who had taken sanctuary in their country following the revolution. Iran was ensuring that it also gained from its operatives' schemes.

Islamic Jihad's main condition for the release of the hostages depended upon the fate of a group of prisoners held in Kuwait. They were known as the Kuwait 17 and had been charged with orchestrating a devastating bombing campaign. On 12 December 1983, six weeks after the attacks on the multinational forces in Lebanon, a chain of explosions had rocked the Gulf state of Kuwait. Six key foreign and Kuwaiti installations were the targets in what might have been the worst terrorist attack of the century had the bombs' rigging not been faulty. Six people died and more than eighty were injured. Two of the bombs exploded at the US and French embassies. The other four bombs

---

★ See *Hostage*, Con Coughlin

went off at Kuwaiti installations, including the country's main oil refinery and water-desalination plant, the control tower of the airport, the Electricity Control Centre and the living quarters of American employees of the Raytheon Corporation. A seventh car bomb was planted in front of Kuwait's Immigration Bureau and was discovered and defused by police after the foreboding voice of Islamic Jihad in Beirut claimed responsibility for the attacks and boasted that another device was still to explode.

The Kuwaiti attacks shook the country and its neighbouring states to the core. A nationwide manhunt was launched and twenty-one men were charged, four *in absentia*. They had tracked down the perpetrators thanks to one gruesome piece of evidence: the thumb of the human bomber who had blown himself up at the US embassy. The human bomber was Raad Mufteen Ajeel, a twenty-five-year-old Shiite Muslim Iraqi. He and his brother had been active underground members of the al-Dawa party in Iraq. His brother had been picked up and arrested during Saddam Hussein's 1982 crackdown against pro-Iranian sympathisers, which targeted al-Dawa members. He was executed along with hundreds of Shiites. Raad, who was also under a death sentence, escaped to Iran.

The al-Dawa party, the largest and oldest Shiite extremist group in the Middle East, had made its headquarters in Iran since Khomeini's 1979 Islamic Revolution. Al-Dawa, which had had members in Lebanon, Iraq and the Gulf states, was one of the main Shiite revolutionary groups which the Guards adopted and sponsored. Its members were vehemently opposed to Saddam's regime and the Guards recruited them to carry out attacks against Saddam Hussein's Baathist regime and against the rulers of some of the oil-rich Gulf states. Iran bore a particular grudge against Kuwait for the support which it gave Iraq during the Iran–Iraq war.

The perpetrators were accused of belonging to the al-Dawa party, which had been outlawed by Kuwait. Two of the men charged were Lebanese, three were Kuwaiti and two were of unknown identity. The rest were Iraqi.

During the six-week trial, the word 'terrorism' was omitted

from the indictments and the Iranian connection was disregarded. Sheikh Jaber al Ahmad al Sabbah, the Emir of Kuwait, revealed that his government had been threatened with further terrorist attacks if the men were not released. Tehran Radio meanwhile broadcast regular warnings from the al-Dawa, threatening grave consequences should the defendants be harmed.* One of the Lebanese defendants was Hussein Youssef Musawi, a cousin of Hussein Musawi who had split from Amal and had allied his newly founded group, Islamic Amal, to Iran and the Guards in the Bekaa. The second was Mustapha Youssef Badredeen who was travelling under a false Christian identity in the name of Elias Fuad Saab. Badredeen was sentenced to death along with five of his accomplices, but the Emir of Kuwait did not sign their death sentence and the men were never executed.

Badredeen was well connected: he was the brother-in-law of Imad Mughniyeh. The two men had carried out the MNF bombings together in Lebanon, and Mughniyeh wanted Badredeen and his comrades released. According to Naiim Qassem, deputy secretary-general of Hezbollah: 'It [Kuwait 17] was the starting point for the idea of hostages, to impose pressure for the release of prisoners in Israel and elsewhere.' Terry Anderson frequently discussed the issue with his kidnappers. During his captivity, he had a number of encounters with a figure known as the 'Hajj'. 'Hajj' is a title given to those who have completed the pilgrimage, *Hajj,* to Mecca; it is also used as a term of respect. Imad Mughniyeh was known as Hajj Imad. Many believed that the 'Hajj' who visited the captives was Mughniyeh, but it later transpired that the figure was a highly placed guard. In one conversation, the 'Hajj' told Terry Anderson that he and the other hostages had been abducted to gain the freedom of their seventeen comrades in Kuwait. Anderson recalled:

---

* See *Hostage,* Con Coughlin, pp. 78–9

I sat with the Hajj for about two hours and he talked about their brothers in Kuwait and how they would negotiate with us. He spoke about how frustrated they really felt and that they were not really horrible people. He justified their deeds in terms that it was necessary 'in our war and we do what we have to do'. He objected to a newspaper report which labelled them terrorists. 'We are not terrorists,' he said, 'we are fighters.' I said, Hajj, you are a terrorist, look it up in the dictionary. You are a terrorist, you may not like the word and if you do not like the word, do not do it.'

We had lots of discussions like that, but they didn't mean anything. One particular thing, always peculiar when you think about it, but very true, was that virtually all of them, even the worst of them, wanted to be liked. They would come in and beat the shit out of you and then come the next morning and wonder why you were still mad at them.

Anderson would always quiz the 'Hajj' on his visits as to why he and his fellow captives were still being held hostage. 'I would say things like, "You want your guys out of Kuwait, why don't you get the Kuwaitis?" An assassination attempt had in fact been made on the Emir of Kuwait and Kuwait Airlines had also been the victim of hijacks. The 'Hajj' would insist that Kuwait was the puppet of the United States and argued that if America was against the release of the prisoners then Kuwait would not release them.

It seemed that the 'Hajj' was not alone in his suspicions about the US's political intervention and power of influence over its allies. Even Terry Waite was a little cynical about the reasons and possibilities for his continuous failed attempts to be granted a visa to Kuwait, where he sought to discuss the fate of the seventeen prisoners with the oil-rich country's representatives.

Although Waite could not categorically say that the American authorities had indeed asked the Kuwatis to block his attempts to visit Kuwait, he nevertheless suspected that they did nothing to encourage the Kuwait government: 'What I would say was that I doubt whether they pursued my claim or whether anybody with any power pursued my claim with any degree of enthusiasm. I don't know, but it seems to me a reasonable surmise because if I had had good backing from America, particularly with Kuwait, they would have said well, yes, okay, let him come along. I think that if America has the power to persuade Iran [to make deals] it has the power to persuade Kuwait. That's all I would say.'

When Terry Waite began negotiating for the release of the hostages, the kidnappers asked him to secure the release of the Kuwait 17. Waite, the Archbishop of Canterbury's envoy, first became involved in the crisis when he was approached by the Presbyterian Church in 1984, on behalf of Benjamin Weir's wife. At first, his efforts appeared successful when Weir, Jacobsen and Jenco were released in 1985 and 1986. However, when the Iran–Contra scandal broke, Waite's credibility suffered: he had originally appeared to be instrumental in securing the hostages' release, but in the wake of the scandal he was cast as the frontman for Oliver North's illegal operations. Nevertheless, Waite returned to Lebanon, determined to salvage his reputation and to prove that he was operating independently. Instead, he was taken hostage on 20 January 1987. Waite had not even been able to get a visa to Kuwait to satisfy the kidnappers' demands. As Waite said:

> The reason I went back [to Lebanon] was in fact personal. I went back out of a personal standard conscience to say I maintain faith with Hezbollah as well as to maintain faith with the western hostages. I could not have gone back that last week if I was not clear of it [Iran–Contra]. From my side, my principal reason was to stand by the hostages, to maintain my integrity and the integrity of those who sent me. People can believe what they like, but the truth of the matter is that when everything collapsed because of the inept deal by the Americans and the Iranians, and you have said that you are working for the release of the hostages, but then everybody else is walking away, I believed

131

that the church should be the last people to walk away. That was my view.

Waite's meetings with the kidnappers were arranged through a Shiite doctor, who worked at the American University Hospital with David Jacobsen who was the director of the hospital. The doctor was dean of the medical school and had contact with senior figures in the community. When Jacobsen was kidnapped in May 1985, the doctor lobbied for his release and the kidnappers began to use the doctor as an intermediary. He agreed to speak for this book about Waite's kidnap for the first time since the events took place, on condition that he remain anonymous, even though his identity has been revealed in the past. Waite had been introduced to the doctor in November 1985, on his second visit to Lebanon. Waite had already made contact with the kidnappers and had asked them to prove that they were the party involved in the hostage crisis. They sent him to the doctor, who had letters from Jacobsen which the kidnappers had delivered. The doctor's clinic became the meeting place for Waite and the kidnappers' representatives. Many have claimed that Mughniyeh himself met Waite at the clinic, but the doctor denies this. There was, however, a senior member of the kidnapping ring waiting outside across the street and the representative who was meeting with Waite would sometimes leave the building to confer.

The doctor's account of Waite's last hours before he was abducted not only reveals how Mughniyeh set up a trap for him, but the extent of the kidnappers' influence. When Waite returned to Lebanon for the last time, there were reports that the kidnappers had warned him against coming, unless he had something concrete to offer regarding the Kuwait 17. One of the kidnappers' representatives paid a visit to the doctor at the hospital. 'He told me, "Our friend is back in town. Has he been in touch with you? Has he told you why he has returned? And why is he here?" ' recalled the doctor. When Waite got in touch with the doctor, a meeting was arranged with the kidnappers. 'Waite told him that he had something new,' said the doctor. 'He said that he now had a very good and important contact with the Kuwaiti government and that he thought he could now get some way by having the death sentences commuted to life imprisonment instead, lesser sentences for some of the others and perhaps even the release of some of the prisoners.'

The kidnappers' representative told Waite that the hostages were depressed and that they would very much like to see him. This was Mughniyeh's bait. Mughniyeh had heard all the declarations from the Kuwaitis regarding Waite's attempts to visit their country and their refusal to deal with him or submit to pressure and he had come to accept that Waite would not be able to resolve the problem. Moreover, the Church envoy had not been able to deliver on his earlier pledges of providing letters and news on the welfare and state of the prisoners in Kuwait. Mughniyeh had furthermore heard the reports on Waite's alleged links with North and the American administration. He had given up three of his hostages in return for Iranian arms and was still no nearer to gaining freedom for his comrades. Simply put, Mughniyeh was not happy.

He did not believe that Waite's alleged high-level contact with the Kuwaitis would bear any fruit and regarded the envoy's trip to Beirut, and his claim that he was bringing them some new development, as a mere publicity stunt aimed at exonerating himself from any involvement in the Iran–Contra affair. If anything, the man who had so coldly and professionally masterminded the bombings of the multinational forces and abductions saw Waite's return to Beirut as a challenge to the warnings which he had issued against his return.

And so the trap was set. Mughniyeh knew that the Church envoy's ultimate hope all along had been to see the hostages. He knew how important the issue was for Waite and how much it would have meant had he been able, at any one time, to declare that he had seen the hostages. So he knowingly made Waite an offer that he could not refuse – a meeting with the hostages.

It was 7.00 p.m. and Waite was prepared to go with the

kidnappers immediately, but the doctor advised against it: 'The city was in a bad state at the time. There had been an explosion in Ouzaii [central road to the suburbs] and the country was in a rough situation with Druze and Amal militiamen clashing here and there. So to take someone as big as Waite at such a time, what with all the checkpoints around, was simply not practical.' At six feet eight inches, Waite cut an imposing figure and the doctor feared he would not be able to travel incognito on his sensitive mission. Another meeting was arranged for the following day at the clinic. 'After the man left he [Waite] came down to my apartment, since I live one floor below the clinic, and we had a few drinks. He was jubilant, he was very happy and he told me: "I think this will win me the Nobel prize, when my picture appears all over the world's media, flanked by the two hostages," ' the doctor added wryly.

The following day, Waite appeared early at the doctor's clinic as arranged to wait for the kidnapper. But there was no sign of him. At 6.00 p.m., the kidnappers telephoned the doctor: they had decided to collect Waite in the evening since they would then not have to blindfold him to prevent him from identifying the location and they would not have to worry about anyone recognising him. The meeting was rearranged for 8.00 p.m. Waite returned to his hotel, held a press conference and announced that he was coming close to meeting the hostages. He returned to the clinic accompanied by the Druze Progressive Socialist Party bodyguards who attended him on his trips. Waite told his bodyguard to leave him at the clinic and not to try and follow him under any conditions. According to 'the Baron', Mughniyeh had installed his men in different locations around the clinic to ensure that Waite was indeed alone and that he was not being followed:

Security was his expertise and Mughniyeh had been planning the ambush for some time. He was only going to carry it out when he was perfectly satisfied that Terry was in fact alone and at their mercy. He was taking no risks here and the whole operation was designed on the basis that Waite would go with the kidnappers willingly. Unlike all the other hostages, Waite was not going to be kidnapped and dragged at gunpoint. This was a big man and the plan had to ensure that he went of his own accord.

When Waite arrived at the clinic, the doctor was called away to attend to the delivery of a baby at the hospital. He asked Waite to accompany him, but Waite declined. 'When I came back from the hospital, I noticed that the lights were still switched on in the clinic and the door was locked. I went into the clinic and did not see anything wrong; nothing was disturbed or messed about, there was no sign that any violence had taken place. Nothing suspicious at all. So, I closed up and went home thinking, "Great, all is well." '

The next day the Druze official, Akram Shehayeb, who was responsible for protecting Waite, paid the doctor a visit. Waite had not returned. Shehayeb managed to keep the press at bay by informing them that Waite had finally gone to hold face-to-face talks with the Western hostages and the story was duly reported by the media. Meanwhile, Shehayeb and the doctor went to see Sayyed Fadlallah to explain the situation and seek his advice. The doctor was a close friend of Fadlallah's and was part of the scholar's following. The news was not good. Having heard what had happened and listened to the concern of the two men, the cleric could immediately read the situation and did not waste much time with them: he confirmed that their fears were well founded. It would not have been surprising if Fadlallah had already been informed of the incident, since he was in a position to know when such events occurred.

'Doctor,' pronounced Fadlallah, 'I am afraid that no one can free him now except the Iranian intelligence. The only person in Beirut who is capable of doing anything about this is the chargé d'affaires of the Iranian embassy. Do not waste your time with anything else.'

For the Druze, Waite's abduction was an insult to their honour and a challenge to their authority. Mughniyeh had not only succeeded in conning everyone, he had also dealt a direct blow to the militia leader Walid Jumblatt, who had become the leader of the Druze after his father Kamal's assassination in 1977. Mughniyeh had snatched Waite away from the Druze: in Lebanon this could spell trouble and in most cases war. If need be, Jumblatt would start a fight with Hezbollah, Iran's allies in Lebanon. Jumblatt knew that they were aware of the dealings of Mughniyeh and his lot. Like most officials in Lebanon, he too knew that the Party of God was providing protection to the kidnappers and their hostages and was covering up for them. Furthermore, Jumblatt also suspected, like many, that the hostages where mostly being held in the southern suburbs of Beirut, where Hezbollah and its leadership nested.

Jumblatt immediately got in touch with the Iranians and a meeting was set up for Shehayeb with Mughniyeh. They met at the Summerland hotel for about six hours. Mughniyeh claimed that they had taken Waite only to interrogate him and that they would return him as soon as they had finished with him; most probably later that evening. Until then at least Shehayeb had no choice but to accept Mughniyeh's promise of freeing Waite later that day as his word of honour. There was nothing more he could do but wait.

When the story of Waite's disappearance broke, the doctor's name was leaked, but he refused to give interviews or to comment. He went to seek the help and advice of Ghazi Kanaan, Syria's chief of military intelligence in Lebanon, who confirmed Fadlallah's words: 'Doctor, these are hunting dogs who are asked to bring targets and they obey and go out and hunt their prey which they bring back. They are the hunting dogs of the Iranians. The Iranians are the prime movers in this and they move them around.'

The doctor has been haunted for years by the results of his mediation:

I feel I was used by the people who brought me the letters [from Jacobsen] in the first place. They used this. My concern to free Jacobsen then was for the sake of the

136

university. I asked them to distinguish him from the rest of the hostages for the sake of the university and so that Washington would regard and view the American University in Beirut differently. But to use my office to kidnap the man, my premises and my name, was mean and not honourable. I only agreed to participate in this because I thought I was being a good Samaritan.

While Shehayeb waited that day for the return of Waite as promised, Mughniyeh calmly left the country. 'That final day we found out that Mughniyeh had left Lebanon and had fled to Iran. This was also direct proof that he was the mastermind and the stooge of the Iranian Guards' regime here,' said the doctor.

In one of history's more ironic moments, it was none other than Saddam Hussein who succeeded where Terry Waite had failed: when the Iraqis invaded Kuwait in 1990, they unwittingly released the Kuwait 17 from prison. Before Saddam could even realise the value of these prisoners, his occupying soldiers in Kuwait had already opened the prison cells and freed the inmates.

A few of the men were reported to have stayed behind for a while to help the Kuwaiti resistance against the Iraqi occupying forces, while Badredeen and Musawi sneaked out to Iran instead. According to Giandomenico Picco, this inadvertent act was the catalyst for the release of the hostages.

Hussein was a great help in the releases, by opening the prisons in Kuwait. When that happened, half the job was done and anyone knowing the situation would have jumped on that, which I did. I knew that we had that and the rest was peanuts, so to speak. I mean if you have a little imagination and some cards to play and you are prepared to take some risks then you are there.

Waite's mistake, he believes, was to have associated himself with the West in the eyes of the kidnappers. Waite's trips between

Beirut and Cyprus had been noticed. When David Jacobsen was released, Waite flew to Beirut from Cyprus in the company of Oliver North. Picco was very careful to make Iran, the East, his starting point.

However the hostages were not released immediately. 'By the time the fifteen [two of the prisoners in Kuwait had been released in 1989] came home or were released, my group would have been happy to send us home the next day,' recalled Terry Anderson. 'They said so. The "Hajj" came to us and said: "I have good news for you. Our friends in Kuwait are free. Well, I would like to send you home, we have gained what we wanted, but it is going to take a bit more time. Not now, but soon." ' Anderson believes that while Imad Mughniyeh was behind his abduction and those held by Islamic Jihad, he had full control of their fate only in the early stages and years of the crisis. By the time Anderson was released, in his opinion, the situation had changed. Various factions had allied themselves with one another and could no longer act independently. They had to consider each other's demands and conditions regardless of whether a particular group had reached a stage where it was willing to free its hostages.

One faction which was particularly reluctant to release its hostages was under the control of Abdel Hadi Hamadi. His group, Holy Warriors for Freedom, was allied to Islamic Jihad and abducted three West German nationals in retaliation for the arrest in Frankfurt of two of his brothers. The first, Mohammed Hamadi, was arrested on 13 January 1987 for his role in the TWA hijack in June 1985. Four days after his arrest a West German national Rudolf Cordes was kidnapped in Beirut by the clan. Mohammed was given a life sentence. On 26 January, the second Hamadi brother, Abbas Ali, also arrived at Frankfurt airport and was arrested on explosives charges. He was tried for the abduction of Cordes and a second West German. He was given a thirteen-year prison sentence when the court heard that the kidnappings were undertaken to win freedom for Mohammed. The hostages would later be released, but the group then kidnapped two others. They were the last

138

hostages to gain their freedom. It took Picco seven months after the rest of the hostages had been released to negotiate their freedom, during which time he was threatened by Hamadi. Picco said drily:

> Mr Hamadi does not like me very much. He never did and he actually wanted me dead. I think he still wants that. The reason for this was that, in the deal I was offering, freedom for his two brothers was not part of it. I was offering him everything under international law. Visitation rights, better conditions and that sort of thing, including leniency if they behaved well, but he wanted their immediate release.

In the case of Abdel Hadi Hamadi, the line between Hezbollah and the kidnappers grows distinctly fuzzy: Hamadi was a member of Hezbollah's security apparatus. He was also a personal friend of Mughniyeh and the Iranian Revolutionary Guards. However, his actions were widely believed to be independent of the Party of God's authorisation and leadership. Hezbollah officials have admitted on several occasions that Hamadi's behaviour was linked to his brothers' arrest and insisted that his actions were taken as a separate measure by the family clan and not as a result of the group's policy. The kidnappers themselves also steered clear of Hamadi's personal vendetta. Picco claimed that even those kidnappers who had met him to talk about the release of their hostages refused to participate in the Hamadi issue. 'They said they did not want to have anything to do with it and that there was nothing they could do. They said this was out of their mandate. "This is a Hamadi family affair with nothing to do with us and we can't help you with it." '

A question mark hangs over Hezbollah's involvement in the hostage crisis. Like the kidnappers, it was a protégé of the Iranian Revolutionary Guards and had links with the al-Dawa party. Hezbollah was well aware of the figures behind the kidnappings and knew the details of their enterprises. The group provided safe cover to the kidnappers in areas under its control, it defended their methods and policies and even found religious arguments or edicts to justify their actions. Hezbollah has continued to stick to its cryptic official line: 'We are neither directly nor indirectly responsible for the taking of the hostages.' Even to this day, it is a subject they usually prefer not to discuss at length on the basis that their agenda amounts to more than the West's regard of them as a bunch of kidnappers.

According to the group's deputy secretary-general, Naiim Qassem, 'The issue of the hostage crisis was basically a result of the West's general performance. Their handling of issues concerning our region sparked a reaction against the West. For example, they brought the multinational forces and then used them to pressure us to accept certain conditions.' Qassem cites the West's support of Israel, the prisoners held in Israel's jails without trial and the West's 'consistent attempts to tighten the noose around us, in every aspect, and their persisting negative dealings with our area' as additional factors which contributed to the emergence of groups in Lebanon who considered that the only solution lay in imposing pressure on the West through taking hostages.

While Terry Waite agrees with the 'no deal' position that the British government insisted on maintaining throughout the hostage crisis, he insists that very little has been done by the West to try and understand the problems which inspired groups like Islamic Jihad to resort to the taking of hostages.

> I think it is much better to get to the point of knowing the roots of the problem and to ask the question why is it that people take hostages in the first place. In other words to deal with the fundamental root of the problem . . . Now I am not saying that they [problems] necessarily justify later inflicting penalties and misery on the innocent, but what I am saying is that if you wish to prevent hostage taking and minimise acts of violence you should address yourself in the first place to the fundamental grievances that people are expressing and attempt to deal with them because

sometimes there is something being said in these grievances.

So I think the lesson to be drawn from the Beirut hostages and the various other hostage situations in the world is for governments to get engaged much more in what I term basic diplomacy and for voluntary agents to become engaged in this . . .

Hostage taking is very symptomatic, you can't pretend that if hostages are released then you have significantly touched the roots: you haven't. The root problem is still there in the Lebanon even though the hostage crisis has ended: it has not been resolved. Saying that, saying that I have sympathy with some of their grievances, does not mean to say that I am in agreement with their tactics, and I have always said so, but I am in sympathy.

Also turn the argument around and you can see of course that is open warfare. On the one hand Hezbollah have employed a variety of tactics such as kidnappings and bombings and so on, when in fairness, they have employed the same tactics that have been employed by other intelligence services against Hezbollah. So in fact you have a running warfare in the middle of which innocent people are caught and that is wrong. It is very difficult to get a balanced view of the mistakes and people don't like having a balanced view.

If you only look at the hostage situation you will only see a symptom, and if you only see a symptom, like saying a body is diseased and never get to the root of it, then you are in trouble.

I have suffered at the hands of terrorism, yet I understand why people do so, I understand why Hezbollah does that, I understand. I say you must get behind the problem, you must understand it more completely. The whole issue at the end of the day is power and power brokering and self interest.

'Hezbollah did not take any decisions regarding this nor did it have any role with regard the hostage issue,' said Naiiem Qassem.

'Now the fact that these groups who carried out these acts were part of the Islamic trend does not automatically mean that they are members of Hezbollah; not everyone who is part of this Islamic tenor is necessarily a member of Hezbollah.'

A close network of clans and family members appears to have been involved in the kidnapping. Terry Anderson and his fellow hostages estimated that the number of Lebanese who saw them in captivity may have been as high as 300. As Anderson said:

> An amazing number considering no one was nearer to finding or locating the hostages – and many did try. The reason for this well-kept secret was due to ideological and religious loyalties and fear. First of all, they are two-thirds family. Most of them are convinced both ideologically and theologically, in other words they are homogeneous in their beliefs or pretty close to it. And the danger to the family who broke the secret was extreme. If they ever found out that anybody had leaked information about us, they would kill him, his brother, his sister, his wife, his mother, his father and their dog. You know that that is the way they operate. It is really extremely difficult to penetrate that kind of structure.

It did not perturb Qassem that his group remains accused of responsibility for the hostage crisis. Nor did it matter to him that evidence indicated that his group was an accessory to the act:

> Now the question as to why we did not prevent them [the abductors] when they were in our areas and [the charge] that the names of some of the people involved were regarded as part of our party, the truth is that we did not know each and every person involved. The second question is, who were we supposed to have served in preventing these people [kidnappers]? Were we supposed to serve the Americans or others in this issue? The answer was,

why should we? Let them [the US and West] pluck their own thorns. The third issue here was, should we have started a conflict with these groups for the sake of the Americans? Again the answer was, why should we have?

In order for us to have done something regarding this issue it meant that we would have had to tackle the groups involved, who obviously had a different view to ours. That would have had a price. Our view was why should we pay the price and for whose sake would we be paying this price, as well as who would benefit from us doing so? The arena was loose then and just as we had people in the arena so did others who also did nothing about this issue. No one was willing to tackle these groups then, so, all in all, the situation dictated for us not to interfere in this issue altogether.

Ultimately it was Syria and Iran who decided to interfere. At the end of the Gulf War, Assad needed US backing for his political role in Lebanon while Rafsanjani, a moderate, was determined to open his country up to the Western world to rescue his battered economy. The two men exerted pressure on the extreme militant wing in Iran headed by figures like Mohtashemi, who not only ran the Guards in Lebanon, but channelled the funds necessary for their operations. President Rafsanjani cleansed his government of the militants and isolated the fundamentalists opposed to his policy. His actions were a clear message to the Lebanese camp that things must change.

Despite Tufeili's and Qassem's willingness to discuss the hostage crisis, the subject remains a highly sensitive issue. A member of Hezbollah's security apparatus warned, during an interview, that there were three 'red lines' which should not be crossed in this book: 'details of Hezbollah's internal security', 'the security of the Islamic Resistance' and the 'hostage issue'. When Hezbollah's leadership heard about the warning which had been made, they asked their press officer to apologise: their security officer had, apparently, not been acting with their authorisation.

An expert on Hezbollah claims that the group would be willing to take the blame for the hostage crisis under the banner of 'protecting the higher interest of Islam'. In this case, the higher interest of Islam amounts to Khomeini's Islamic Republic and the Iranian Revolutionary Guards. Hezbollah therefore remains prepared to defend and protect the Iranians and their agents even at the price of personally being held responsible for the whole affair. It is a heavy burden.

5

Necessities of Life

Have you considered him who calls the last judgement a lie? That is the one who treats the orphans with harshness and does not urge [others] *to feed the poor. So woe to the praying ones, who are unmindful of their prayers, who do* [pious deeds] *to be seen and withhold the necessities of life.*

Surat al-Maun, 1–7, The Quran

When the Shiites began fleeing north from the war zone of South Lebanon, they settled in the southern suburbs of Beirut. It was once a middle-class, residential district, but as the numbers of refugees grew, the population expanded into areas that were not designed for living. The Shiites began to build their makeshift homes in the vicinity of the city dump and Beirut's common sewer. The suburbs gained a reputation as the Shiites' slums, commonly referred to as the 'Belt of Misery'. Piles of garbage, mixed with sewage from burst pipes, littered the streets and emitted an offensive stench. During Lebanon's torrential winter rainfall the roads flooded, cars sank into the mud and pools of filthy water attracted flies and rats. With each passing season, the area appeared to have deteriorated and always threatened further decline. Electricity was a luxury, ninety per cent of the district lacked running water and the few existing telephone cables no longer functioned. It was hard to fathom how the residents survived in such a desolate environment.

The government felt threatened by the influx of refugees and did not lift a finger to improve the situation. It ignored the Shiites' presence and hoped that they would disappear. The Sunni Muslims also resented the newcomers from the South, as Beirut was historically their patch. Meanwhile, the Belt of Misery expanded at an alarming rate and earth tracks were cut to link the shantytown's growing neighbourhoods. Residents of the luxury apartments on the periphery of the slum remained oblivious to the wretchedness on their doorstep. As the years passed, the poverty, discrimination and injustice fuelled the wrath of the Shiites and ultimately led to the explosive birth of Lebanon's Islamic militancy. By the early eighties, the suburbs had become a Hezbollah bastion, where its leadership lived and worked.

Government officials, many of whom were also the heads of Lebanon's warring militias, were too engrossed in their struggle for power and new territory to bother about the plight of so many hundreds of thousands of refugees. Christian leaders concentrated on improving their own areas: they built roads and highways, extended flyovers and secured basic services for their communities. Walid Jumblatt, leader of the minority Druze faction, used his influence and ministerial position in charge of Public Works to improve his community's districts. Tarmac highways connected the villages of the Druze's Chouf mountains, lush forests were planted in the hills and valleys surrounding the scenic area and the most basic amenities were secured. The Sunnis, on the other hand, lived within the security of Beirut. Despite suffering power failure during the civil war, the city maintained most of its amenities and had an infrastructure which, while needing modernisation and maintenance, still functioned.

Although the Shiites' deteriorating conditions were largely a result of the government's neglect, their own leaders had done little to help the community even before the civil war. Those in positions of power rarely used their influence to get government concessions for their people. They came from a handful of wealthy families, whose sole interest revolved around protecting their privileges and barring other Shiites from social advancement. They had discouraged education among the peasants and kept them trailing behind the rest of the country, politically, socially and economically. They believed themselves to be superior to the rest of their community and behaved accordingly.

Hezbollah maintains that the lack of government spending, coupled with the long policy of neglect, left it with no choice but to tackle the situation itself. With Iran's help, it embarked on an ambitious enterprise to build an entire social welfare infrastructure for the Shiite community. Iran saw the Shiites' dire circumstances as fertile ground for exporting its revolution and channelled millions of dollars worth of aid and financial assistance to Hezbollah. It was a move that would not only provide help for the destitute, but would secure the allegiance of the Shiite population to Hezbollah and its Iranian mentors.

A counterpart of Iran's construction organisation, Jihad al-Binaa (JAB), Construction Jihad, opened in 1984 and the Islamic Health Committee (IHC) was launched the same year. In 1987, Iran's home-grown social welfare operation, the Relief Committee of Imam Khomeini (RCIK), opened a branch in the Hrat Hreik neighbourhood in the southern suburbs of Beirut. It was launched at the personal request of Ayatollah Khomeini. In a clear reprimand to Israel and the West, Khomeini hoped that the organisation 'would alleviate the pain of the Lebanese oppressed who had not only suffered at the hands of the colonialists, but were further afflicted, impoverished and orphaned by the civil war and the wars of opportunists seeking to overtake their country'. His personal blessing raised the organisation's standing in the eyes of Hezbollah and its Shiite followers.

The Relief Committee has since grown into a giant social welfare organisation, whose services vie, even now, with the

Lebanese government's efforts for the Shiite community. With the exception of the Christian Maronite militias, who levied taxes to improve Christian neighbourhoods, none of Lebanon's parties had ever attempted such an undertaking. The Relief Committee has branches in eight regions of Lebanon: western Bekaa and the eastern Bekaa; Tripoli and the Hirmel area in north Lebanon; Sidon, Tyre, Nabatiyeh and Jebaa in the South. Tripoli and Sidon are predominantly Sunni areas, while regions of the Bekaa and the Hirmel are Christian. Hezbollah boasts that, although its social welfare system was first instigated to cater for the need of its Shiite brethren, it is also available to the poor of other religious sects. In a country where sectarian divisions and hostilities run deep, few Lebanese outside the Shiite community have availed themselves of Hezbollah's numerous welfare facilities, primarily out of fear that it would indebt them to the group.

The Lebanese government was happy to let Hezbollah take responsibility for the Shiites' welfare. The Relief Committee, the Islamic Health Committee and Jihad al-Binaa have official recognition and were all registered by the Interior Ministry in 1988. The Relief Committee is sanctioned by the government to carry out charitable, humanitarian and social work as well as any business ventures, health and educational programmes aimed at terminating 'ignorance, poverty and sickness'. Its brief is that of several government ministries combined. It is licensed to construct clinics, hospitals, schools, centres for higher education, research institutes, orphanages and centres for the physically handicapped. In addition, the Relief Committee is qualified to initiate investments from which all proceeds must be returned to fund its activities. It has departments licensed to issue school and university loans and to encourage the growth of handicraft, manufacturing and agricultural ventures. It grants financial assistance to young married couples as well as housing and business loans. There is no interest to pay on Hezbollah's loans, since interest is not permitted in Islamic law.

The Relief Committee declares that its goals are: 'To help families reach a level of self-sufficiency, to raise the educational and social levels of families and the needy, and to equip them with knowledge and education as a means of confronting the future complexities of day-to-day demands.' Some families are provided with equipment or livestock to start their own businesses, which can range from knitting machines to herds of cattle and beehives. The Relief Committee has opened the first employment office in the country and formed several handicraft and technical institutes, where some women have learnt a trade for the first time in their lives. Those who complete the courses successfully are then awarded certificates or prizes for their achievements by the general manager of the Iranian mother organisation in a ceremony attended by Hezbollah officials. It is an exercise which not only marks the graduates' achievements, but to some extent it is also a reminder of whom they have to thank. The Relief Committee freezes aid when families succeed in reaching a level of self-sufficiency. There were 6,261 such cases in 1992.

From the beginning, the Relief Committee researched the areas it would cover in order to identify the families and individuals in need of its help. Those seeking its services are thoroughly investigated for proof of their neediness since the organisation insists that only those who are poor, orphaned, needy, destitute, widowed, divorced, sick or handicapped benefit from its services. It classifies them into three categories, each receiving different forms of assistance: families without bread-winners, 'Monthly Families'; families with health problems, 'Continuous Health Families'; and families with unexpected financial burdens, 'Miscellaneous Families'. Each of these categories is further subdivided into different groupings. Families in need of consistent help are classified separately as 'Oppressed Families'.

A team of representatives from the organisation personally visits the families concerned and hands them their monthly payments. In 1992, the Relief Committee distributed 1,988,670.87 dollars* to 6,885 families in these categories. The

----

* All figures quoted are US dollars

149

organisation also provides food, household supplies and clothing to the families it supports. Clothes are usually donated, but the food supplies are bought by the Relief Committee from local wholesalers and it has its own reserve warehouses for emergencies. Blankets, mattresses, kitchen utensils and furniture are often provided brand new. The Relief Committee has an additional method of assistance, called 'Financial Lump Sums', for those who suddenly find themselves in dire financial difficulties: 916,149.45 dollars were advanced to 14,151 families in this category in 1992.

Hezbollah financed its enterprises without any contributions from the official Lebanese authorities. None of its schemes would have been possible without the backing of Iran. The financing of the Relief Committee and Jihad al-Binaa is directly taken care of by the mother companies in Tehran. The Lebanese branches apply directly to them if they require additional financing for special projects or emergencies. Iran also has offices in Beirut to pay the salaries of the employees and to oversee the general management of the institutions. 'To deny the Iranian aid issued to Lebanon's Hezbollah would be like denying that the sun provides light to the earth. Who can deny such a thing?' says Sheikh Subhi Tufeili, Hezbollah's first leader. Despite Tufeili's frankness, Hezbollah is coy about revealing the sums it has received from Iran. In the early days, the chief source of finance was the Iranian ambassador to Syria, Hojjatoleslam Ali Akbar Mohtashemi. He played a major role in helping the Lebanese clerics create the Party of God and Tufeili describes him as Hezbollah's intellectual founder.

Only a few senior Hezbollah officials and a handful of their financial advisers know the exact amounts that were received from Tehran in the early years. Reports have spoken of figures ranging from five to ten million dollars per month, but it is possible that Hezbollah received larger sums. It is only in recent years that Iran has decreased its aid. When Hashemi Rafsanjani came to power in 1989, after the death of the Ayatollah Khomeini, Iran's policy changed. The radical factions lost power; Hezbollah's sponsor Mohtashemi fell out of favour and Iran began negotiations with the West for the release of the hostages. A sure sign of Iran's swing towards a more moderate stance was the presence of the leader of Amal Nabih Berri at the mourning ceremonies for Khomeini.*

Iran's theological leadership also supports Hezbollah financially. These contributions have always been independent of those made by the country's official authorities. According to Islamic law, every Muslim in the world is under a religious obligation to pay religious taxes: *zakat*, a tax on assets and *khoms*, a tax on net income. The taxes are paid to the *marja al-taqleed*, a religious leader who advises Shiites on the application of Islamic law, and distributed to charitable organisations and religious leaders around the world to spend on the poor and oppressed. Sums can also be endowed to Islamic organisations for their political advancement. Hundreds of thousands of Shiites in Lebanon and around the globe, who strictly adhere to this duty, pay such amounts on a yearly basis. The total sum of the collections is never made public. According to Hajj Hussein al-Shami, head of Hezbollah's social welfare programmes, the sum can equal the domestic budget of a wealthy nation.

Hezbollah receives considerable sums from these 'legal rights or alms', as they are known. Some of the money is sent directly to the group's leadership which in turn allocates it to specific projects and transfers funds to the directors of Hezbollah's charitable organisations to finance the social services. The group also has collection boxes distributed in shops, neighbourhoods, banks, on street corners and in mosques all over Lebanon. Between the money pouring in from Iran and those from the legal alms which are specifically allocated to the group's personal use, Hezbollah has succeeded in investing in enterprises and businesses beyond its charitable organisations.

Hezbollah's aim is to become self-sufficient and to reach a

---

* See *After Khomeini: The Iranian Second Republic*, Anoushiravam Ehteshami

stage when its business enterprises and investments can sustain it independently of outside support. It is also conscious that Iran may not always be in a position to finance it. The group's investments are already taking care of a large part of its costs with the exception of the funds needed to finance its war against the Israeli occupation in South Lebanon. In this respect, Hezbollah still heavily relies on Iran's military contributions. 'I cannot say that Hezbollah has the financial capability of covering and financing the costs of the continuing battle with the Zionists,' says Tufeili. 'The battle takes huge, enormous capacities and Hezbollah has not got those yet. Even in our financial activities we are experimenting and some experiments work, others don't.'

Rich Lebanese Shiites are a further important source of income. In some cases, Hezbollah will advertise certain projects and call on interested parties to join them in a financial partnership. These deals usually work on a percentage basis: the partner receives a share of the profits while Hezbollah reinvests its own percentage into the project or into another charitable service. Hezbollah has also successfully struck deals with the owners of sites which the group wishes to develop for welfare projects.

Hezbollah has entered into large-scale business operations by opening co-operative supermarkets in the suburbs and other areas of the country. It has revenue coming in from school fees, as well as bookshops, stationers, farms, fisheries, factories and bakeries. It manufactures Islamic clothing, which it exports to the expatriate Lebanese Shiite community in Africa, the US and South America. The group has also entered the booming property market in Lebanon. Despite the great number of high-rise apartment blocks in Beirut, there is a severe housing crisis due to the lack of affordable accommodation. Hezbollah has developed housing projects to address the need for low-cost housing. Their flats are sold on long-term leases at no interest and are proving popular with young married couples.

Hezbollah also has direct contacts with Muslim Shiite businessmen in Europe, who are sympathetic to the Party of God's work. Some of these tycoons hold close relationships with the group's leaders and have established investment companies from which Hezbollah buys stocks and shares of commodities. Hezbollah's financial transactions can, in theory, be conducted within the framework of their Islamic ideology. Over the past thirty years, Islamic banking has become the fastest-growing sector in Middle East finance. The prohibition of interest is the fundamental premise of the system: Saudi Arabia has based its banking on interest-free deposits while Iran and Pakistan have both attempted to build economies based on interest-free systems. Alongside Islamic banks, there are now also investment institutions such as Kuwait's International Investor, which opened a branch in London in 1994. Operating within the confines of Islamic law can prove problematic and some Western analysts believe that Islamic banks have managed to accommodate the prohibition on interest through adept chicanery. Islamic bankers have, however, taken great pains to create a system which fulfils the religious injunctions. Some institutions, for example, have developed equity funds which only contain stock from interest-free sources.*

The demand for a financial system based on Islamic ethics was first made by the Muslim Brotherhood in Egypt in the 1930s. An immensely influential movement, the Brotherhood set the agenda for the current Islamic revival. The group was founded in 1928 by Hassan al-Banna when Egypt was still struggling for freedom from British domination. Hassan al-Banna saw Islamic reform as the path to liberation from Western influence and as a viable alternative to communism and capitalism. He believed that social change was the means to realise an Islamic society and set up an extensive welfare network which included commercial enterprises and hospitals. Like Hezbollah, the Muslim Brotherhood entered the political arena. As an opposition group, it has come into conflict with the

---

* See 'Islamic Banking', Edmund O'Sullivan, *MEED* 26 August 1994, Vol 38 No 34; 'Arab Banking', Colin Barraclough, *Institutional Investor*, July 1995; *Islamic Banking and Interest*, Abdullah Saeed, p. 9

political establishment in Egypt and its militant splinter group, Gamaa Islamiya, remains a thorn in the side of President Mubarak.*

The Brotherhood served as a model for the Palestinians in Gaza, who set up the Mujama, Islamic Congress, in 1973, to provide social and educational services. While the Palestinian and Egyptian groups are Sunni Muslim, like Hezbollah they were facing occupation when they launched their institutions and all share an Islamic vision, founded on the belief that Islam is a comprehensive system embracing every aspect of existence, from religion and social welfare to politics and economics. Like Hezbollah, the Mujama was funded by alms, in addition to receiving outside support from the Gulf states, Jordan and expatriate Palestinians in America. Even Israel supported the Mujama and registered the organisation as a charity in an attempt to undermine support for the PLO. As in Lebanon, Israel's political tactics failed: Hamas and the Palestinian Islamic Jihad, both vehemently opposed to the peace process, are offshoots of the Mujama.** The two groups have offices in Beirut and maintain close links with Hezbollah.

Lebanon was still at the height of its civil war when Hezbollah's welfare services were launched. In a country where the government was powerless against the reign of the warring militiamen and where the most basic services needed for survival were absent, the organisation found itself inundated. In the late eighties and early nineties, during the 'War of Liberation', the southern suburbs suffered acutely. The war was launched in 1989 by General Michel Aoun against the Syrian presence in Lebanon. Aoun was a former commander of the Lebanese army who had been appointed head of an interim government by

---

* See *The Islamic Threat: Myth or Reality?*, John L. Esposito, p. 120f
** See *Islamic Politics in Palestine*, Beverley Milton-Edwards, pp. 98–101; pp. 146–7; 'Modern Islamic Reform Movements: The Muslim Brotherhood in Contemporary Egypt' Abd al-Monein Said Aly and Manfred W. Wenner, *Middle East Journal*, Vol 36, No 3, Summer 1982

the outgoing President Amin Gemayel. The intermittent fighting carried on for nearly two years before the Syrians and their Muslim allies launched a major offensive to oust Aoun from power. During that time, however, Aoun's government turned off all water and electricity supplies in West Beirut and the suburbs in an attempt to force the Muslims into submission. Lack of drinking and running water had long been a problem for the residents and had already been exacerbated by the increase in population. For the inhabitants of the ill-equipped and poorly constructed southern suburbs, Aoun's war was a catastrophe.

Hezbollah's organisation Jihad al-Binaa launched an initiative to tackle the crisis and opened an office to direct the new project. Iran provided funding, paid the salaries of the employees and sent hundreds of water tanks to Lebanon. Hezbollah's slogan and the Iranian flag were painted on the sides of the tanks, along with pictures of Khomeini and Khameini.

The project initially concentrated on the suburbs and has currently been expanded to cover other neighbourhoods of Beirut which were inaccessible during the fighting. Approximately seventy water tanks were distributed throughout the suburb's neighbourhoods and another twenty are currently stationed in Beirut and the environs of the capital. Seven huge water tankers transfer water supplies twice a day to the tanks. The quality of the water is tested three times a day by lab technicians. Since the project began, it has become common to see people queuing to fill their plastic containers for their daily needs. It might not be the most practical solution, but the move has brought relief to thousands of families. Between 1990 and 1994, the water tankers delivered more than 20 million litres of water to the suburbs and Beirut at a cost of 960,000 dollars.

Before this campaign, Hezbollah's own water tankers, accompanied by vans carrying mobile generators, were frequently seen parked in front of high-rise buildings, pumping water into household reservoirs. Even at the height of the water shortage in Beirut, the Lebanese government failed to provide practical assistance. Families were forced to buy their water supplies or travel to other neighbourhoods which could spare the precious commodity. Some resorted to filling up their containers with the water which poured from burst pipes.

In addition to dealing with the immediate crisis, Jihad al-Binaa dug wells, repaired sewers, collected garbage, built power stations and laid electricity cables. The organisation built twenty-five power stations between 1988 and 1993 and dug twenty-one wells between 1988 and 1992. Its services also extended to the South and the Bekaa. Some areas and villages had lived without electricity for years. These were the areas and villages in Lebanon which were known as the 'oppressed regions'. They were not only Shiite areas: they included remote villages in Christian and Sunni districts in the far north of the country, where the inhabitants still relied on candles and oil lamps. Although the government had been working towards extending power stations and cables to these regions, it had changed its priorities once the civil war began.

The social welfare of the Shiites in the South is a particular concern to Hezbollah, since the region is the arena of its conflict with Israel. A further exodus of villagers to Beirut suits neither Hezbollah nor the Lebanese government. The continued presence of civilians in the area is vital for the movement and protection of Hezbollah's fighters: the success of the Islamic Resistance depends upon the co-operation and hospitality of the villagers as well as their support. Hezbollah therefore demands that civilians remain in their homes and villages in the face of Israeli threats and reprisals. In return, it guarantees them assistance and ensures that they are provided with all the requirements necessary for their day-to-day survival.

When Hezbollah's Resistance fighters carry out attacks against Israeli soldiers, the civilian population of South Lebanon often bears the brunt of Israel's reprisals. Israel claims that Hezbollah launches its attacks from the villages and that its reprisals are aimed at Hezbollah strongholds, but the damage inflicted on the villages suggests that Israel has targeted civilians in an attempt to turn them against the Islamic Resistance. In an effort to counter any such eventuality and maintain the villagers' support, Jihad al-Binaa has permanent teams ready to enter areas of destruction and repair the damage. One of Jihad al-Binaa's first large-scale projects was to rebuild the village of Maydoun, which had been abandoned by its villagers in 1985 after a major Israeli ground and air assault. Hezbollah believes, in common with many Lebanese, that Israel harbours plans of expanding the territory which it already occupies. In 1992, following the Israeli assassination of Hezbollah's former leader Sayyed Abbas Musawi, the villages of Kafra and Yater came under fierce attack from the Israelis and Jihad al-Binaa stepped in once again. By the end of the year the organisation had rebuilt 957 homes. In its annual report for 1992, Jihad al-Binaa declared that its aim was not only to ensure the population's support for the Islamic Resistance, but to 'foil the enemy's dreams and plans of expansion in a bid to settle its Jewish communities'. Hezbollah fears that, if villages are abandoned, Israel may take the opportunity to occupy the area and populate it with Israeli settlers, as has happened in the Golan Heights and the West Bank. The belief, whether justified or not, provides a further incentive for the civilians to return to their villages.

Hezbollah's methods appear to have been successful. Every step that the group has taken to rebuild Israel's destruction in Lebanon has encouraged people to remain in their villages. Even families who had disliked Hezbollah's policies and had distanced themselves from the group have accepted their aid. The failure of the Lebanese government to offer reimbursement or assistance has also served to magnify Jihad al-Binaa's efforts in South Lebanon. Hezbollah even assiduously tracks down absentee owners whose property requires repair. In one example, a resident of Nabatiyeh, who lives in London, received a telephone call from his village in South Lebanon shortly after the 1996 Israeli offensive. Part of his property had been destroyed and the caretakers of his residence had been visited by a Hezbollah team who wanted to know whether the owner would allow them to repair the damage. The owner, somewhat surprisingly, refused their assistance: not through any ideological objections, but because Hezbollah was not prepared to replace the marble floors and expensive tiles.

The Islamic Health Committee (IHC) has similarly put the Islamic Resistance and the southern Shiites high on its agenda. The Health Committee's stated commitments include providing health care to injured members of the Resistance and supporting Lebanese civilians who are subjected to shelling and dispossession in the South. To this end, the organisation has built health clinics and centres.

In the village of Jebaa, in South Lebanon, a major health centre was opened in 1987 to provide assistance to the surrounding villagers who regularly endure Israeli shelling. It is also regarded by Hezbollah as a vital centre for the medical treatment of its Resistance fighters in the South. Open on a twenty-four-hour basis, the centre has an emergency ward and a daytime clinic for general health problems, paediatrics and gynaecology. Its dispensary issues patients with free medication. In 1993, the centre treated 17,866 patients.

There are also five clinics in South Lebanon. Each covers most of the surrounding villages, while a mobile clinic caters for those villagers who live on the border of the 'security zone'. The mobile clinic is particularly popular with the civilians. It has successfully delivered medical treatment to nine villages, most of whose residents prefer not to travel frequently for fear of being caught in the fighting. In 1993 the mobile clinic in South Lebanon dealt with 7,250 cases at an average of 600 per month. Another two such mobile clinics exist in the Bekaa Valley and treat the residents of seventeen remote villages.

Health care was perhaps one of Hezbollah's main challenges when it started its welfare programmes in Lebanon. The poor and illiterate Shiite population had little awareness of health issues and lacked access to affordable treatment. Lebanon does not have a national health service and medical insurance remains a luxury. The few government hospitals in the country which catered for the needs of the less fortunate had poor reputations. To address these problems, the Health Committee opened more than forty health centres and clinics in Beirut, South Lebanon and the Bekaa Valley. The centres are divided into three types: general medical centres, clinics and first-aid posts, and dental centres. Five of the clinics are based in Beirut and three in the southern suburbs. The main clinic in Beirut dealt with 15,272 patients in 1993. Hezbollah has also established subsidised pharmacies and several well-equipped hospitals to provide medical services to those in need. Its two major hospitals were built with Iranian money: the Bir al-Abed hospital on the Beirut airport road and the Imam Khomeini Hospital in Baalbeck.

Many of the doctors and surgeons who staff Hezbollah's hospitals and clinics qualified in French and American medical schools. Most are politically affiliated to Hezbollah. They regard the group as one of the few political parties that has started in Lebanon along a defined political course and which has continued to work sincerely towards its goals. Lebanese law does not permit Hezbollah's health care to be given free of charge, but the fees are approximately a quarter of the government's charges. Some of the medical prescriptions are provided free of charge while the majority are heavily subsidised. Iran sends a large proportion of medicines, while others are received through the International Red Cross, UNICEF and other foreign humanitarian organisations in Lebanon.

General medical centres are miniature hospitals. In addition to providing general health care, they have delivery wings and care for the newly born, laboratories, X-ray departments, specialist care for women and children, a vaccination section which also provides general health advice, a blood bank and dispensaries. One of the largest general centres is the Dar al-Hawraa, which first started in 1984 as a childbirth centre in an apartment in the southern suburbs. Since then it has become one of the largest general centres for mothers and their children. Many Muslim women in the southern suburbs prefer to have their babies delivered there. The centre charges about 125 dollars for its services, a third of the Ministry of Health's fees. Under Islamic law, women are not allowed to be treated by male gynaecologists except in situations where their lives or that of their baby are in danger. The Health Committee's centres are the only ones in Lebanon which have a policy of fulfilling this religious requirement.

Hezbollah's welfare system has undoubtedly brought about an increase in support for the group and won it a better standing in society. Hezbollah's leaders vehemently refute charges that their welfare system was largely developed to recruit people to their party and deny any suggestion that they impose conditions on families benefiting from their social assistance. They claim that they are acting, first and foremost, out of an Islamic obligation which demands that all Muslims help the less fortunate and give aid to the destitute. Some commentators have described Islam as the prototype of the welfare state, since the obligation towards the poor is embodied in Islamic ritual practice through the payment of religious taxes.

Many Lebanese and Western observers believe that Hezbollah demands service in the Islamic Resistance in return for its welfare assistance. It is, however, unlikely that the group needs to resort to such tactics: in the past few years, the Islamic Resistance has become an increasingly attractive option for many young Muslim men. Since the Israeli attacks on Lebanon in 1993 and 1996, the group's fighters have won the status of national heroes and a greater sector of the population has come to support the Resistance. The Islamic Resistance's improved military performance in the South has further increased its prestige and the group has the backing of Syria and the Lebanese government in its war with Israel. Hezbollah's television station dedicates a great deal of airtime to promoting the Islamic Resistance's activities, which has also served to raise the level of recruitment.

Hezbollah does, however, expect the families dependent on their welfare to adhere to an Islamic way of life. The Relief Committee's practice of visiting its beneficiaries to hand them their monthly payments certainly allows it to maintain a personal link and remain updated on changing circumstances and any pending problems as the Committee claims. However, one cannot ignore the fact that it also allows the organisation to maintain control over its wards. The representatives and volunteers who visit these families deliver sermons on Islamic law and the teachings of Khomeini. They emphasise the Arabs' historical animosity towards Israel and warn of the dangers of adopting the 'decadent' traditions and social behaviour of Western societies.

Many female members of the families being supported by Hezbollah have taken to wearing the *chador*, the Iranian-style black cloak. The trend for wearing the *chador* began to grow after 1982, in the immediate aftermath of the birth of Hezbollah. It had not previously been common for even the most devout Muslim women in Lebanon to wear it and the party has been accused of imposing the practice. Stories circulated that the Party of God was paying between 100 and 250 dollars a month to women who agreed to wear the *chador*. Hezbollah denied the charge and insisted that the women concerned did so of their own accord. It is certainly possible that the Islamic faction did not attempt to impose the practice. The group had, after all, bitterly learnt from past mistakes that imposing conditions only served to alienate the community. Moreover, many Hezbollah women and a number of female Hezbollah officials do not wear the *chador*, but cover their heads with regular scarves and wear a long baggy coat over their clothes.

Hezbollah's female officials are part of the group's 'Women's Association' and are chiefly involved in social welfare schemes. This includes the Jihadic Committee for the Support of the Islamic Resistance, which collects donations and provisions for the fighters, and literacy programmes. In a notable instance, Hezbollah has proved itself a champion of women's rights and used its muscle to defend the wives of its martyrs in family disputes. Known as *Armalat al-Shaheed*, the martyr's widow, these women are placed in a special category. Hezbollah looks after their financial needs and housing problems as well as ensuring that their children receive a full education.

Martyrs' widows are usually treated with particular respect by the community, but have often been caught powerless in family disputes. According to Islam, the father-in-law of a widow becomes the guardian of her children. The home of a martyr's widow usually belongs to her husband, and the father-in-law would frequently reclaim the property on the basis that it was costly to maintain two homes. Either he would demand that the mother and children come and live in his household or he would often move into his daughter-in-law's home. In some cases, the fathers-in-law used the pretext that it was not socially fitting for the widows of their sons to continue living on their own. Under such circumstances, many widows suddenly found themselves living under the rule of their in-laws. If the women had rebelled and opted to move elsewhere, they would have been forced to give up their children to the legal guardians. Eventually, many women could not tolerate the situation and complained to Hezbollah.

Hezbollah defended the position of the women. It felt that they were not being treated fairly and that they had endured enough suffering following the loss of their husbands. The group decided that while tradition was important in society, it should not be used to suffocate individual freedom or the right to self-determination. It felt that the behaviour of some of the martyrs' families embodied a rigidity which needed to be abolished for the sake of the community's future. After lengthy deliberation, Hezbollah came up with a solution which allowed women the independence they sought: it decided to build homes for widows with such problems. The houses are legally registered in Hezbollah's name, which releases the widows from their in-laws' control. If the women decide to remarry and move house, the homes are automatically transferred to Hezbollah's widows' trust.

Hezbollah has also secured its influence within the community by building schools. Lebanon has always boasted of its educational standards, yet illiteracy is on the rise at the poorer end of the social scale and is particularly high amongst the Shiites. Hezbollah has made education one of its priorities, arguing that illiteracy and ignorance have contributed to the Shiites' lack of social and political progress in the country. A famous incident in South Lebanon epitomises the long neglect of the Shiites by their own traditional leaders. One of the most powerful Shiite families was the al-Assad family, whose most famous member is Kamel al-Assad. Some villagers once approached Kamel al-Assad's father to petition his help in building a school for the local children. The patriarch was outraged at the request: 'Why do you need a school for your children?' he thundered. 'Kamel is already getting an education.' Kamel grew up to become the speaker in the House of Deputies and proved to be a chip off the old block: he was a vigorous opponent of Musa Sadr's struggle for the rights of the Shiites.

The government has launched a campaign, directed at the poorer communities, to promote the importance of education. In Lebanon, schooling is not provided free and many Lebanese have had to remove their children from school either because they could no longer afford to pay for their education or because they required their children to contribute towards the family's income. Many villages in the remote western Bekaa and South Lebanon have only had schools built in the last decade. Some families have had to send their children to nearby cities or towns to be educated, others could not afford the costs of the daily journeys or found the effort involved in arranging their children's education too burdensome.

In an attempt to address the problem, Hezbollah embarked on a project of building and rehabilitating schools in remote villages and towns. Hezbollah is not permitted to offer free education, but their schools are cheaper than the government institutions and this has proved to be one of their chief attractions. The construction department of Jihad al-Binaa renovated twenty-four schools between 1988 and 1994, of which four were in the Bekaa and fifteen were in the South. Hezbollah has subsidised the schools in an effort to provide poorer families with an affordable option. It also sponsors children and grants scholarships. The political importance of Hezbollah's course of action is stated clearly in the aims of the Relief Committee. The welfare organisation has declared that it intends to focus on the Shiites' cultural development 'in order to improve the level of maturity amongst the community so that it will not remain vulnerable to opportunists'.

Among the main schools which Hezbollah's Jihad al-Binaa has built in co-ordination with the Relief Committee are the Imam Mehdi schools, named after the Twelfth Imam. This includes the Sharqiyeh school in the South which was inaugurated in January 1993. The school caters at present for 450 pupils and there are plans to expand and accommodate a student population of 1,350 after completion. Construction has cost 350,000 dollars to date. The Majadel school, also in South Lebanon, and the Ouzaii school, in Beirut's southern suburbs, both opened in 1993. In the western Bekaa Valley, the Educational Centre of the Martyr Bojeiji opened in 1992 in the village of Mashghara, a stronghold of Hezbollah and the Islamic Resistance. It has nineteen sections covering both nursery and elementary classes and also serves the children of seven neighbouring villages, which border Israel's 'security zone'. The school aims to expand into another two buildings to cater for secondary and advanced classes. Construction has cost 500,000 dollars to date, excluding the running costs of administration and equipment.

Not only Hezbollah supporters send their children to the schools. A Lebanese father in South Lebanon, who works for UNIFIL and is known more for his affiliation to Amal, has placed his little boy in a Hezbollah school:

Many of us are not Hezbollah, nor are we in the least affiliated with their ideologies or political views, but we cannot deny them their achievements and we realise that their schools are currently better than anything else in the area. Not only is my son getting a better standard of education, but at a young age he was practically reading the English alphabet on some of the English adverts and billboards as we drove past one afternoon. I could not believe it, but they place as much emphasis on the teaching of foreign languages as they do Arabic, despite all their rhetoric about the West.

Hezbollah's schools may already be the best in the South, but they face stiffer competition in Beirut where there are many private schools with high standards of education. The curriculum of Hezbollah's schools is approved by the Ministry of Education. The schools are increasingly attracting a wide spectrum of the population; many are fully booked in advance and newcomers are being placed on waiting lists.

Hezbollah has used huge resources in an effort to make its schools attractive. It considers schooling in Lebanon to have become increasingly Westernised and therefore a source of corruption to the minds of children. It introduces its pupils to the Quran and Islam from an early age in a bid to start them on what it believes to be the right path. Western dress and behaviour are frowned upon and prayers are obligatory. The schools adhere to the Islamic code of behaviour and classes are segregated after the age of seven. On reaching that age, girls are encouraged to cover their heads with scarves. Islamic studies occupy a central position on the curriculum.

When Khomeini blessed the birth of the Relief Committee, he clearly expected Hezbollah's social welfare programme to be a means of spreading Islam amongst the Lebanese: he trusted that the care provided by the organisation would 'embrace the oppressed in the hope of leading them to Islam'. Many Lebanese, especially from the Christian community, are wary of the group's Islamic ideology.

Hezbollah is careful to emphasise that its Islamic vision should not be interpreted as an intention to impose an Islamic society on the Lebanese. It claims that it has never attempted to enforce an Islamic way of life, despite its early history of coercion in South Lebanon. Its opening manifesto calls for an Islamic system to replace the current multi-confessional government, but qualifies the demand by stipulating that the Lebanese should be allowed to choose a political system best suited to their beliefs. Since the Shiites have grown to form the largest sect in the country and popular support for Hezbollah is threatening to outstrip Amal, it is likely that a referendum on Lebanon's political system would realise Hezbollah's dream. Nevertheless, despite their confidence in having a strong following, Hezbollah's leaders are the first to admit that an Islamic republic is unlikely to become a reality in Lebanon. In the 1996 elections, a concerted effort was made by the Lebanese political establishment to limit Hezbollah's power.

The group can, however, spread Islam at grassroots level and has devoted a large proportion of its funds to the construction of mosques and Husseiniyahs, mourning houses which also serve as social centres. Since 1991, Jihad al-Binaa has built at least thirteen mosques and renovated another fifty-three in Beirut, the Bekaa and the South. Mosques and Husseiniyahs are not only religious sites in which Muslims perform their religious obligations towards God, they are also vital for the group's mission to indoctrinate the public. It is here that the Imams and Sheikhs win the minds of their populace and where they have preached some of their most fervent sermons. It was from such mosques that Hezbollah first made itself known. The Friday sermons given by religious leaders are particularly important: they are the source of many edicts affecting the population and people look to them for political guidance. The sermons are perhaps one of Hezbollah's most important links with its followers and a constant source of new recruitment.

Although Qom, in Iran, and Najaf, in Iraq, are the Shiites' two main centres for higher theological studies, Hezbollah has also started several theological schools in Lebanon for those seeking to specialise in religious studies and become clerics. Hawzat al-Imam al-Muntathar, the Theological School of the Awaited Imam, in Baalbeck, cost 3 million dollars to build. It covers 7,500 square metres and includes dormitories for boarding students, lecture halls, administrative offices, a mosque and gardens. A huge fence separates the compound from the outside world.

The current Lebanese government has begun to address the long neglect of the Shiites. Rafiq Hariri's 'government of reconstruction' was elected in 1992 and aims to spend 32 billion dollars on rebuilding the country. In addition to its education programme, the government is building a hospital, which promises to be the first attempt of its kind to provide top-quality treatment for the thousands of Lebanese who can no longer afford private hospitals and clinics. The government has also been careful to present a united front with Hezbollah's welfare operations: in 1994, Lebanon's Health Minister Marwan Hamadi issued a statement on the Islamic Health Committee's tenth anniversary in which he showered praise on the organisation's achievements and included them as partners in the government's own healthcare drive.

Following the two major Israeli air and artillery blitzes of July 1993 and April 1996, the Lebanese government began to match Hezbollah's efforts for the civilian victims in the South. After the Israeli offensive in 1993, 'Operation Accountability', Hariri launched the first major government compensation programme for the southern Lebanese. Nevertheless, it fell short of satisfying the population. Although the programme compensated families whose homes were destroyed during the attack, many felt that the amounts offered were insufficient and still had to rely on Hezbollah's teams to ensure the complete repair of their homes. While the government offered financial compensation, Hezbollah's teams rebuilt partially damaged property themselves and bore the costs of material and labour. They also offered financial compensation to families whose homes had been completely destroyed.

Israel's 1993 July offensive against South Lebanon and the western Bekaa sector left a trail of destruction across eighty villages and approximately 6,000 homes. Thousands of displaced families converged on Beirut, putting severe pressure on the Lebanese government. It was a massive exodus and Hezbollah had to evacuate schools and charitable institutions across the southern suburbs and Beirut to house the new refugees. Jihad al-Binaa and all Hezbollah's charitable organisations and volunteers were mobilised to help in the immediate crisis. At the end of the offensive on 6 August 1993, Hezbollah's secretary-general Hassan Nasrallah announced his group's initiative to repair and rebuild all the homes damaged by the

Israeli attacks. Nasrallah assigned Jihad al-Binaa with the daunting task of reconstruction that lay ahead as well as the return of all displaced families to their homes and villages. The initiative was carried out under the slogan 'The hand which works and builds, the Hand of the Resistance'. It received considerable support from Iran and was Hezbollah's biggest undertaking to date, costing an estimated 8.7 million dollars.

During Israel's sixteen-day air, land and sea offensive against Lebanon in April 1996, the Lebanese government became more involved from the start and extended considerable assistance both to the refugees and to the families who insisted on remaining in their homes in the South. It was a historical show of solidarity in which the government mobilised volunteers, humanitarian institutions and even the Lebanese army to provide care for the refugees.

Despite Hariri's efforts, the gap between the rich and poor in Lebanon has continued to grow and there is concern that his government is failing to convince the Shiites that it is addressing the imbalance.* Hezbollah, meanwhile, has gained itself a reputation in Lebanon as a champion of the poor. Its work has made a significant impact on the Lebanese public, many of whom had long feared the group and had shrunk from its extremist image. Lebanese who were previously unwilling to accept that Hezbollah was becoming a fact of life in Lebanon now discuss the group's achievements with open praise. In the words of Hajj Hussein al-Shami, the head of Hezbollah's social services, the group's social work has succeeded in transforming it into something 'larger than a party, yet smaller than a state'.

---

* See David Gardner, Lebanon Survey, *Financial Times*, 16 July 1996

6

The Grapes of Wrath

Mine eyes have seen the glory of the coming of the Lord:
He is trampling out the vintage where the grapes of wrath are stored.
Battle Hymn of the American Republic,
Julia Ward Howe

Thousands of miles away from their Pacific sun-filled island, the Blue Beret Fijian soldiers sombrely stood on the metal and concrete rooftops of their UN base in the village of Qana in South Lebanon. They were paying their final respects at a mass funeral. On 18 April 1996 at 2.08 p.m., Israeli tank fire had attacked the base and killed 109 Lebanese refugees who had taken shelter in the UN compound from Israel's bombardment of South Lebanon.

Other UN soldiers lined up behind the barbed wire that separated the base from the cemetery, in a show of solidarity with the thousands of mourners who had poured into the tiny village, where the Bible recounts that Christ conducted his first miracle of changing water into wine. One of the soldiers had been carrying a baby in his arms when the Israeli 155mm howitzer artillery shells had suddenly begun to land on 18 April.

Seconds later he had looked down to find that he was holding only the upper half of the baby. The infant's body had acted as an indirect shield for the Fijian and had been cut into two by flying shrapnel.

The local children of Qana had grown up around the base and some had even learnt to speak Fijian. The soldiers knew them well. They had often visited their homes and eaten with them. They had also tried to comfort them when they took refuge in the base. One of the locals, known as 'Mama', used to bring the soldiers barrels of pickles and home-cooked food.

As the funeral cortège wound its way into the village, from a distance it looked like a traffic jam of coffins. The level of grief was intense. The crowd screamed and wailed and punched their fists in the air in defiance, chanting, 'Death to Israel'. Some carried placards: 'The massacre of Qana is a real witness of Israeli terrorism.' A band played the national anthem while the mosques broadcast recitations from the Quran. One man's plaintive voice pierced the uproar as he sobbed over and over again: 'Hassan, ya, Hassan!' A woman climbed into one of the graves and refused to come out. Another sat next to a grave clutching pictures of her dead relatives: 'Please talk to me!' she begged them. The crowd was vast, but the number of relatives who had come to mourn their dead was strikingly small for a Shiite funeral: entire families had been wiped out in the attack on the base and few were left to pay their respects.

It was hot. The corpses of the victims had already begun to decompose and the smell was overwhelming. Water was sprayed over the crowd to cool them from the heat of the sun. When the infants were taken out of the makeshift, cardboard coffins for burial, the crowd went berserk. A father jumped into a grave and took out the corpse of his baby, wrapped in a white body bag. He held the bundle high in the air and did a circuit in front of the crowd. Two tiny feet protruded. The crowd screamed, 'Resistance, Resistance, all of us are Resistance! Our children are Resistance!'

The battalion had been garrisoned in the sleepy village of Qana for eighteen years. It was the largest UN post in South

Lebanon. The attack against the base came exactly one week after Israel launched 'Operation Grapes of Wrath' against South Lebanon and the western Bekaa Valley under the pretext of neutralising Hezbollah guerrillas in the area. Israeli military officials announced that the attack on Qana was triggered after several Hezbollah guerrillas fired five Katyusha rockets at an Israeli commando group which had advanced beyond Israel's self-declared 'security zone'. The purpose of the artillery barrage, they argued, was to provide protective fire to their commandos, not to hit the UN base. Very few Lebanese believed Israel's version, while the UN soldiers were even more sceptical. A UN investigation, published the following month, concluded that it was 'unlikely' that the Israelis had hit the base in error. Amnesty International issued its own report in July and declared that the attack had been intentional.

The attack on Qana was a particularly bloody moment from a grim historical repetition that had enveloped the South of Lebanon. 'Operation Grapes of Wrath' was the second time in three years that an Israeli government had launched an extensive military operation against the South to destroy the Islamic Resistance, but Hezbollah had proved to be a more elusive adversary than the Palestinian guerrillas. Once again, Israel's attempts to eliminate the Islamic Resistance were to backfire. The group emerged from the assault with more popular support than it had ever enjoyed.

The tit-for-tat war between the Resistance and Israeli soldiers first climaxed in 1993, when Israel launched 'Operation Accountability', an air and artillery blitz of South Lebanon in response to the killing of eight soldiers. It was Israel's fiercest air and land offensive against the South since its 1982 invasion of Lebanon. For fear of incurring casualties and a repetition of the 1982 mass invasion, in which 650 Israeli soldiers were killed along with thousands of Lebanese and Palestinians, Israel's Prime Minister Rabin had decided to limit his country's operations in Lebanon to artillery, air and sea attacks. 'Operation Accountability', the Israeli government assured the world, was aimed at 'wiping out Hezbollah terrorist bases'.

More than fifty villages were blitzed by air and ground artillery in an assault which killed more than 130 civilians and only a handful of guerrillas.

Hundreds of houses were pulverised, whole neighbourhoods and areas wiped out and more than 200,000 refugees fled north to the safety of Beirut following Israel's latest attempt to depopulate the South. It was clear that Israel was enforcing its old tactic of penalising the residents of the South for the activities of the Islamic Resistance in the hope of turning them against the fighters. It was also obvious that it had failed to fathom that the use of such methods normally backfired.

This time would prove to be no different. The offensive served to bring the people even closer to Hezbollah's Islamic Resistance and they turned their wrath against the occupation instead. It also reawakened a sense of bitterness against the West. Muslims interpreted the Western powers' lack of action as proof of further tacit collusion with Israel. They could not be blamed for thinking so. Israel was once again getting away with its actions in Lebanon. It was only on the fourth day of its frenzied bombardment of the South, during which it had fired about 13,000 heavy artillery shells, that Boutros Boutros Ghali, the United Nations secretary-general, managed to issue a lame criticism of Israel for intentionally pursuing a policy of displacing civilian inhabitants in South Lebanon. The UN Security Council did not even meet to discuss the offensive and the US, unsurprisingly, blamed Hezbollah and Iran for starting the cycle of violence.

Israel's Prime Minister Yitzhak Rabin said that he regretted the suffering which the attack was causing, but vowed to carry on until the Shiite guerrillas stopped their resistance: 'We are steadfast in our decision to continue to act to achieve our aims . . . we will continue this action until we achieve this purpose of ours whether militarily or whether by a military and political combination,' Rabin told a special Knesset meeting to debate the effect of Israel's latest bombardments. He reiterated his conviction that the estimated 200,000 refugees would ultimately pressure the Lebanese authorities and the Syrian government to put an end to Hezbollah's attacks against his troops.

Hezbollah, on the other hand, vowed to continue with its attacks against Israel's 'security zone' and its northern borders. The Lebanese government and Syria declared that they could not ask the Party of God to halt what was internationally accepted as a right to resist an occupation. Lebanon's Prime Minister Rafiq Hariri made his government's position clear when he told the French daily *Libération*: 'Nobody can put the Resistance in jail . . . the duty of the Lebanese army is to guard the security of the Lebanese, not guard the Israeli border . . . it is not the government's duty to stop the Resistance.'

It took a week of intense negotiations to end the Israeli onslaught against South Lebanon. Hezbollah came to an understanding with Israel which stipulated that while the war between the two sides would continue, it would in future be contained between the guerrillas and the Israeli soldiers. Israel undertook not to shell or attack civilian targets and villages outside its occupied zone, while Hezbollah pledged not to fire rockets at Israel's northern border.

The basis of this understanding lasted for three years. Hezbollah claimed that Israel breached the truce and attacked civilian targets 231 times between 1993 and 1996. In return, the Party of God says it retaliated with Katyushas against settlements in northern Israel on thirteen occasions. Both UN military and Western diplomatic sources in Lebanon confirmed Hezbollah's allegations. Hezbollah had meanwhile intensified its attacks against Israel's soldiers and the South Lebanon Army militia (SLA) in the 'security zone'. Between 1993 and 1996, and in the immediate weeks and months before 'Operation Grapes of Wrath', its operations had not only grown in number, but were carried out with new daring, confidence and sophistication.

Since the beginning of 1996, approximately fifty Israeli soldiers had been injured. On 4 March, Hezbollah's Resistance fighters killed four Israeli soldiers in the 'security zone'. Hezbollah also lost one of its fighters in the attack. This was followed on 10 March by another bomb attack, also in the 'security zone', in which one Israeli soldier was killed and four others wounded. On 20 March, a Hezbollah fighter, strapped with explosives, detonated himself against an Israeli convoy near the border with Israel. An officer was killed in the attack. In return, Israel breached the 1993 understanding and shelled the southern village of Yater, outside the 'security zone', on 30 March. Two young men building a water tank by their home were killed and a three-year-old girl was seriously injured. The Israeli Prime Minister Shimon Peres immediately called the attack a mistake and contacted the American Secretary of State Warren Christopher, urging him to seek Syria's intervention to prevent Katyusha reprisals.

Israel's apologies fell on deaf ears in Lebanon. Hezbollah was determined to pay Israel back in kind. It said that it had heard such standard disclaimers too many times and that Israeli promises to hold military inquiries into such incidents in the past had never materialised. Hezbollah fired salvoes of Katyusha rockets into Israel's northern settlements as a reminder to Israel of their 1993 understanding. The message was simple, but blunt. If Lebanese civilians and villages outside the zone were to be hit then Israeli settlements and settlers would bear the consequences. The attack caused material damage but there were no casualties.

The crisis mounted on 8 April, when a bomb blast killed a fourteen-year-old boy in the southern village of Baraachite, outside the 'security zone', and wounded two others. The following day, Hezbollah accused Israel of planting the mine, claiming that the bomb fragments carried Hebrew markings. Once again, it activated its Katyusha batteries, unleashing over twenty salvoes of rockets against the Israeli town of Kiryat Shmona. This time, seven Israelis were wounded and twenty-nine were treated for shock.

Israel's Prime Minister Shimon Peres was also facing war on other fronts. He had taken office following the assassination of his predecessor and long-time colleague, Yitzhak Rabin, in November 1995. The assassination had shaken Israel to its core. An extremist, right-wing Israeli shot Rabin at a peace rally; his intention was to put an end to the peace process. Yitzhak Rabin's government had ushered in a new era of reconciliation in the

Middle East. On 13 September 1993 and 25 September 1995, he had signed the historic Oslo Accords with Yasser Arafat, allowing limited Palestinian autonomy in Gaza and the West Bank. A peace treaty with Jordan followed in October 1994 and negotiations were even under way with Syria regarding the Golan Heights. In the wake of the assassination, there was a surge of popular support for Peres: 59 per cent of the population declared itself in favour of the Oslo Accords.

The Labour government of Rabin and Peres not only faced violent opposition from Israeli extremists, but from Palestinians. Hamas and the Palestinian Islamic Jihad were vociferous in their rejection of the peace process. In February 1996, Hamas launched a series of devastating bomb attacks against Israeli civilians in revenge for the murder of the group's master bomb maker, Yahya Ayash. Hamas adopted Hezbollah's lethal methods and killed sixty-two people in four different human bomb attacks. Peres began to lose support and the leader of the right-wing Likud party, Binyamin Netanyahu, gained a lead in the polls for the first time. Elections were to be held in May and Peres had to act quickly to regain popular backing. His campaign slogan was 'Israel is strong with Peres' and he had to prove it. In a country where security is a cardinal political issue, Peres needed to retain the confidence of the public and he lacked the military background of his predecessor Rabin. Although the Israeli and Palestinian authorities rounded up Hamas and Islamic Jihad officials and actually succeeded in preventing further planned bombings, the damage had already been done.★

Hezbollah was not responsible for the Palestinian attacks and was not solely to blame for the mood of discontent in Israel, but it was still a principal cause of irritation for Israel. Moreover, its sponsor, Iran, was considered to be supporting the extremist Palestinian groups. Peres could not go to war against the Palestinian extremists without enraging Yasser Arafat and

---

★ See *Keesing's Guide to the Middle East Peace Process*, Lawrence Joffe, p. 419

sabotaging the peace treaty; Lebanon, however, was a weak country, where Israel had already exercised its military might. Political analysts claim that Israel was given the go-ahead for its campaign against Lebanon in March, during the anti-terrorism summit at Sharm el-Sheikh in Egypt. The summit was organised by Egypt and the United States in a show of support for Israel following the Palestinian bombings. The emergency conference was attended by twenty-nine heads of state, but did not include Syria or Iran. Iran had called the bombings 'divine retribution'. The summit was intended to isolate Assad and to send him and his Iranian allies a clear message that they should end their support for what the Americans and Israelis regarded as 'terrorist groups'. It was also a warning to Assad that unless he made peace with Israel, both he and his Iranian allies would become pariahs.

Israel left the summit armed with the knowledge that it could seek its revenge against Hezbollah. According to an official in the Clinton administration, who was quoted in *Newsweek*'s 6 May edition, the US had told Israel 'to go ahead into Lebanon', but had warned: 'If things go wrong don't come running to us.' The official continued: 'And then of course they did [go wrong] and now the United States is trying to clean up the mess.'

The United States had its own political agenda in the region. President Bill Clinton was also facing a general election and was not prepared to jeopardise the votes of the Jewish American lobby. Clinton had personally worked towards achieving peace between the Arab countries and Israel and was determined to strengthen Peres's election campaign. Like most Western leaders, he feared the prospect of an elected Likud government and its repercussions on the Middle East peace process. Binyamin Netanyahu opposed the policy of exchanging territory for peace and was expected to bring the peace process to an immediate halt if elected. Until the Qana massacre, the US administration made few remarks and voiced little concern about Israel's activities in Lebanon. When asked about the issue, Clinton's representatives would defend Israel's position by putting the blame on Hezbollah and Iran.

Once 'Operation Grapes of Wrath' was under way, it became apparent that, contrary to Peres's official line that the goal was to end 'Hezbollah's terror', the Israeli Prime Minister had another agenda. There was also an economic aspect to Israel's latest military adventure. Lebanon was in the process of almost miraculously shedding its former image as a city of terror and was attracting foreign investors. The Lebanese government, political analysts and even Israeli economists, charged that Israel's military operation was aimed at hampering the progress which the country had made since the end of the civil war in rebuilding its economy and infrastructure. Two newly built power stations were partially destroyed in the attack.

According to an Israeli economist, Peres used military strikes against Lebanon's newly built infrastructure in a bid to pressure the Lebanese government and Syria into curbing Hezbollah. Contrary to the claim that 'Operation Grapes of Wrath' was 'a military operation aimed against Hezbollah,' the economist argued, 'the assault was aimed at causing economic disarray and confusion in Lebanon.' Foreign investors seeking to participate in Lebanon's reconstruction plan would then be bound to freeze all projects and contributions once a military campaign was under way. Even if a cease-fire took hold, he continued, the economic damage to Lebanon would already have been inflicted. Investors would think twice about making a financial commitment to a country which was clearly under constant threat of future attacks from Israel.

Lebanon's Minister of Trade and Commerce Yassin Jaber echoed the sentiment:

The dice was rolling in our favour in a very big way and I think that was not really well received across the border. If you look at the two countries [Lebanon and Israel] they are in the same location strategically and they are bound to play a similar role as a point of entry to the Near East region. You see, Lebanon flourished since its independence in the forties because it was a gate of entry to the Middle and Near East. Part of this was taken away during the civil war, but there wasn't a city that was able really to replace Beirut fully. Now at that time Israel was not in competition because there was no peace and they had no access to the Arab world. Now things are changing, peace is on the table and they will have access to the Arab world. They already have access to Jordan and they will eventually have access to other areas and it is important to them to keep Lebanon at a disadvantage.

On the military level, moreover, 'Operation Grapes of Wrath' did not achieve its declared aims. Israel had assured the world that it would target Hezbollah camps and armed caches in Lebanon; in fact the campaign killed only thirteen guerrillas and failed to destroy a single Katyusha launcher. Hezbollah's World War Two vintage Katyusha rockets had proved to be a difficult target for Israel's American-made F-16 and Cobra helicopter gunships to eradicate. Many military experts later said that Israeli airstrikes were always doomed to be ineffective against small targets such as the mobile Katyushas. Arieh O'Sullivan, the distinguished defence analyst of the right-wing *Jerusalem Post*, made the same point when he wrote: 'Despite all its bravado and state-of-the-art weapons systems, the IDF's attempts to stop Hezbollah from firing Katyushas into northern Israel is like a tiger trying to catch a mosquito in his teeth.'

The operation did, however, succeed in terrorising and killing over 165 civilians. It also destroyed telephone lines and highways and pulverised scores of villages in the South. The onslaught sought to alienate the Lebanese civilian population from the Resistance in the hope of ending their support for Hezbollah. Peres ignored the example set by Yitzhak Rabin who had embarked on a similar tactic of collective punishment in 'Operation Accountability' in 1993 and had also failed to achieve his aim. As before, the 1996 campaign was in danger of glorifying Hezbollah and of drawing more sympathy towards the group. Many Lebanese saw Hezbollah as the only body determined to fight the occupation and able to challenge the might of the region's superpower.

There was no logic, no precision and most of all no justification for the destruction of the homes, roads, electrical supplies and water tanks of Lebanon. As Israel boasted about its surgical strikes, precision targeting and 'smart' missiles, homes were being ravaged. Between 1982 and 1996, fifteen Israeli citizens had died as a result of Hezbollah's Katyusha attacks. Between 1993 and 1996, more than 300 Lebanese citizens had died as a result of Israel's military operations.[*] While Peres repeated that Israel was not in the habit of deliberately murdering civilians, Lebanese babies, as young as four days old, together with their mothers, sisters and brothers, uncles, aunts and cousins were being slaughtered by his army's military might under the banner of attacking the 'Hezbollah terrorists'. Worst of all, the attacks were being committed with the blessing of the United States, the tacit support of Europe and under the watchful eye of a powerless United Nations. For most Arabs, and in particular the Lebanese, 'Operation Grapes of Wrath' will go down in history as further proof of the West's two-faced policy in the region.

The campaign also raised questions about the accuracy of Israel's intelligence and its supply of aerial maps, which had been plotted with the information gathered from years of daily reconnaissance flights over Lebanon. On checking the targets hit, it was difficult not to wonder about Israel's claim to have details of Hezbollah's hideouts and locations. On the first day of the offensive, at 4.30 a.m., Israeli F-16s dropped gravity bombs on what was described as a 'logistic base of Hezbollah's'. This later turned out to be a garbage dump which continued to burn until the following day. At 10.30 a.m. on that same murky, spring day, Israel returned, with a vengeance, to Beirut, after almost fourteen years. Four of its American-made Apache helicopters, bearing the blue Star of David, flew across the Mediterranean and turned into Dahiya, Beirut's southern

---

[*] See A. R. Norton, 'Israel in the grip of the insecurity zone' in *Lebanon on Hold*, eds. Rosemary Hollis and Nadim Shehadi

suburbs, Hezbollah's bastion and home to many of its leadership. They fired Hellfire missiles into a building which Israel would later claim to be Hezbollah's *Majlis al-Shoura*, the group's nerve centre. Each of the smart bombs carried a nose-cone camera which transmitted the image of its progress right from the second it was fired to the moment it collided with its target. They were pinpoint attacks which should, in theory, take out the target with minimum collateral damage, but the Party of God's high-rise nucleus stood untouched. The missiles hit a nearby residential building instead, killing a sixty-year-old man and injuring several others. Another stray missile hit the parking lot of a hospital located directly across the street from a children's nursery.

Lebanese who had just begun to put the memories of the civil war behind them were immediately jolted back into a nightmare. Wailing ambulances raced to the scene of attack as screeching cars sped out of the neighbourhood. Anti-aircraft batteries were activated while shop owners hurriedly brought down their aluminium shutters. Shelters which had not been used in six years were reopened, mothers hysterically ran to nearby schools to collect their children and Hezbollah fighters in full camouflage fatigues, cradling American M-16s and rocket-propelled grenades, were out in force, directing traffic, advising people to stay indoors and guarding access to Hezbollah offices. Although the attack on Beirut was small and almost symbolic compared to that of 1982, it was nevertheless a major escalation after fourteen years and a line which people had believed Israel would never cross again.

All that day, television broadcasts and radio stations interrupted their programmes with news bulletins on the deteriorating situation. The popular, nationalistic songs of Marcel Khalife and Ahmad Qaabour, both famous for their Resistance anthems and lyrics on the 'heroism' of South Lebanon and the 'steadfastness' of its people against Israeli aggression, dominated airtime. Most of the day, the news was not good. Another smart missile, delivered by another helicopter against yet another 'Hezbollah target', hit a BMW car by the Jiyeh power station on the road north of Sidon, incinerating a twenty-seven-year-old woman. A Lebanese army checkpoint, in the port city of Tyre, was also hit, killing the soldier manning the post. A second helicopter missile hit a Syrian anti-aircraft unit by the international airport, killing a soldier and wounding seven others. The attack sparked fears that Israel was trying to drag Damascus directly into the Lebanese conflict.

Assad could only reiterate that Israel's latest war in Lebanon would diminish the little hope which remained for the progress of the peace initiative. He stressed that it was Israel and not Hezbollah which was breaching the 1993 understanding. The Syrian leader warned the US that it risked losing its role as a mediator in the Middle East after the American administration bluntly defended Israel's strikes and called on Damascus and Iran to curb Hezbollah's attacks. He stressed that 'no honest person', Arab or otherwise, could call people seeking to liberate their land 'terrorists'. Syrian state radio, a mouthpiece for the government, accused the US of exposing the region to 'real dangers' and urged it to keep to its role as an honest broker. 'The American stand is far from having the credibility which a superpower should maintain as a peace sponsor in the world.'

Further air raids, backed by artillery bombardment, were delivered against the South and the Bekaa Valley as Israel gave civilians ultimatums to leave their homes and villages or face the consequences. Israel's proxy, the South Lebanon Army militia (SLA), warned that electricity power stations and water systems would also be attacked, confirming suspicions that Israel's real motive was to coerce Lebanon's government into disarming Hezbollah. Lebanon's Prime Minister Rafiq Hariri warned of the grave consequences of the violence and warned that it could run out of control. He pledged that the Katyusha attacks would stop once Israel ended its occupation and withdrew its troops from the South of the country. Hariri reiterated that the attacks against the Israelis inside the 'security zone' would continue, since the people of Lebanon had a legitimate right and duty to 'resist'. He repeated that neither his government nor Syria had the intention of disarming

Hezbollah until Israel abided by UN Resolution 425 which called for its immediate withdrawal from South Lebanon. Meanwhile, Israel and much of the international media, in particular the Americans, depicted the campaign as a defensive war caused by Hezbollah's Katyusha attacks on northern Israel.

As 'Operation Grapes of Wrath' continued into its second day, Israel laid siege to the ports of Lebanon alleging that it was blocking Hezbollah's shipments of weapons from getting through. Most of the group's weapons in fact come overland from Iran, its main supplier, via Syria. Israel gave the villagers in the South until 2.30 p.m. that day to leave their villages. Its surrogate, the South Lebanon Army, made further threats on its behalf by broadcasting to the population of South Lebanon that 'he who forewarns is excused': Israel would not be to blame for the consequences if the civilians chose to remain in their homes. Within minutes of the broadcasts, the coastal highway linking the South with Beirut became crammed with hundreds of thousands of civilians heading north towards the relative safety of Beirut. Most were in a state of fear and shock and could not believe the fact that they were once again being forced out of their homes. For many of the refugees, it was the fourth occasion since Israel first invaded Lebanon in 1978.

On the third day of the attack, an Israeli helicopter gunship attacked an ambulance packed with fleeing women and children. The picture of the little Lebanese girl lying dead in the ambulance that was taking her to safety shocked the world that weekend, but it did not rouse the West to intervene and end Israel's offensive against Lebanon. Israel immediately claimed that the ambulance was carrying Hezbollah guerrillas and blamed the group for the death of the women and children in the vehicle. As far as it was concerned, anyone who remained in the South and had not adhered to its warnings was a terrorist. It could not understand that many people had remained in their homes and villages, despite the warnings, because they preferred to die in their homes, if need be, rather than become refugees.

Two women and four little girls were instantly killed in the ambulance attack, which was said to be the bloodiest episode since Israel began its blitz against the Islamic militants. The vehicle was hit just as it drove past a United Nations checkpoint, and was hurled off the road through a garden and into the front of a house about 20 metres away. Najla Abu Jahja, a photographer working for Reuters news agency, was less than 20 metres away when the hovering helicopter fired its missile, and she described the scene:

> It was awful. The girl's head was leaning out of the window. Another girl of about eleven came out of the ambulance and ran towards me screaming: 'I want my brothers.' She then rolled on the ground wailing even louder, 'My sister's head blew apart, I want my sister, I want my sister. Oh God, Oh God.'
>
> Two other small children were still alive inside the ambulance. I tried to talk to them to keep them awake. There was a woman aged about fifty and another about thirty. Both were leaning against each other – dead. A child of about three lay on the stomach of the young woman – dead.

A video-tape of the event was broadcast in Lebanon and the rest of the world that evening. It showed a man who had lost his wife and two of his daughters in the attack, running with blood pouring down his face. He carried his three-month-old injured baby girl and another wounded infant in his arms, screaming for help. His name was Abbas and he was one of the men Israel claimed were Hezbollah 'terrorists'. Abbas had lived and worked in Germany during the civil war and had only returned to Lebanon and his home village of Mansourieh at the end of 1995, in the belief that all was now well back home. Since his return, Abbas had been working as an ambulance driver. During the lull on that doomed day, he had piled his wife and three children, along with a few neighbours, into his ambulance. His village had come under direct shelling and he was concerned about the safety of his household. The few who did not fit in the ambulance went in his car. He had arranged for a neighbour to drive the ambulance. He thought that by driving in front of the ambulance, his vehicle would take the first hit should things go wrong and thus act as a shield for his wife and children following behind.

The ambulance was a white Volvo estate car, a make commonly used as ambulances. It sped behind Abbas's car with its siren blazing and its red light flashing. Abbas thought that the Israelis would respect the ambulance signs and not attack the vehicle. It also carried the red logo of *Rissalat al-Kashaf al-Islamiyah*, the Islamic Scout's Mission, which is run by Amal. There was to be no remorse from the Israelis who later said: 'If other individuals in the vehicle were hit they were being used by the Hezbollah as cover.'

Abbas's youngest daughter, the three-month-old baby he was seen carrying out of the ambulance, died later that evening from severe head injuries as she was being transferred from Tyre to Beirut for more specialised neurological treatment. For twelve days, his wife and three girls lay in a morgue in Tyre's Najem hospital, while he and his two surviving little boys took refuge in Tyre: 'I need to put them to rest because I know they are tired and their souls are not in peace where they lie in the morgue,' he said, sobbing softly at his loss. 'Allahu Akbar, God is greater, don't they fear God? How can Israel claim we are terrorists? Doesn't the intentional killing of innocent children come under the definition of terrorism, please someone answer me? What is the world going to do about this?'

No one could answer Abbas's heart-wrenching questions. It was hard for anyone to explain to the bereaved father and husband that even the simple demand for a joint UN and world condemnation of Israel's acts against Lebanon had become impossible to achieve, thanks to the US decision to block any such moves for fear of offending Israel or endangering Peres's chances of winning the elections. Certainly no one could explain to Abbas why the lives of his murdered wife and children were not as worthy as the votes sought by politicians campaigning for the forthcoming elections. No arguments could justify to the anguished husband and father why his family's lives were not considered as important as the lives of the Israeli civilians whose deaths, in four chilling bombings, had sparked world-wide censure only two months earlier.

Abbas was not alone. A similar incident had taken place the previous day, but had not made the international headlines simply because of the lack of media coverage in the area at the time. Two families were instantly killed by an Israeli missile as they evacuated their village following an Israeli ultimatum. Ibtissam Youssef had left the capital with her five children and moved to her hometown village of Suhmor, in the Bekaa Valley. The cost of living in Beirut had soared since the end of the civil war and it had become too expensive for her family to live in the capital. Ibtissam's husband, Mohammed, had stayed behind to carry on working in a furniture showroom. His modest salary, the couple agreed, would stretch further in the village. Their children's schooling would also be cheaper in the local school which was subsidised by the government. On 12 April, Mohammed called his wife and told her to return with the children to Beirut following the deteriorating situation in the area. She refused for the very reasons that had driven her out of the city in the first place and instead promised to leave the village and to head to the lakeside town of Qaroun, also in the Bekaa Valley, which was not under attack. Israel had given Ibtissam's village a deadline to evacuate Suhmor or face the consequences. It ran out at 6.00 p.m.

Ibtissam called her uncle's family, who agreed that they should all leave together. He arranged to pick them up and drive them in his Mercedes to Qaroun. At precisely 2.00 p.m., her uncle, his sister, wife and daughter collected Ibtissam, her five children and her sister, who was staying with them. On the way out of the village a helicopter fired its first missile which landed in front of the vehicle, bringing it to a halt. The car broke down and Ibtissam, in fear for her family's lives, decided to split them up. It is a habit which many Middle Eastern families follow when travelling, on the basis that should something happen to one party at least the others will be safe. Perhaps it was her intuition or maybe it was sheer traditional superstition, but her instincts proved correct. Ibtissam's sister went one way with the two eldest children and they all agreed to meet later in Qaroun. The mother stayed with her three younger children, her uncle, his sister, his wife and their daughter. They took shelter in the garage of a building where they decided to wait for a lull in the shelling before moving on.

The area was under attack and a missile fired by the heli-copters was directed at the entrance of the building. The sister of Ibtissam's uncle was the only survivor. She recovered, some fifteen minutes later, to find the remains of her family's bodies. Injured and unable to stand up, she began to crawl out of the garage in an attempt to get help. As she inched her way out, she stumbled into some electricity cable which had been hit by the shelling. The neighbours heard her scream of pain from the shocks and rushed to her aid. A terrible scene of carnage awaited them. Ibtissam, her three children, her brother, his wife and child all lay dead in a big pool of blood.

The bodies were transferred to one hospital and the injured woman to another. Ibtissam's husband had meanwhile decided to come to Suhmor to fetch his wife and children. On arriving at the entrance to the village, which had been sealed off during the ferocious bombardment, he received the horrifying news of his family's fate. When he reached the hospital and saw the spectacle of his dismembered family, Mohammed passed out. Stricken by grief and unaware that two of his children had survived, Mohammed then attempted to kill himself. 'Life is not worth living any more, I cannot go on without them, I have no reason to live any more,' he cried. His friends used all their powers of persuasion to convince him that suicide was not the answer, especially when he still had two surviving children. Both were still alive and well and had made it safely with Ibtissam's sister to Qaroun.

The two massacres inspired a chilling response from Hezbollah. Sayyed Hassan Nasrallah appealed to the Muslims for a general mobilisation, a call which had in the past drawn thousands of young men and fighters from other parties and militias to support the Party of God's regular army. Nasrallah issued a statement, his first since the Israeli military operation had begun, in which he threatened revenge. It was a grim message in which he warned Israel and Peres to expect the group's forthcoming wrath: 'The day will come and very shortly when Shimon Peres will regret having pushed matters to such an extent as to attack the capital [Beirut] and the southern suburbs. We shall continue along the course of the Resistance which we have chosen until liberation and victory.'

In an unprecedented move, Hezbollah distributed a spectacular film showing more than seventy 'human bombs' taking their last vows and pledging to carry out missions to avenge the deaths of their fellow countrymen. The men were shown in military fatigues, with plastic explosives at their waists, linked to detonators. They proclaimed their allegiance to God and their Imam Khomeini and sealed their vows by kissing the Quran. Hezbollah said the men shown in the footage were only a sample of more than 300 guerrillas who had volunteered for such acts.

'Every country has its secret and special weapons. We do not have the latest high-tech armaments that the Israelis and other countries have, but we do have these faithful strong men who can compete and are more effective than any of our enemy's equipment,' a Hezbollah official proudly boasted. Shortly after the film was shown, the human bombs were scattered along the front lines with one mission in mind: they were to blow themselves up against any Israeli convoys or soldiers in the event of an Israeli ground assault.

Following the attack on the ambulance, the UN Security Council finally agreed to convene. Lebanon had lodged a complaint against Israel's military activities and asked for an urgent meeting to discuss the crisis. The official meeting was scheduled for Monday 15 April at 6.00 p.m., New York time. A UN diplomat in the Lebanese mission to New York declared: 'This was a triumph for Lebanon. Would you believe it? It was a victory for us after a lot of hard work just to get an agreement to be heard and to have the Council convene on our country's behalf. So many times before we were unable even to get our government's complaints against Israeli actions in Lebanon submitted to the Council, let alone have them assemble on our behalf.'

The American ambassador to the UN, Mrs Madeleine Albright, asked Lebanon's ambassador to the UN mission, Samir Habib, to delay the date of the requested meeting. The Americans' argument was that a delay would allow their Middle East envoys Dennis Ross and Warren Christopher more time to discuss the conflict with the Lebanese, Syrians and Israelis. The Lebanese felt that requests for further delays were largely aimed at allowing Israel more time to carry out its military operation in Lebanon and refused the US's request.

Albright then asked for a brief on the schedule of complaints which Lebanon intended to submit to the Council. She was apparently unhappy to discover that the Lebanese were determined to request the UN Council to order Israel to halt all its attacks on Lebanon, to appeal for an official condemnation of Israel and to call for the implementation of Resolution 425. The Lebanese also requested that international aid and humanitarian assistance be extended to the country.

It came as no surprise to the Lebanese mission when Western intermediaries informed them that the US was determined to use its right of veto against any moves which might be made against Israel. The Americans' argument, the Lebanese were told, was that if Israel was to be condemned then Hezbollah should be condemned as well. Lebanon objected to this on the basis that it could not allow a legitimate resistance to be treated in the same manner as the country launching the aggression; to allow Hezbollah to be condemned would set a precedent for the condemnation of any future resistance against Israel. They argued that Hezbollah's Katyusha attacks were a response to Israeli strikes against Lebanese civilians and that Lebanon had a legitimate, recognised international right to resist the occupation of its territory by a foreign country and should not be denounced for taking action against that occupation. The Lebanese mission's argument was a remarkable recognition of

Hezbollah's legitimacy. Prior to 'Operation Accountability', the Lebanese government had disputed the merits of the Islamic Resistance. The Lebanese public had also voiced criticism of Hezbollah's attacks on Israel's northern border and the government had deployed the army in the South in an attempt to disarm and control the guerrillas. In the wake of 'Operation Grapes of Wrath', Lebanon was prepared to defend Hezbollah's right to exist before the world.

On the day of the scheduled meeting the population and government of Lebanon harboured no great expectations. They were all too familiar with the outcome of UN decisions when it came to Israeli–Lebanese issues and on this occasion they were even told in advance not to expect any action to be taken against Israel nor even to hope for a UN resolution or statement condemning Israeli attacks on Lebanon. The Lebanese mission, however, did not wish to be seen to succumb to American and Western pressure. It considered that if it adhered to the Americans' wishes it would, in effect, be giving Israel and the US a licence for future intimidation.

After four hours of discussion and debate, the Council issued a five-line statement agreeing that the fighting should end in Lebanon:

> The one conclusion I think I can draw as President of the Council from this debate is that all who have spoken are concerned that the fighting, violence and bloodshed should cease once and for all, that the humanitarian needs of the civilian population should be addressed and that the peace process must be sustained.

Instead, the fighting and violence intensified. All was going well for Israel: it had suffered no military casualties and world opinion remained largely unmoved. Michael Portillo, Britain's Minister of Defence, spoke out in support of Israel. At a press conference in Jerusalem, on a pre-scheduled visit to Israel during 'Operation Grapes of Wrath', he said:

I would not describe the Israeli reaction as disproportionate. My view is that we look to Israel to take measures which are measured, considered and which are proportionate. I believe Israel has taken measures to ensure civilian casualties are kept to a minimum. I think it is enormously distressing to all of us to see those casualties and see people made refugees and homeless. Clearly the cause of that is terrorist operations carried out in the midst of a civilian population, terrorist operations that count upon a human shield provided by the local civilian population.

No one is pretending that the problem could be solved militarily. But what we face at the moment clearly is a terrorist threat to undermine the peace process. Israel is facing a very substantial terrorist threat from Hezbollah.

Portillo's remarks both surprised and shocked the Arab world and in particular Lebanon. The United Kingdom had in the past been seen as an advocate of the Arab cause and had been frequently criticised by Israel and the Jewish community in Britain for being pro-Arab. Portillo's words provoked a hostile response in Lebanon against Britain. Several British journalists in Beirut were verbally attacked for their country's position.

An overjoyed Peres expressed his gratitude for British support. 'We cannot ignore the moral side of the story,' he said. 'We were forced to do what we are doing. We were left with no alternative. Every country has the right to defend itself and the life of its citizens.'

Israel's defence, it seemed, was also threatened by a 300-yard strip of the Beirut–Sidon–Tyre coastal highway, 15 miles south of Beirut. On the sixth day of the offensive, three Israeli gunboats which had been laying siege to the port of Beirut targeted the highway. Israeli officials claimed that the naval blockade along the coastal highway was aimed at obstructing Hezbollah's supply lines and deterring it from sending reinforcements South. The argument did not convince the Lebanese: the Islamic Resistance, which was mainly based in South Lebanon, did not depend on daily supplies from Beirut and would not have used the Beirut–Sidon highway in any case. Moreover, as an underground Resistance waging a guerrilla-style war against Israeli occupiers, its members were already based in the areas and villages in which the conflict was taking place. Hezbollah later claimed that Israel's artillery bombardment of Lebanon's roads failed to damage its system of communication. The attack on the coastal highway was no more and no less than another means of terrorising the civilians. It was also intended to put more pressure on the government by hindering its efforts to bring aid to the thousands of people who were trapped in their homes and to the refugees who had followed Israel's orders and had left their villages to seek refuge in Sidon and its vicinity.

Journalists travelling on the coastal highway were also shelled, despite the huge signs across their vehicles bearing the word 'Press' in big letters, which were designed to be seen at a distance. According to the official Israeli line, individual cars were being targeted based on 'intelligence information'. They explained that the aim was to make it clear that anyone driving supplies to Hezbollah ran the risk of being shelled. So Israel's 500-ton naval might flexed its muscles against unarmed civilians in their saloon cars, vans and even ambulances.

It was not until the eighth day of the offensive on Thursday 18 April that Western countries suddenly became anxious to find ways of establishing a cease-fire. The day began with more Katyusha salvoes raining down on northern Israel, which had been evacuated by the Israel Defence Forces. At about 7.00 a.m. that morning Israeli helicopter gunships fired several smart missiles at a three-floor building, in the southern front-line town of Nabatiyeh, where a family of eleven had taken refuge. The attack killed a mother, her seven children and her intended son-in-law. The youngest was Nour, whose name means 'Light'. Baby Nour was only four days old and the youngest victim of Israel's campaign. She had come into the world in the early hours of Sunday 14 April to the thud of artillery. She was tiny, tinier than the size of the 155mm Howitzer shell which killed her, her three sisters, three brothers and mother. Rescue workers who lifted her from beneath the rubble broke down and cried at the sight of the baby, still tightly enfolded in the garments in which the mid wife had wrapped her earlier that week. They worked feverishly with their bare hands under the scrutiny of Israel's drones which flew overhead, clearing the debris and rubble to reach the remaining family. There were two survivors in Hassan al-Abed's household: fifteen-year-old Ibrahim and his eighteen-year-old sister Noujood. Ibrahim's bloodied face, peeping through the rubble as he called out to rescuers to help him, made the front pages the following day. Noujood's fiancé was killed in the attack. Rescuers at the scene recall hearing her voice from under the rubble as she repeatedly called out the names of her mother, brothers, sisters and fiancé, unaware that they had all been killed. The horror of what was to follow will haunt the young woman for life – rescuers pulled out her eight-year-old sister Houda, whose brains fell out of her head when they lifted her on to the stretcher. Then came her two dead sisters, Lulu and Nada. The three girls were placed on top of each other on the same stretcher as the search for the remaining family members continued. Fawzieh, the mother, came next, followed by her three sons, Ali, twelve, Mohammed, thirteen and Mourtada, four. They had all perished in less than a few minutes.

Hassan had moved his wife, six children and new born baby from their home the previous day. He was due to travel to Saudi Arabia the next day to perform the Muslim pilgrimage to Mecca and he believed that his family would be safer in the lower floor of their friend's abandoned home. Their own home was close to an Israeli position. They were still asleep, that morning, when Israel's warplanes fired five rockets in retaliation for a mortar attack at a nearby village which had caused no Israeli casualties. The building collapsed like a deck of cards. Hassan was still at the airport waiting to board the Middle East Airline plane, when news of the attack broke. He was informed by airline officials who immediately arranged for his transport back to Nabatiyeh.

It was a terrible start for Lebanon that day. But Thursday 18 April had worse in store. Lebanon would plunge into its darkest moments later that afternoon during the Israeli artillery assault on the UN outpost in Qana. For exactly seventeen minutes, the UN base of the Fijian contingent was pounded by seventeen incoming Israeli shells, thirteen of which landed directly inside the base and hit the two makeshift shelters under which 850 civilians had taken refuge from Israel's military offensive against their homes and villages. As well as the 109 civilians, mostly women and children, who died in that attack, more than 150 were injured, including four Fijian soldiers, and an estimated twenty other people were declared missing, presumed dead. It was an attack of such magnitude that it prompted President Clinton to call for an immediate cease-fire. The American President's call was echoed by Western diplomatic circles.

President Clinton was on official visits to Tokyo and Russia and dispatched both his Secretary of State Warren Christopher and Dennis Ross. Warren Christopher, who had been conducting discussions on the telephone with both Syria's Foreign Minister Farouq al-Sharaa and Israel's Foreign Minister Ehud Barak, started out on a round of shuttle diplomacy.

The American administration had little choice but to reverse its previous tolerance of Israel's campaign. The repercussions of the Qana massacre suddenly threatened its policy in the region, leaving its credibility in the Middle East in tatters and jeopardising the hegemony which it had enjoyed since the end of the Gulf War. America's continued backing of Israel's campaign not only threatened the US-sponsored peace process, but was undermining the international support which its administration had won for Israel at Sharm el-Sheikh. Russia's Foreign Minister Yevgeny Primakov was said to have had a rancorous meeting with Israel's Prime Minister at which he said: 'If you sought to convene the Sharm el-Sheikh conference today, the heads of state would not come.'

Syria, which only a month earlier had looked hopelessly isolated, found itself back in the centre of affairs. Before Israel had launched its campaign against Lebanon, the new order which was being created in the Middle East had left Assad politically encircled. To his south, King Hussein of Jordan had allowed the US to set up a temporary 1,000-man airforce base on its territory. To his north, Turkey had signed a military pact of co-operation with Israel. Other Arab countries were also establishing diplomatic ties with Israel, while Assad's own negotiations with Israel over the Golan Heights had come to a dead end and looked likely to remain stalled at least until after the Israeli and American elections.

The Qana massacre suddenly changed everything. Washington knew that a cease-fire agreement could not be worked out between Hezbollah and Israel without Assad's intervention and Clinton sent his most senior emissaries to Damascus. Washington was alarmed to see Iran also breaking out of its previously isolated position, as the Iranian Foreign Minister Ali Akbar Velayati held discussions in Damascus with his Russian and French counterparts.

Clinton's call for an immediate cease-fire forced Shimon Peres to modify his position radically. Two days before the attack on Qana, the Israeli Prime Minister had said: 'It is too early to negotiate.' The Israeli government had sought to bargain with Lebanon and Syria while keeping them under the pressure of artillery bombardment. In a manifest change of policy, Peres announced after an emergency cabinet session on the evening of the Qana massacre: 'It is also possible to conduct the negotiations for new understandings when there is a cease-fire on the ground. We do not have to be firing.'

Warren Christopher, who had constructed the truce between Israel and Hezbollah in 1993, was expected to join forces with the French Foreign Minister Hervé de Charrette, who had unsuccessfully embarked on a lone mission to negotiate a cease-fire. Charrette had been dispatched earlier in the week by President Jacques Chirac: Lebanon's Prime Minister Rafiq Hariri was a close friend of the French leader and had requested France's intervention. Earlier that month, before 'Operation Grapes of Wrath' was launched, Chirac had been the first Western leader to visit Lebanon since the end of the civil war. Chirac had addressed parliament and Nabih Berri, the leader of Amal and speaker of parliament, had compared the Islamic

Resistance to the French Resistance of the Second World War.

The Lebanese and the Syrians were initially dismayed to find that the US proposals made no reference to the 1978 UN Resolution 425 which called on Israel to withdraw from all Lebanese territory. The US initiative involved securing a cease-fire based on an agreement between Hezbollah and Israel to halt all attacks against civilians. It also called for Hezbollah to be disarmed and for an end to its resistance against Israeli troops in the 'security zone'. Provided that no attacks took place for nine months, Israel would then commence discussions on its military withdrawal from Lebanon.

The proposal was automatically rejected by both Syria and Lebanon, who considered it to be a realisation of the aims which Israel had attempted to pursue in its military campaign. The Lebanese government had repeatedly stated that it was not prepared to take action against Hezbollah while Israeli troops still occupied South Lebanon, as to do so would be taking sides against a legitimate resistance to occupation and would most certainly plunge the country into civil war. Assad was also not willing to lose the strongest card which he held at his disposal in his negotiations with Israel over the Golan Heights. Further-more, neither he nor the Lebanese government trusted Israel's word on timetabled withdrawals: they had already seen it fail to keep to its schedule with Yasser Arafat. Their lack of trust had been further underlined when the late Israeli Prime Minister Yitzhak Rabin had proclaimed, after signing the peace treaty with Arafat, that timetables were not sacred.

The French proposals, on the other hand, mentioned the UN Resolution 425 and considered that any truce to end the current crisis would be a preliminary step towards a later withdrawal of Israeli troops from the South. The French did not call for Hezbollah to be disarmed before an Israeli withdrawal; nor did it call for an end to the group's military activities against the Israeli troops in the 'security zone'. It did stress, however, that both sides should not attack civilians.

Israel's tactics in Lebanon had backfired once again. It had not succeeded in increasing Peres's standing in the opinion polls or his chances of winning the 29 May elections, but it had served to give new status to Hezbollah's Resistance. Despite the great destruction inflicted on Lebanon by 'Grapes of Wrath' and despite all the fanfare about ending Hezbollah's Katyusha attacks against northern Israel, the number of rockets raining down on Galilee appeared to have increased during the military operation. Hezbollah's military apparatus was intact: the guerrillas whom Israel was set on destroying at the start of the campaign had suffered few casualties and their popularity had risen. For the first time since the group had come into being, Lebanese of all religions, sects and classes rallied around the Party of God's Islamic Resistance in an unprecedented show of support and solidarity. Even Israel's old-time allies of 1982, the Christian Maronites, who are perhaps the staunchest opponents of Hezbollah's Islamic ideology, managed to put aside their political differences.

Twenty-four-hour radio chat shows were inundated with telephone calls from residents of Lebanon's northern and eastern Christian-dominated areas, wishing to relay messages of support and solidarity with the Islamic Resistance. Young boys went on air complaining that their families would not let them participate in the fighting. Others asked the radio stations for the location of Hezbollah's nearest recruitment centres. Some of the most talked-about cases were the number of Christian, as well as Muslim, telephone callers who contacted the radio stations asking about the cost of Katyushas and where they could send money to Hezbollah.

A few days after the offensive, advertisements had begun to appear in the local papers. A little square on the front page carried the following message:

In defence of our land and people, in defence of our women and children, in confronting the sinful Zionist aggression against Lebanon, be partners of the Resistance, contribute towards the price of a rocket [missile]. The Islamic Resistance's Committee of Support calls on the Lebanese people to participate in the Resistance through the following projects:

1   The Resistance's fund.
2   The monthly contributions.
3   General contributions.
4   The Islamic legal contributions.
5   Participating towards the cost of a bullet.
6   Participating towards the cost of a rocket [missile].
7   Fitting out a *mujahed* [guerrilla fighter]

The advertisement listed telephone and fax numbers. It was a novel idea and the group's methods were beginning to be much discussed amongst the Lebanese. Many Lebanese were amazed by the group's professionalism. Others discussed the latest reports and stories circulating about the women and men who had contacted the group with large offers of money to contribute towards the purchase of Katyushas. People in general were caught up in the fever of the Resistance. Each day they checked how many Katyushas the Resistance had fired into northern Israel while the switchboard of Hezbollah's press office, which continued to function twenty-four hours a day at its usual location, was inundated with telephone callers demanding that the group take further reprisals for the Israeli massacres.

A Christian woman who had sent Hezbollah a cheque for 15,000 dollars went on a radio station identifying herself and said that she had contributed the money on condition that Katyushas be bought with the sum and fired at Israel's settlements in her name. She said:

Our people in the South have as much right as the Israelis to lead a safe and secured life, and if Israel insists on carrying out its policy of displacing them, then we too will apply that same policy and displace their northern settlers. We, as a people at large, regardless of our religion and sects, are one hundred per cent behind the Resistance and if need be those of us who can afford it will help finance its needs in order to help it carry on defending our people.

A man donated the sum of 25,000 dollars to one of Hezbollah's offices and also asked specifically that Katyushas be bought with his money. His demand amused Hezbollah's officials who said that they had a difficult time convincing him that they could not follow his instructions to the letter:

> Imagine, he wanted us to buy these rockets and then fire them in salvoes of five, fired consecutively at a specific time each day and to announce later that they had been fired. Our problem with his demands, as we explained to him, was that we could not fire them in fives as he requested, because our military tactics dictated that we do not send the same number of missiles in each salvo. We could not stick with a regular pattern when firing these rockets in order not to allow the enemy to know what to expect each time we fired a salvo.

Those were good days for Hezbollah in Lebanon, despite the military pressure. It was clearly overwhelmed by the public support it had gained and for the first time in its history it even allowed itself to display a certain amount of pride and joy in its achievements. On one occasion, two of the group's top press officials were visiting a Lebanese media centre in the heart of Ashrafiyeh, a Christian neighbourhood. As they got out of their Range Rover, an old Christian man spotted them from across the street. He raised his arms in greeting and shouted to the embarrassed officials, 'Hezbollah, Hezbollah, we are all Hezbollah. We are all behind you, God be with you, you have made us proud.'

The official, who recounted the incident with some amusement, choked with emotion when he explained how he was taken aback by the old man's declaration:

> I just stood there feeling overwhelmed by his words, especially because of the area in which we were in. Part of

me initially panicked at his public shouts of the word Hezbollah in the midst of this Christian enclave and another part was filled with emotion when I saw the other pedestrians and shoppers look at us with smiles of acknowledgement and acceptance. I knew then that we had come a long way as a group and, more importantly, as a people, so I waved back to the old man and carried on with my journey.

Joint demonstrations were held by Christians and Muslims. Joined by politicians, they met along Beirut's infamous Green Line which not so long ago had divided the capital into Christian East Beirut and Muslim West Beirut. The two sectors had for decades represented the deep divisions within the Lebanese community. Schoolchildren, teenagers and university students flooded the streets of Beirut carrying donation boxes labelled: 'Help the Islamic Resistance' and 'Help the Resistance be steadfast'. Men and women from all walks of life contributed generously towards the Resistance. Some of the boxes collected donations for the refugees while others were clearly for the Resistance. But that made little difference to the supporters. For most, the issue had gone beyond Hezbollah itself: Israel and the US were attempting to force Lebanon to comply with their strategies in the region, by means of waging a war against Lebanon's right to resist an unlawful occupation. The unprecedented public outrage against Israel's offensive, shared by Lebanon's Christians and Muslims alike, was at last giving the country a long-awaited sense of national unity.

Israel's image, meanwhile, was fixed as an aggressor and occupier. Moderates in the region who had supported the move towards peace with Israel were now beginning to question the nature of the peace on offer. In Saudi Arabia, Sheikh Salem bin Hamid, Imam of the Grand Mosque at Mecca and a member of Saudi Arabia's highest Consultative Religious Council, denounced Israel's campaign when he addressed some one million Muslim faithful on the last day of the pilgrimage to Mecca. Sheikh bin Hamid asked the United States, which he said was preoccupied with the causes of fundamentalism, how it expected to prevent 'terrorists and extremists' from emerging from the piles of corpses and rubble. The theologian said that the military operation would only 'sow hatred and revenge' that would 'not be confined to one party or one organisation, but affect Arabs and Muslims everywhere'.

The Sheikh also appeared to justify Hamas and Hezbollah's human bomb attacks when he said that no blame could fall on 'the oppressed who resisted and chose death'. The Sunni sect generally condemns the practice and it was an unprecedented defence. Bin Hamid's sermon was broadcast by the Saudi media both locally and abroad.

Sheikh bin Hamid's statement echoed others around the Arab world and added to a communal sense of Arab guilt. Lebanon's Arab allies in the Arab League and the Arab Collective Security Pact had failed to fulfil their moral and legal obligation during Israel's campaign. During the sixteen-day offensive, the Lebanese newspapers had run banner headlines asking where the Arabs were, and Lebanon's people had publicly spoken out against the Arab regimes for ignoring their plight and behaving as 'puppets' of the Western world.

Lebanon, an eternal victim of Israel's military might, had once again been left to face the consequences of the Arab–Israeli conflict alone. The Arab countries sent no help other than the usual rhetorical words of condemnation, warning and denunciation. Sheikh bin Hamid asked how long it would be before the 'silence of people' and the 'subjugation of the oppressed' erupted: 'The times are pregnant and history has a thousand returns,' he warned.

He was not alone in posing the question. The editor of Egypt's *Al-Ahram* newspaper, mouthpiece of the Egyptian establishment, also addressed the US when he warned that Israel's actions in Lebanon were 'making it impossible to continue controlling the reactions of the Arab people, who are bound to rebel against the humiliation of their national ethos'.

Perhaps the most striking denunciation came in a live message from an old Muslim Lebanese woman who said she had fled her village in South Lebanon with no money in hand and walked for three days to get to Beirut, where, seething with anger, she had headed for a radio station to broadcast 'a message to President Clinton who accuses us of terrorism' on its live talk show. She began sarcastically:

> Clinton, you are accusing these few Hezbollah men, who have formed a resistance to defend their land and integrity, of terrorism and Israel is not committing any terrorism? America is the master of terrorism because it continues to support Israel which terrorises us and does what it does to us. I also extend a message to the Arab leaders who are crawling and begging to make peace with Israel and who leave us alone when they know that our country is weak and unable to take on the Israeli army.
>
> I am from the South of Lebanon and I have walked for three days to get here. This is a message for America, Britain and France, but mainly the US which is the master of terrorism and which has taught the world the art of terrorism and corruption. Where are you Hosni Mubarak, or you King Hussein? If you have an ounce of blood and conscience left, you should have come and seen the women who were removed by the kilo [from the UN post in Qana]. How can you both face your people? And how do you expect to face your God?
>
> I say how can you accept what has happened and how can you remain silent about it? For ten days now we have been killed like cockroaches, we have not even been slaughtered like sheep. Where is Clinton and who is this Christopher? Let them know that we pray to God to destroy them. Let them see what is happening to us. They remain silent but have the audacity to ask Hezbollah to stop firing their Katyushas. I tell them, we should all detonate ourselves against Israel and America. Please pass on this message to them. Get the foreign media, this is not addressed to the Lebanese this is addressed to the people of America and the West.

What have we done to deserve what they are doing to us? They are fighting Hezbollah? Hezbollah is defending its land and its integrity. Where are the collective security pacts between us and the Arabs who are supposed to defend us? Let Clinton hear this from a woman who has seen her family members, friends and neighbours being removed from Qana by the bagfuls.

The woman's statement, delivered in the raw, immediate dialect of the South, made a deep impression on the Lebanese. Her sentiment was becoming typical and was a reflection of the new hatred brewing amongst Lebanon's southerners against Israel and the United States.

Iran, Syria and Hezbollah knew that the continuation of the campaign would cause more harm to Israel and the US than to their own cause. Israel's objectives were no longer attainable and Peres needed a cease-fire deal that would extricate him from Lebanon without damaging his credibility any further. His army had promised to deliver him two prizes in the military operation and had disastrously failed: it had guaranteed an end to Hezbollah's ability to fire Katyushas into northern Israel and it had promised to eliminate the group altogether. They had pledged to do the job using their newly acquired 'smart' bombs and high-tech equipment which were expected to hit targets without causing civilian casualties. Nearly 650 air raids and 24,000 artillery shells later, Hezbollah was still firing salvoes of Katyushas, at a rate higher than when the sixteen-day offensive began and it continued to do so until the cease-fire deadline came into effect. More than 150 civilians had been killed, including four massacres which not only drew international outrage, but damaged Israel's military reputation and under-mined the image of the Israel Defence Forces' professionalism.

It took Warren Christopher six days of intense shuttling between the Syrian capital and Israel, including a brief stop-over in Lebanon, to clinch a cease-fire agreement between the parties concerned. It was not the ideal agreement that Israel had hoped for: Syria and Lebanon had rejected Israel's demand for immunity for its troops in the 'security zone' and the right to fire against civilian villages, if its forces were attacked. Following the Qana massacre, Peres knew that he was no longer in a position to demand his former goals and had to settle for less. While polls showed that the sixteen-day offensive had not lost him votes in Israel, they also proved that he had not gained much. Although he had paid a heavy political price by alienating the countries who only a month earlier had convened in Sharm el-Sheikh to show solidarity with his country, he had not incurred any military or civilian losses in the whole operation. Only seven civilians were injured by the Katyusha rockets and Peres could claim that he had indeed stopped the Katyusha rockets from raining down on Galilee, at least until after the elections, which was all he needed to deliver.

The final deal was similar to the 1993 understanding. Both sides agreed not to attack civilian targets and a committee of representatives from the US, Syria, Israel, Lebanon and France was to be formed to supervise any violations across the border.

Israel's occupation of Lebanon continued: no reference was made in the agreement to the UN Resolution 425 which calls on Israel to withdraw from the Lebanese territory it occupies. Damascus was back as a main broker in the peace process and Hezbollah's right to continue its resistance against Israel's occupying forces had been recognised.

On the face of it, the latest accord brought an end to one war and legitimised another. The danger of further military escalation remains a threat given the nature of the tension in the area. The core of the problem has once again been left unresolved. So long as the problem of Israel's occupation of the South is ignored and Israel's demand that Hezbollah guerrillas be disarmed has not been achieved, there is no reason why the bloodshed of 'Operation Grapes of Wrath' should not be repeated. In a nice turn of phrase, Augustus Norton has called the 'security zone' in South Lebanon Israel's 'insecurity zone'.

Once the cease-fire took hold, Hezbollah continued with its operations against Israeli occupying forces and their South

Lebanon Army militia within the 'security zone'. On the day of the Israeli elections, the Islamic Resistance carried out two attacks in the occupied heartland of Marjayoun. Four Israeli soldiers were killed and seven others were wounded in the two attacks which also injured several SLA militiamen. Israel retaliated and, in its first breach of the agreement, attacked a civilian area in the Bekaa Valley injuring two people.

Shimon Peres lost the elections. The mass grave at Qana has become a pilgrimage site.

Epilogue

When the Israelis went to the polls in May 1996, the Middle East held its breath. Since the end of the Gulf War, peace had at last appeared to be a possibility. In 1993, the PLO and Israel's Labour government had achieved the unimaginable. In an historic ceremony on the lawns of the White House, Yitzhak Rabin had shaken hands with Yasser Arafat, the man whom Israel had denounced as a 'terrorist' and attempted to destroy in 1982. The following year, the Israeli army had begun its withdrawal from the Gaza Strip and from part of the West Bank. It seemed that it would only be a matter of time before Palestinian autonomy would give rise to a Palestinian state. Despite the violent protests of Israeli and Palestinian rejectionists and the Israeli government's own belligerence in Lebanon, peace remained an objective. Israel had begun to break out of its long years of isolation in the Middle East. A peace treaty was signed with Jordan in 1994 and relations were being established with Morocco, Qatar, Oman, Tunisia and Turkey. Even Syria, Israel's staunchest enemy in the region, had come to the negotiating table. It was the last piece in the jigsaw: if Israel and Syria could come to an agreement on the Golan Heights, which Israel had occupied since 1967 and annexed in 1981, then Israel's occupation of Lebanon was also bound to be resolved.

Binyamin Netanyahu's victory in the Israeli elections changed everything. As the leader of the right-wing Likud party, he was elected on a platform which was opposed to the establishment of a Palestinian state and to the return of the Golan Heights. His triumph was a blow to the Clinton administration, which had sponsored the peace process. It also dismayed the Arab world which could only watch impotently as Ariel Sharon, architect of the Israeli invasion of Lebanon in 1982, and Rafael Eitan, chief of staff during 'Operation Peace for Galilee', returned to power in Netanyahu's cabinet.

Since his election, Netanyahu has indicated that he would be prepared to make a deal with Lebanon, known as 'Lebanon first', as the basis of negotiations with Syria. According to the terms of the deal, Israel would be prepared to withdraw from Lebanon once Hezbollah has been disbanded and the Lebanese army deployed in the 'security zone'. Syria and Lebanon have rejected the proposal as a bluff designed to conceal Netanyahu's opposition to reaching an accommodation with Syria and Lebanon, which makes Syria appear to be the party hindering negotiations. Analysts in the Middle East have assessed Netanyahu's offer as no more than public relations.

Netanyahu may yet surprise everyone, but for the moment the stalemate in South Lebanon appears set to continue. Lebanon demands that Israel adhere to UN Resolution 425 and withdraw from its territory, while Israel attaches conditions to its withdrawal. Not only does Israel want to see an end to Hezbollah, it also wants guarantees for the safety of its proxy militia, the South Lebanon Army. Israel would like to see the SLA incorporated into the Lebanese army.

While Lebanon remains unable to effect Israel's withdrawal, it has however begun to take action against the SLA. Hezbollah has mounted a campaign to woo Shiite members of the SLA away from the militia and back into the fold and makes daily broadcasts on its television station, 'Al-Manar', calling on the militia's members to repent before any peace settlement is reached or face the consequences in the future. Hezbollah regards the militiamen as traitors. A number of SLA members have already deserted and the Party of God claims that Shiite deserters are in the process of being rehabilitated. It is not possible to confirm, as yet, whether Hezbollah is in fact truly prepared to integrate the SLA renegades into its community or whether it plans to exact punishment.

As a result of the intensity of Hezbollah's campaign and the persistence of its members in the Lebanese parliament, the government has also taken action. It has made intensive investigations and collected evidence against the militia. It has publicly confirmed Hezbollah's views that membership of the SLA is a treasonable offence and has issued summonses ordering members of the SLA to come to trial. None have obeyed. Court martial proceedings began in March 1996 and resulted in Lebanon's military prosecutor indicting at least eighty-nine SLA officials and militiamen *in absentia* with life imprisonment on charges of 'collaborating with Israel'. On 6 December 1996, the military prosecutor also charged Antoine Lahad, head of the SLA militia, with a long list of indictments for his activities against Lebanon and its citizens. He has been sentenced to death *in absentia* for treason and collaboration with Israel.

The SLA are paid, trained and equipped by Israel. Some of their families work in Israel and in the event of a peace settlement a few might find refuge there, but the majority would be left to their fate. Some have already begun to leave the country. Reports from the area suggest that morale is low among the SLA militiamen. The Lebanese government has also begun to invest considerable funds in updating the infrastructure in the 'security zone', in a bid to reassert its authority in the region.

Will Hezbollah ever accept peace with Israel? In public, Hezbollah's leaders have not softened their position. Hezbollah's deputy, Naiim Qassem, declares:

We shall not be a part of the peace treaty signed by Lebanon or anyone else. We shall announce this both politically and practically and we shall scream and not stop. Even in our worst days and moments we shall not say that these [Israelis] are our friends.

Even if it [Israel] withdrew from Lebanon it will never end as an enemy which is occupying Palestine. If it withdrew from South Lebanon we would have achieved a certain victory. But the problem in the region would not have finished.

Such wholesale rejection indicates that Hezbollah could become an obstacle to a peace settlement. However, it is also possible that the Party of God may not wish to be seen deviating from its ideological line until all the players in the peace negotiations have laid their cards on the table. Despite its rhetoric, Hezbollah knows that its military resistance would be terminated once Israel withdraws from South Lebanon. The Lebanese government, which has supported Hezbollah's struggle in South Lebanon at great cost to the country's infrastructure and economy, has continued to defend the Resistance on the basis that the Party of God's military presence in Lebanon will cease once Israel terminates its occupation.

The leadership of Hezbollah has in fact departed from its manifesto by declaring that the goals of liberating South Lebanon and al-Quds, Jerusalem, are two different enterprises. It stipulates that armed struggle is the only way to deal with the occupation of South Lebanon, but concedes that the question of Jerusalem is a Palestinian issue. The leadership now talks of co-operating with the Palestinian rejectionists instead of chanting that it will fight until Jerusalem is liberated.

'I am saying that I am hostile to Israel. How I translate this animosity is another issue,' adds Qassem enigmatically.

Subhi Tufeili, however, who represents Hezbollah's most militant trend, is not afraid to make his hardline views known in public. During the commemoration of Ashura, the Shiites' most sacred festival, in 1995, Tufeili delivered a passionate speech. In the days leading up to Ashura, Shiites attend nightly religious gatherings at which Lebanese and Iranian clerics preach to the congregations. The atmosphere at this time is charged as Shiites collectively mourn their supreme martyr, Hussein. The mosques and Husseiniyahs are not large enough to contain the crowds and chairs are laid out in the open air in front of a stage, setting the scene for a dramatic performance.

Tufeili took full advantage of the occasion to reinforce his opposition to any compromise with Israel. He addressed a vast crowd of men and women who had gathered to hear him:

> Some people have asked me what our plans are for the Resistance if peace is realised. Will they [the Resistance] remain in Jabal Amel, the South, and the Bekaa, or not? Do you think our work is seasonal? That there is a season for the Resistance and that when that season is over we just pack up and move on like the Bedouin [nomads] do? If we really believe that these Zionists are rapists and that the land is ours and that Palestine is the home of the Muslims and that we must return this land to its rightful people and follow the Imam's [Khomeini's] decree that [Israel] is a cancerous growth that must be cut out, then how can the Resistance cease? No, the Resistance will not cease.
>
> It is very important that you listen now, for who knows whether I will be able to speak to you again when the [Lebanese] government decides that it will make peace with the Zionists and begin to ban people from saying such things and maybe threaten us with imprisonment should we preach about this subject?
>
> If peace is made tomorrow with the enemy and you had a chance to kill the Zionist [Israeli] ambassador in Beirut, then it is your duty to do so. You should not hesitate to undertake such a feat. The Resistance will be alive and you should know that the Resistance is continuous whether peace is made or not. We shall shred the peace documents and humiliate those rulers of ours who agree to sign them. We shall not be the supporters or helpers of the Zionists and we shall never permit the loss of our rights. We shall never allow the humiliation of our people and we shall never grant Palestine to the Jews.

Tufeili no longer represents the mainstream. Despite his rhetoric, the Resistance cannot yet operate independently of its powerful sponsors. Military supplies from Iran come into Lebanon via Syria and if Assad decides that the time for peace has come, Hezbollah may have no choice but to lay down its arms. 'It is important for them to survive and they won't do anything without Syria's assent,' comments the political analyst Michel Nawfal, who is a Christian convert to Islam. 'Hezbollah is a vital card which the Syrians will not play until they get their deal in the strategic negotiations.'

Many in Lebanon who are opposed to the group's ideology believe that when Syria decides to curtail the Resistance, Hezbollah itself will come to an end as a movement. This expectation is based on the belief that the Party of God depends upon the Resistance as its source of power and popularity. The Resistance was certainly once Hezbollah's *raison d'être*, but since the Party of God made its entrance into politics in 1992, it no longer depends solely on its military force for its identity.

In its first four years in parliament, Hezbollah established a significant voice. It refused to pass a vote of confidence in Rafiq Hariri's government on two occasions and it also rejected the 1996 budget. It has presented itself as a champion of the oppressed and has attacked government corruption. Despite its Islamic identity and its calls for an Islamic republic in its manifesto, its deputies have not focused on Islamic issues since they were elected.* Politicians and analysts in Lebanon are generally impressed by Hezbollah's performance as a political party.

'The presence of such a respectable number of Hezbollah's parliamentarians is proof that it has indeed joined the political game,' comments Salim al-Hoss, former prime minister of Lebanon and a Sunni Muslim:

They have been very active in parliament. It [Hezbollah]

---

* See May Chartouni-Dubarry, 'Hizballah: From militia to political party' in *Lebanon on Hold*, eds. Rosemary Hollis and Nadim Shehadi, London, 1966, p. 61

is distinguished from other parties in the fact that its dealings with people are in general morally upright. Many of the previous parties collapsed because of the transgressions that their military wings committed. To a large extent, Hezbollah has succeeded in not falling into this trap. Hezbollah has shown that it is in total harmony with itself and in its position of opposition to the government in general. Its stance on the various issues debated in parliament is also clear and united.

As a political party, however, one must question the goals of this group. For if Hezbollah is determined to work for the establishment of an Islamic republic in Lebanon, then we must disagree with it on this issue. For Lebanon is a multi-confessional nation, in which many different religions and sects co-exist. So any suggestion of establishing an Islamic republic contradicts the multi-faceted nature of this nation. Despite our disagreement over this ideology, we consider that Hezbollah has the right to a political role within a democratic framework in order for it to achieve any goal that it adopts.

Michel Nawfal believes that Hezbollah has successfully struck a balance between its Islamic ideology and the realities of the Lebanese political arena. 'More important is their achievement with Damascus,' he observes. 'They have a very solid relationship with Damascus and Syria has an interest in accommodating them because they represent a fundamental trend in Lebanon.'

In the elections of 1996 Hezbollah lost two seats: one in Beirut and another in Mount Lebanon. The party then recovered ground in the South and in the Bekaa and ultimately lost only one seat in parliament. Mount Lebanon is a staunchly Christian area which includes part of the southern suburbs in its constituency. The Christians had boycotted the elections in 1992 and their decision to enter the elections in 1996 contributed towards Hezbollah's defeat in Mount Lebanon. Despite the immense general popularity which Hezbollah enjoyed following

'Operation Grapes of Wrath' it clearly still depends on the support of the Shiites for its seats in parliament.

During the elections, Hezbollah's rivalry with Amal was much in evidence. Both parties were summoned to Syria to sort out their differences and to ensure that they ran on the same list in the South and in the Bekaa. Not even 'Operation Grapes of Wrath' had served to unite the parties. It had in fact exacerbated their competition for leadership of the Shiite community. Amal, which had once enjoyed the position of being the Shiites' first and only representative, was again reminded that it was in danger of losing its claim. Amal deeply resented the glory which Hezbollah's Islamic Resistance won during 'Operation Grapes of Wrath'. It also appeared to have lost its position as spokesman: for the first time, foreign journalists, who had once not dared to approach Hezbollah, were courting the Party of God's press officers and hanging on their every word.

Amal and Hezbollah even clashed over the arrangements for the funeral at Qana. During a time of supposed national unity, their dispute was an indication of how far relations between them had degenerated. The clash took place on the day before the funeral when Hezbollah representatives began to hoist their flag next to Amal's and alongside the national flag on the roads leading to Qana. Amal's officials in the South argued that Qana was their territory and that Hezbollah had no right to display their flag. Amal had also participated in the resistance to Israel's military operation and was determined to assert its presence and draw attention to its contribution towards the defence of the South.

Angry words were exchanged and Amal officials fired a few warning rounds into the air. Hezbollah's officials ultimately walked away from the argument and its representatives did not appear at the funeral. The officials of both parties made light of the incident, but it proved that friction between the two factions is continuously in danger of erupting into conflict and that Syria is still very much needed as an arbiter. Their quarrel is also a reflection of the differences which still run deep between a number of other Lebanese factions, both Christian and

Muslim. Although many would like to see Syria leave the country, its presence does serve to contain simmering conflicts and perhaps even prevent war.

While Hezbollah has continued to consolidate its position in Lebanon through its political, social and military endeavours, its reputation abroad remains demonic. Since the end of the Cold War, fear of Islamic militancy appears to have replaced the former dread of communism in the popular consciousness. Not only have Western governments fostered the climate of mistrust, but Arab regimes have also contributed in fear of the challenge which the Islamic trend poses to their legitimacy. In this atmosphere, many deeds are laid at Hezbollah's door and it has become closely identified with its Iranian sponsor. Its name continues to evoke images of bearded men shouting anti-American and anti-Western slogans, scenes of embassies ablaze, human bombs, hijackers and kidnappers. It is seen as part of the monster of 'Islamic fundamentalism' whose tentacles extend beyond Lebanon and the Middle East. It is related to each and every newly born organisation with a grievance against the West and the United States and often tops the list of suspects when acts of terror are committed. It has even been linked with the South African Muslim vigilante group PAGAD.

The Party of God considers itself to be an Islamic movement whose ideology travels beyond the boundaries of Lebanon, but its arena of operations is domestic. It may ultimately envisage a larger role for itself in the world, but it is a young movement which is still fighting for its own space and consolidating its identity at home.

Yitzhak Rabin once ruefully commented that Israel's invasion of Lebanon had 'let the Shiites out of the bottle'.* He declared that the Shiites had the potential 'for a kind of terrorism that we had not yet experienced. If, as a result of the war in Lebanon, we replace PLO terrorism with Shiite terrorism we have done the worst thing in our struggle against terrorism.'

---

* Cited in *Sacred Rage*, Robin Wright, p. 233

So long as the West and Israel continue to regard the problem as a crusade against terrorism they are in effect denying their own responsibility for fostering the conditions which gave rise to Hezbollah. Israel can continue to deny Hezbollah's cause any legitimacy by branding the Resistance as 'terrorists' and it can conceal its illegal occupation of South Lebanon under the euphemism 'security zone', but as long as Israel continues to defy the international decree which calls for the end of its presence in South Lebanon, there is very little hope that the circle of violence will end.

Bibliography

Sources written in English:

Agha, Hussein J., and Khalidi, Ahmad S., *Syria and Iran: Rivalry and Co-operation,* London, 1995

Ajami, Fouad, *The Vanished Imam: Musa Sadr and the Shia of Lebanon,* New York, 1986

BBC World Service Newspack, *Foreign Hostage Crisis in Lebanon,* Cyprus, 1991

Chomsky, Noam, *The Fateful Triangle: The United States, Israel and the Palestinians,* London, 1983

Coughlin, Con, *Hostage,* London, 1993

Dekmeijan, R. Hrair, *Islam in Revolution,* New York, 1995

Ehteshami, Anoushiravam, *After Khomeini: The Iranian Second Republic,* London, 1995

Esposito, John L., *The Islamic Threat: Myth or Reality?,* New York, 1995

Fisk, Robert, *Pity the Nation: Lebanon at War,* Oxford, 1992

Hiro, Dilip, *Islamic Fundamentalism*, London, 1989

Hiro, Dilip, *Lebanon: Fire and Embers*, London, 1993

Hollis, Rosemary, and Shehadi, Nadim, (eds), *Lebanon on Hold*, London, 1996

Izadi, Mostafa (Ed.), *Extracts from Speeches of Ayatollah Montazeri*, Tehran, 1988

Joffe, Lawrence, *Keesing's Guide to the Middle East Peace Process*, London, 1996

Katzman, Kenneth, *The Warriors of Islam: Iran's Revolutionary Guard*, Boulder, Colorado, 1993

Kramer, Martin, 'Hezbollah's Vision of the West', Washington Institute Policy Papers, Number 16, Washington, 1989

Kramer, Martin (Ed.), *Shi'ism, Resistance and Revolution*, Boulder, Colorado, 1987

Mallat, Chibli, *Shi'i Thought from the South of Lebanon*, Oxford, 1988

Milton-Edwards, Beverley, *Islamic Politics in Palestine*, London, 1996

Momen, Moojan, *An Introduction to Shi'i Islam*, New Haven and London, 1985

Pintack, Larry, *Beirut Outtakes*, Lexington, Massachussets, 1982

The Quran, translated by Shakir, M. H., Tehran

Saeed, Abdullah, *Islamic Banking and Interest*, Leiden, 1996

Salibi, Kemal, *Crossroads to Civil War: Lebanon 1958–1976*, New York, 1976

Schiff, Ze'ev, and Ya'ari, Ehud, *Israel's Lebanon War*, London, 1985

Seale, Patrick, *Asad: The Struggle for the Middle East*, Berkeley, Los Angeles, 1988

Wright, Robin, *Sacred Rage*, London, 1986

Yann, Richard, *Shi'ite Islam*, Oxford, 1991

Yapp, M. E., *The Near East since the First World War*, London, 1991

Sources written in Arabic:

Al-Khadi, Adel, and Ahmad, Ahmad, *Dunyaa al-Shabaab*, Beirut, 1995

The Arab Centre of Information, *Al-Amaliya Al-Istishhaadiya*, Beirut, 1985

Fadlallah, Hassan, *Al-Khiyar Al-Akhar*, Beirut, 1994

Sourour, Ali Hassan, *Tahaddi al-Mamnua*, Beirut, 1992

Chronology

1920	France receives the mandate for Lebanon and expands the boundaries to include the Bekaa Valley, South Lebanon and part of the coastal region.
1943	Lebanon gains independence from France.
1948	State of Israel founded. Palestinian refugees arrive in Lebanon.
1958	Civil war breaks out in Lebanon between Christians and Muslims.
1959	Musa Sadr arrives in Lebanon.
1967	Musa Sadr creates Lebanese Shiite Higher Council; Six Day War: Israel occupies West Bank, Gaza Strip and Golan Heights.
1968	PLO begins to make guerrilla raids against Israel from Lebanon.
1970–71	PLO expelled from Jordan – bases its operations in Lebanon.
1975	Civil war breaks out in Lebanon; Amal is formed.

1976   Syria first despatched troops to Lebanon at the request of the Christian Maronites, who sought military help for fear of being overtaken by the Moslem and leftist militias.

1978   Israel invades Lebanon 'Operation Litani'; UNIFIL arrives to implement UN Resolution 425; Musa Sadr vanishes.

1979   Islamic Revolution in Iran.

1981   Israel annexes Golan Heights.

1982   **June–September**: Israel invades Lebanon; Lebanese resistance begins against Israeli occupation; Hezbollah is conceived; Iranian Revolutionary Guards arrive in Lebanon; four Iranians abducted by Lebanese Forces; David Dodge is kidnapped; multinational forces arrive; PLO evacuated from Beirut; massacre of Palestinian refugees in Sabra and Chatila.
November: first human bomb attack destroys Israeli military headquarters in Tyre.

1983   Hezbollah forms first *shoura*, council;
April: bombing of US Embassy; **May**: Israeli–Lebanon peace accord; **September**: Israel withdraws to Awali River, north of Sidon; **October**: clash between Israeli troops and Shiite civilians in Nabatiyeh, followed by call for civil resistance; bombing of multinational forces; **December**: bombings in Kuwait, 17 men charged.

1984   **February**: multinational forces leave; start of hostage-taking; Sheikh Ragheb Harb assassinated; **June**: first issue of Hezbollah's newspaper *Al-Ahed*; Jihad al-Binaa and Islamic Health Committee founded.

1985   **February**: Israel withdraws to Litani River; Hezbollah declares its manifesto and birth of Islamic Resistance; **March**: Khalil Jarradi assassinated; **June**: Israel completes three-stage withdrawal to self-declared 'security zone'; **August**: first missiles in arms-for-hostages deal delivered to Iran; **September**: Benjamin Weir released.

1986   **November**: arms-for-hostages, Iran–Contra, scandal breaks.

1987   Relief Committee of Imam Khomeini opens its branch in Lebanon.

1988   **February**: Lieutenant-Colonel William Richard Higgins kidnapped; 'Battle for the Supremacy of the South' breaks out between Amal and Hezbollah.

1989   **January**: Damascus Agreement between Amal and Hezbollah, sponsored by Syria; **March**: 'War of Liberation' between Michel Aoun and Muslims backed by Syria; **June**: Ayatollah Khomeini dies; **July**: Sheikh Abdul Karim Obeid abducted by Israel; **October**: Taif Accord ends civil war in Lebanon.

1990   Saddam Hussein invades Kuwait.

1991   Gulf War.

1992   **February**: Sayyed Abbas Musawi assassinated – Hassan Nasrallah becomes secretary-general of Hezbollah; **June**: last Western hostages released; first parliamentary elections for 20 years held in Lebanon.

1993   **July**: Israel launches 'Operation Accountability';

September: Yitzhak Rabin and Yasser Arafat sign peace accord.

1995　　**May**: Salah Ghandour makes human bomb assault on Israeli convoy; **September**: Yitzhak Rabin and Yasser Arafat sign final agreement on Palestinian autonomy; **November**: Yitzhak Rabin assassinated.

1996　　**February–March:** Hamas bombings in Israel, 62 dead; **April**: Israel launches 'Operation Grapes of Wrath'; **May**: Binyamin Netanyahu wins Israeli elections; **September**: Lebanese elections.

Glossary

Amal: Shiite militia founded by Musa Sadr's followers. Current leader Nabih Berri.

Al-Amaliya al-Istishhaadiya: Martyr's attack. Hezbollah's term for human bomber missions.

Ashura: Shiites' most sacred religious festival. Commemorates martyrdom of Hussein, grandson of Mohammed.

Belt of Misery: Common name for southern suburbs of Beirut.

Al-Dawa: Islamic party which originated in Iraq.

Fatwa: Religious edict.

Husseiniyah: Shiite religious centres named after Hussein, also serve as mourning houses and social centres.

IDF: Israel Defence Forces.

IRGs: Iranian Revolutionary Guards. Unit created to export Iran's Revolution. Dispatched to Lebanon in 1982. Brains behind Hezbollah's Resistance.

Khoms: Religious tax.

LNR: Lebanese National Resistance. First official resistance organisation to fight against Israeli occupation in South Lebanon. Dominated by Amal.

Majlis al-Shoura: Hezbollah's council.

Mujtahid: Religious scholar qualified to make judgements on points of law.

Muslim Brotherhood: Most influential Islamic group in modern Islamic revival. Founded in Egypt in 1928.

'Security zone':   Israeli term for the area which it occupies in South Lebanon. The zone covers ten per cent of Lebanon's territory.

Sharia: Islamic law.

SLA: South Lebanon Army. Israel's proxy militia in 'security zone'.

Taqiyya: Doctrine which permits Shiites to dissimulate their religion when their lives are in peril.

Twelfth Imam: One of rightful leaders of Shia Islam. According to tradition, he disappeared and is believed to be in occultation. He is expected to return before the Day of Judgement.

Ulama: The religious class.

UN Resolution 425: Passed by UN Security Council in 1978, it calls for the withdrawal of Israel from South Lebanon.

UNIFIL: United Nations Interim Force in Lebanon. Arrived in Lebanon in 1978 to supervise Israel's withdrawal.

Wilayat al-Faqih: Government of the religious class under the authority of a supreme religious authority. Basis of Ayatollah Khomeini's Islamic Republic.

Zakat: Religious tax. Also known as 'poor-rate'.

Maps

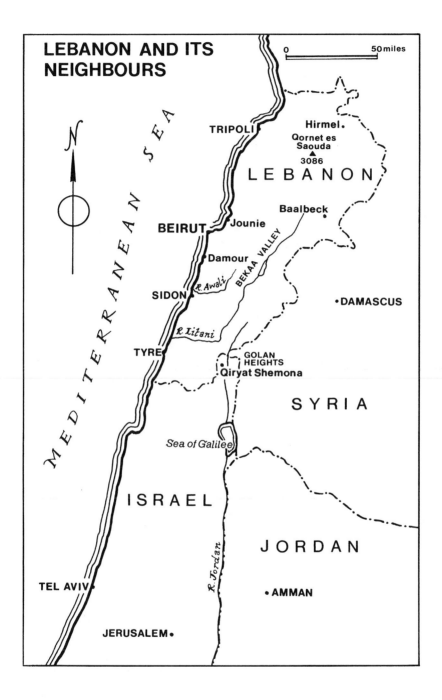

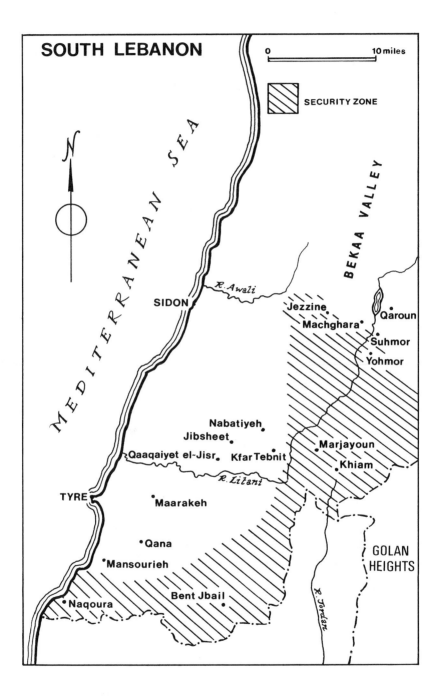

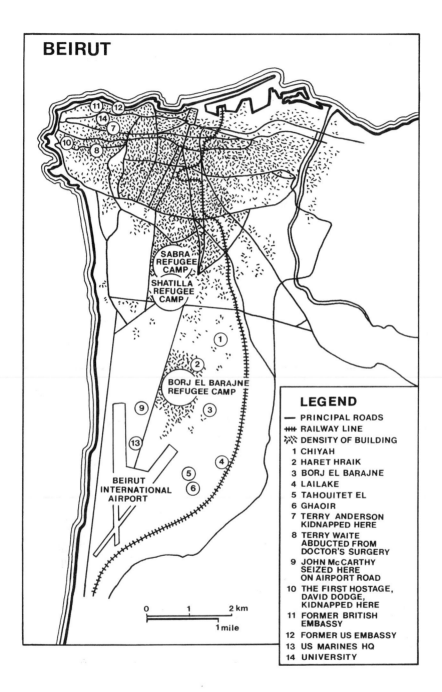

BEIRUT

SABRA REFUGEE CAMP

SHATILLA REFUGEE CAMP

BORJ EL BARAJNE REFUGEE CAMP

BEIRUT INTERNATIONAL AIRPORT

LEGEND

— PRINCIPAL ROADS
╫ RAILWAY LINE
DENSITY OF BUILDING
1 CHIYAH
2 HARET HRAIK
3 BORJ EL BARAJNE
4 LAILAKE
5 TAHOUITET EL
6 GHAOIR
7 TERRY ANDERSON KIDNAPPED HERE
8 TERRY WAITE ABDUCTED FROM DOCTOR'S SURGERY
9 JOHN McCARTHY SEIZED HERE ON AIRPORT ROAD
10 THE FIRST HOSTAGE, DAVID DODGE, KIDNAPPED HERE
11 FORMER BRITISH EMBASSY
12 FORMER US EMBASSY
13 US MARINES HQ
14 UNIVERSITY

0   1   2 km
1 mile

Index

231